Tourist information

TEWKESBURY ABBEY ✠	**Abbey or priory**
WOODHENGE ⊞	**Ancient monument**
SEALIFE CENTRE 🐬	**Aquarium or dolphinarium**
CITY MUSEUM AND ART GALLERY ✕	**Art collection or museum**
TATE ST IVES 🅖	**Art gallery**
1644 ⚔	**Battle site and date**
WWT SLIMBRIDGE WETLAND CENTRE 🦅	**Bird sanctuary or aviary**
⌂	**Camping site**
🚐	**Caravan site**
NUNNEY CASTLE ▦	**Castle**
EXETER CATHEDRAL ✝	**Cathedral**
ST NONNA'S CHURCH ⛪	**Church of interest**
UPTON 🌉	**Country park**
ROYAL BATH & WEST SHOWGROUND ⚲	**County show ground**
HOME FARM 🐄	**Farm park**

PRIOR PARK GARDENS ❀	**Garden, arboretum**
ST ANDREWS ⛳	**Golf course** – 18-hole
LANHYDROCK HOUSE ⌂	**Historic house**
SS GREAT BRITAIN ⚓	**Historic ship**
MONTACUTE HOUSE ⊞	**House and garden**
RURAL LIFE MUSEUM ⊞	**Local museum**
DAWLISH WARREN 🍃	**National nature reserve**
⚓	**Marina**
THE TANK MUSEUM ⚓	**Maritime or military museum**
CASTLE COMBE ▦	**Motor racing circuit**
ROYAL CORNWALL MUSEUM 🏛	**Museum**
Ⓟ	**Picnic area**
WEST SOMERSET RAILWAY ▦	**Preserved railway**
WINCANTON 🐎	**Racecourse**
WITCOMBE ROMAN VILLA ▦	**Roman antiquity**

🅘	**Tourist information centre** – open all year
🅘	– open seasonally
STEAM ⬭	**Transport collection**
LEVANT MINE ◆	**World heritage site**
BRISTOL △	**Youth hostel**
PAIGNTON ZOO 🐘	**Zoo**
BUSH FARM BISON CENTRE 🦬	**Other place of interest**

Speed Cameras

Fixed camera locations are shown using the ㊵ symbol.

In congested areas the ㊵ symbol is used to show that there are two or more cameras on the road indicated.

Due to the restrictions of scale the camera locations are only approximate and cannot indicate the operating direction of the camera. Mobile camera sites, and cameras located on roads not included on the mapping are not shown. Where two or more cameras are shown on the same road, drivers are warned that this may indicate that a SPEC system is in operation. These cameras use the time taken to drive between the two camera positions to calculate the speed of the vehicle.

Key to map pages

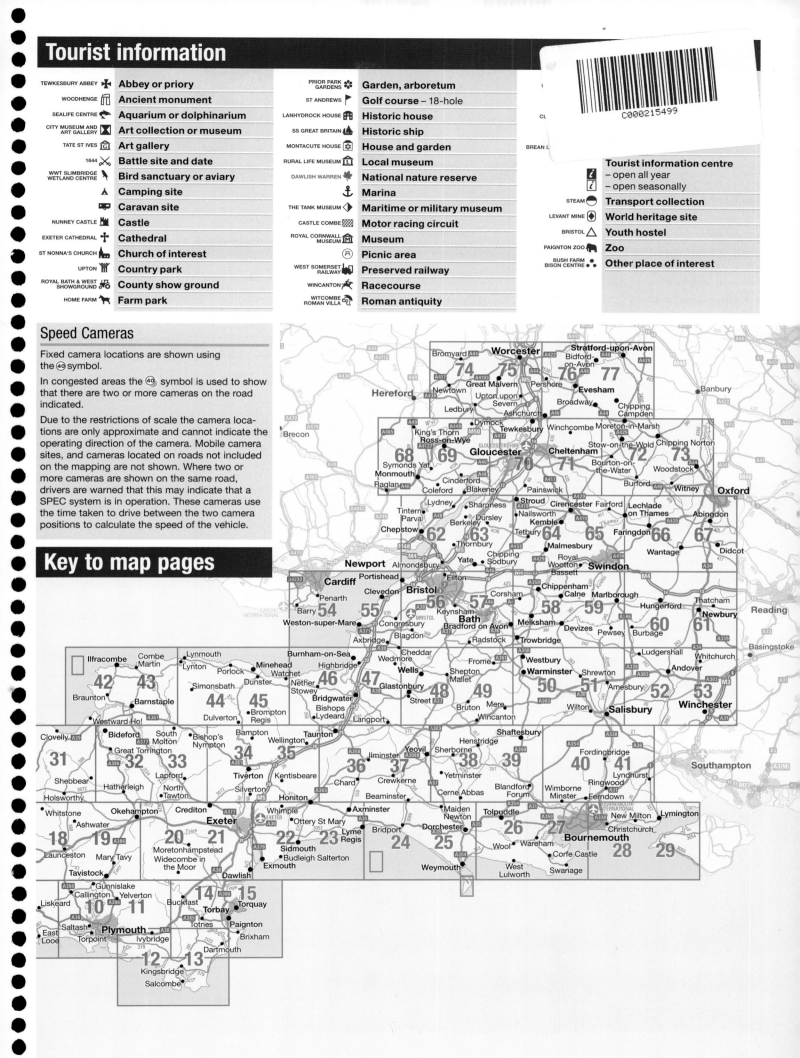

Best places to visit

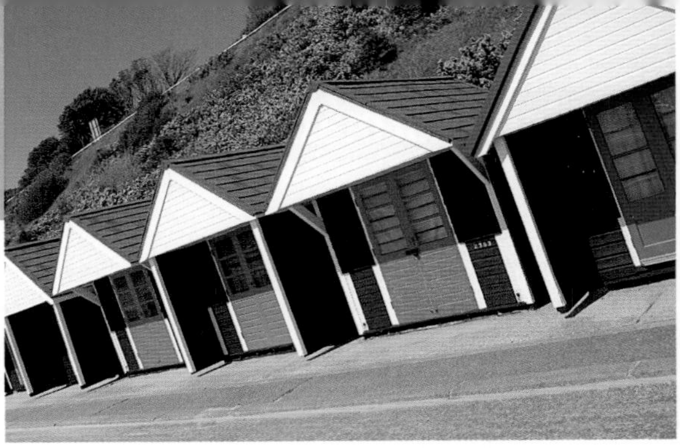

Outdoors

Animal attractions

Listed here is a wide range of selected activities for both children and adults – and many are suitable for both. Some do not need advance booking, but it is always best to telephone first to check both availability and opening times.

Bristol

Bristol Zoo Gardens *Bristol* Animals and plants from around the world, aquarium and ZooRopia high-level rope walk. 0117 9747399 www.bristolzoo.org.uk **56 B3**

Horse World *Whitchurch, Bristol* Equine rescue centre. 01275 540173 www.horseworld.org.uk **56 C4**

Cornwall

DairyLand Farm World *Newquay* Winner of four national awards. Real working farm. Adventure playground, milking parlour, horse-rides and nature trails. www.dairylandfarmworld.com 01872 510246 **7 D8**

Monkey Sanctuary *Looe* (0) 844 272 1271 www.monkeysanctuary.org **9 E8**

National Seal Sanctuary *Gweek* Britain's largest seal rescue facility. 01326 221361 www.visitsealife.com/Gweek **4 E2**

Newquay Zoo *Newquay* Feedings and displays. 0844 474 2244 www.newquayzoo.co.uk **7 C7**

Paradise Park *Hayle* Collection of rare birds, American river and Asian otters and JungleBarn indoor play area. 01736 753365 www.paradisepark.org.uk **3 C7**

Porfell Animal Land *Nr Lanreath* Wild and domestic animals in natural environments. http://porfellanimalland.co.uk 01503 220211 **9 D6**

Screech Owl Sanctuary *St Columb* Care and rehabilitation for sick and injured owls, as well as meerkats, ponies, pygmy goats, emus and play area. 01726 860182 www.screechowlsanctuary.co.uk **8 C1**

Shire Horse Farm and Carriage Museum *Treskillard* All three breeds of heavy English horses. Over 40 horse-drawn vehicles. 01209 713606 **4 C1**

Springfields Fun Park & Pony Centre *Nr Newquay* Large all weather family fun centre. Pony rides and farm animals. www.springfieldsponycentre.co.uk 01637 881224 **8 C1**

Tamar Otter & Wildlife Centre *Launceston* 01566 785646 www.tamarotters.co.uk **18 C2**

Tamar Valley Donkey Park *Gunnislake* Children's centre; petting area and donkey rides. 01822 834072 www.donkeypark.com **10 A4**

Devon

Big Sheep *Bideford* Farm-based attraction with indoor and outdoor activity areas. www.thebigsheep.co.uk 01237 472366 **42 F3**

Canonteign Falls *Nr Chudleigh* England's highest natural waterfall. Wildlife and woodland nature reserve. 01647 252434 www.canonteignfalls.com **21 D6**

Combe Martin Wildlife & Dinosaur Park *Ilfracombe* Safari park. 8-ha (20-acre) home to otters, gibbons, etc. Life-size dinosaur models including a 6.7-m (22-ft) Tyrannosaurus Rex. 01271 882486 www.devonthemepark.co.uk **43 B7**

Dartmoor Otters & Buckfast Butterflies *Buckfastleigh* Tropical garden housing exotic butterflies and moths. Large, landscaped otter enclosures. www.ottersandbutterflies.co.uk 01364 642916 **14 B2**

Dartmoor Zoological Park *Plymouth* More than 1000 creatures in 12 ha (30 acres) of Devonshire countryside. www.dartmoorzoo.org 01752 837645 **11 D7**

Exmoor Zoo *Bratton Fleming* 170 species. 01598 763352 www.exmoorzoo.co.uk **43 C8**

Miniature Pony Centre *Moretonhampstead* Animals and adventure play area. 01647 432400 www.miniatureponycentre.com **20 D4**

North Devon Farm Park *Barnstaple* 15th-century farm house. Farm park and rare breeds centre. 01271 830255 www.farmpark.co.uk **43 E7**

Pennywell Farm & Wildlife Centre *Buckfastleigh* Shire horses, falconry displays, pets corner and play areas. www.pennywellfarmcentre.co.uk 01364 642023 **14 C2**

Quince Honey Farm *South Molton* Watch Watch honey bees at work through glass booths; leaf-cutter ants and play area. www.quincehoney.co.uk 01769 572401 **33 A7**

Shaldon Wildlife Trust *Shaldon* Many rare and endangered species. 01626 872234 www.shaldonwildlifetrust.org.uk **15 A6**

The World of Country Life *Exmouth* Falconry displays, deer park safari. Farm centre, petting area and nursery. Historical exhibits and play areas. 01395 274533 www.worldofcountrylife.co.uk **22 D2**

Dorset

Abbotsbury Children's Farm *Abbotsbury* Ancient barn and children's farm animal-petting area www.abbotsbury-tourism.co.uk 01305 871817 **25 D6**

Abbotsbury Swannery *Abbotsbury* World-famous swan sanctuary. www.abbotsbury-tourism.co.uk 01305 871858 **25 D6**

Farmer Palmer's Farm Park *Organford* Feeding, milking demonstrations. Tractor-trailer ride. Indoor and outdoor play areas. www.farmerpalmer.co.uk 01202 622022 **27 B5**

Kingston Maurward Gardens and Animal Park *Dorchester* Children can feed unusual animals. 01305 215003 www.kmc.ac.uk/attractions/gardens **26 B1**

Monkey World Ape Rescue Centre *Wareham* 01929 462537 www.monkeyworld.org **26 C3**

New House Farm *Mosterton* Llama trekking. 01308 868674 www.ukllamas.co.uk **37 E7**

Putlake Adventure Farm *Langton Matravers* Bottle-fed lambs and goats (Mar-Oct), alpacas, horses, chickens and ducks, pets area, picnic and play areas, crazy golf and tractor-trailer rides. 01929 422917 www.putlakeadventurefarm.com **27 E7**

Gloucestershire

Birdland Park & Gardens *Bourton-on-the-Water* 2.8 ha (7 acres) inhabited by more than 500 birds, including flamingos, pelicans and penguins. Also tropical, temperate and desert houses. Small nature reserve. 01451 820480 www.birdland.co.uk **72 C2**

Cotswold Falconry Centre *Moreton-in-Marsh* Breeding and conservation. Eagles, hawks, owls and falcons. 01386 701043 www.cotswold-falconry.co.uk **72 A2**

Cotswold Farm Park *Cheltenham* Gloucestershire Rare breeds conservation. Adventure playground, pets corner. www.cotswoldfarmpark.co.uk 01451 850307 **71 B8**

Folly Acres *Stroud* Working farm, Rural Conservation area. 01452 766822 **64 A2**

Folly Farm Waterfowl *nr Bourton-on-the-Water* Also farm animals, llamas and rheas. 01453 766822 **71 C8**

International Birds of Prey Centre *Newent* World-leading centre for conservation of birds of prey and owls; more than 60 species; daily flying displays. 01531 820286 http://icbp.org **69 C8**

Prinknash Bird and Deer Park *Cranham* Unusual birds from all over the world. Other animals including deer and African pygmy goats. 01452 812727 **70 E3** www.thebirdpark.co.uk

The Butts Farm *South Cerney* Working rare breeds farm with animal feeding, pony rides, petting area and farm shop. http://thebuttsfarmshop.com/thefarm 01285 869414 **65 C6**

North Somerset

Court Farm Country Park *Banwell* Working farm with animals, play areas, trailer rides and other activities. www.courtfarmcountrypark.co.uk 01934 822383 **55 D7**

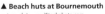

Somerset

Alstone Wildlife Park *Highbridge* 01278 782405 **47 B6**

Animal Farm Adventure Park *Burnham on Sea* Farm animals, pets' corner and play areas. 01278 751628 www.animal-farm.co.uk **55 F6**

Exmoor Falconry and Animal Farm *Allerford* Animal handling, flying displays, falconry days and riding. 01643 862816 www.exmoorfalconry.co.uk **45 B5**

Ferne Animal Sanctuary *Chard* Home to 300 abandoned animals, set in 20 ha (50 acres) of countryside. 01460 65214 www.ferneanimalsanctuary.org **36 E3**

Heaven's Gate Farm Animal Rescue Centre *Henley* Rehoming centre for variety of animals and fowl. 01458 252656 www.nawt.org.uk/somerset/about.asp **47 E8**

Home Farm *Carhampton* Small livestock farm. www.homefarmblueanchor.co.uk 01984 640817 **45 C7**

Swindon

Roves Farm *Swindon* Bottle-feed and see a variety of farm animals. 01793 763939 www.rovesfarm.co.uk **65 E9**

Torbay

Paignton Zoo Environmental Park *Paignton* One of England's largest zoos with more than 1300 animals, and more than 300 species within 30 ha (75 acres). www.paigntonzoo.org.uk 0844 474 2222 **15 D5**

Seashore Centre *Goodrington* Aquaria and organised rock-pooling sessions (check availability/times) 01803 528841 **15 D5**

Wiltshire

Bush Farm Bison Centre *West Knoyle* Herds of bison, elk and guanacos, as well as prairie dogs and raccoons. 01747 830263 www.bisonfarm.co.uk **50 E1**

Farmer Giles Farmstead *Teffont* Working dairy farm, with pets corner, llamas and indoor adventure play area. 01722 716338 www.farmergiles.co.uk **50 E4**

Longleat *Warminster* Safari park, adventure castle, King Arthur's Mirror Maze, safari boats, Longleat railways, butterfly gardens, world's longest hedge maze and pets' corner. 01985 844400 www.longleat.co.uk **49 C8**

Beaches and resorts

Cornwall

Bude Small unspoilt resort town. Popular beaches for families and surfers. Annual jazz festival. www.bude.co.uk **30 E4**

Carbis Bay Sheltered bay ideal for families and surfers. **3 C6**

Constantine Bay *Constantine* Wide beach with pale sands. **16 F2**

Crackington Haven Coastal village with good beach and cliff walks. Cornwall's highest coastal point. **17 A7**

Crantock Long, peaceful sandy beach backed by sand dunes. Good for surfing. **7 C6**

Crinnis, Carlyon Bay *Nr St Austell* Popular sandy beach backed by cliffs. **8 E4**

Duporth Shingle and rocky beach in a sheltered bay. **8 E3**

Fistral Beach *Newquay* Sandy beach partly sheltered by dunes. One of the top surfing spots in Europe. **7 C6**

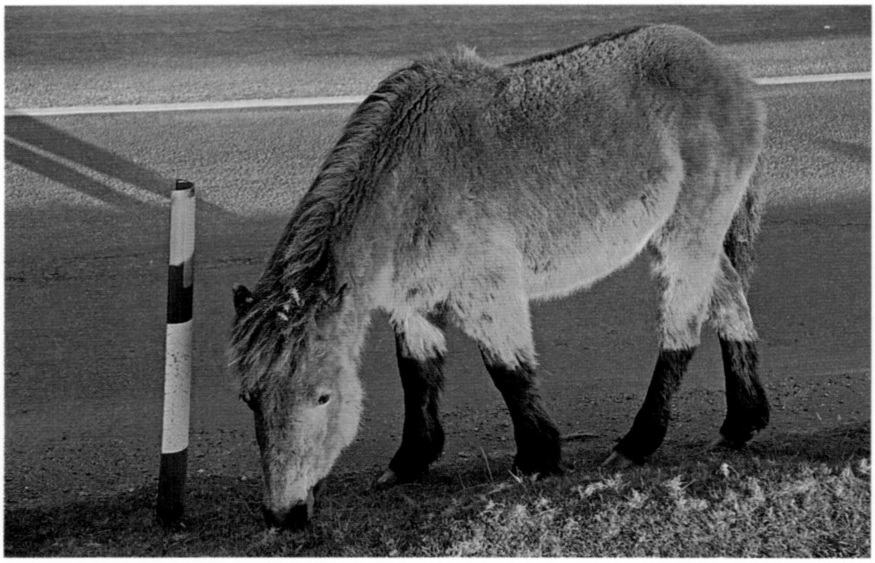

◀ A Dartmoor pony near Haytor. The ponies roaming free on Dartmoor are owned by Dartmoor Commoners.
Moorefam /iStockPhoto.com

▲ Beach huts at Bournemouth
mrtom-uk / www.iStockphoto.com

Godrevy *St Ives* Extensive sandy beach to east of St Ives Bay, lighthouse island featured in Virginia Woolf's 'To the Lighthouse'. **3 B7**

Great Western *Newquay* Popular family beaches in sheltered coves. **7 C7**

Gyllyngvase *Falmouth* Main resort beach for Falmouth. Small, wide, sandy beach. **4 D4**

Holywell Bay *Newquay* Sandy beach with dunes. Good surfing. **7 D6**

Kennack Sands *Nr Coverack* Two sheltered sandy beaches. Part of National Nature Reserve. **5 G2**

Kynance Cove (NT) *Lizard* Famed beauty spot. Sheltered sandy coves and caves at low tide. **5 H1**

Millendreath *Looe* Lively beach resort. **9 E8**

Mother Ivey's Bay *Padstow* Isolated rural beach accessible by coastal path. **16 E2**

Newquay Cornwall's most popular and lively holiday resort. 11 km (7 miles) of beautiful sandy beaches. UK's main centre for surfing. www.newquayguide.co.uk **7 C7**

Parr Sands *Nr St Austell* Extensively sandy beaches. **8 E4**

Pendower *Roseland* Long sandy beach. Cliffs and rock pools. **5 C6**

Perranporth Lively beach resort. Village End beach and Penhale Sands are both sandy beaches with good surfing in places. **7 E6**

Porth Joke *Newquay* Attractive bay with sandy beach. **7 C6**

Porthpean *Nr St Austell* Safe, sandy cove. Popular with families. **8 E3**

Porthtowan North coast rural family resort. **6 F4**

Portwrinkle *Nr Torpoint* Sandy beach with rocks in a rural setting. Popular with surfers. **10 E3**

St Ives Bay *St Ives* 6 km (3¾ miles) of golden sandy beaches bordered by fishing resort of St Ives. The best stretches include Carbis Bay and Porthminster Beach, with Godrevy Lighthouse. www.stives-cornwall.co.uk **3 B6**

Swanpool *Falmouth* Small sand and pebble beach. **4 D4**

Tolcarne *Newquay* One of Newquay's most popular beaches, close to the town centre. **7 C7**

Treyarnon Bay *Treyarnon* Wide sandy bay in an Area of Outstanding Natural Beauty. **16 F2**

Vault Beach *Gorran Haven* Gently shelving sandy beach on National Trust land. Good for families. **5 B8**

Watergate Bay *Watergate* 3 km (1¾ miles) of golden sands. Lots of activities and rival to Fistral Bay for surf. **7 B7**

Widemouth Sand *Widemouth Bay* Large sandy beach with low cliffs and rock formations. Good surfing because of reef. **30 F3**

Devon

Bantham Sandy beach backed by sand dunes. Popular with surfers. **12 D4**

Bigbury-on-Sea Sandy beach at the mouth of the South Devon Avon. Connected to Burgh Island by a causeway at low tide; at high tide a sea tractor transports passengers. **12 D4**

Blackpool Sands *Blackpool* One of the most picturesque beaches in Devon. Crescent sands backed by cliffs and fields. European blue flag award and Seaside awards. **15 F5**

Challaborough Sheltered sandy cove; rock pools at low tide. **12 C3**

Croyde Beach *Croyde* One of the best surfing beaches in the country. **42 D3**

Exmouth Beach *Exmouth* Exmouth has remained a popular resort since its Victorian heyday. The sandy beach is backed by a wide promenade. **22 D2**

Hope Cove *Nr Salcombe* Sandy beach. Safe swimming area. **12 E4**

Ilfracombe (Tunnels) Beach *Ilfracombe* Grey sand and shingle backed by cliffs with small bays and rock pools. Swimming and scuba diving. **42 B5**

Ness Cove *Shaldon* Sandy cove backed by red sandstone cliffs. **15 A6**

Putsborough Beach *Putsborough* 5 km (3 miles) of golden sands. Excellent surfing towards the two headlands. **42 C3**

Salcombe North and South Sands *Salcombe* Sandy, family beach. **13 E5**

Saunton Sands *Saunton* Superb beaches with miles of sand dunes. **42 D3**

Slapton Sands *Slapton* Long, straight shingle beach backed by Slapton Ley freshwater lake (NT). **13 D7**

Thurlestone North and South *Thurlestone* Owned by the National Trust. Popular sandy beach. **12 D4**

Wembury Small cove surrounded by low cliffs. **11 F6**

Woolacombe Village Beach *Woolacombe* 3.6 km (2¼ miles) of golden sands backed by hills and downs. Water sports. Regular surfing competitions. Woolacombe Sands is within the Heritage Coastline and is backed by National Trust land. **42 C4**

Dorset

Bournemouth One of the most popular resorts in the south. Bournemouth town has lots to do and has numerous sandy beaches. **28 B1**

Charmouth Ideal for family holidays. Sandy beach with café and beach huts nearby, as well as Heritage Coastal Centre. Famous worldwide for its fossils. **24 B2**

Christchurch Friars Cliff and Highcliffe Castle *Christchurch* Sand and gravel beaches. Backed by promenade and beach huts. **28 B4**

Church Ope Cove *Portland* Sheltered beach with limestone pebbles. Private beach huts. **24 D2**

Durdle Door *Nr Wareham* Famous for Durdle Door Arch, a naturally formed arch in the headland. The beach is narrow and shingly. **26 D3**

Kimmeridge Bay *Kimmeridge* Sandy beach with fossil-bearing shale. Popular with surfers. **27 E5**

Lyme Regis Known as the Jurassic Coast because of the number of fossils. Site from which ships sailed to meet the Spanish Armada. **24 B1**

Shell Bay *Studland* Beautiful beach on tip of Studland Peninsula. Part of Purbeck Heritage Coast. **27 C7**

Weymouth, Home to the 2012 Olympic sailing events; award-winning, sheltered, safe sandy beach with donkey rides, children's fun fair and sand sculpting. **25 D8/E8**

North Somerset

Weston-Super-Mare Resort with wide sandy beach. **55 D6**

Poole

Sandbanks, Harbour Lake *Poole* Popular sandy beaches. **27 C7**

Somerset

Burnham-on-Sea Traditional family resort. 11 km (7 miles) of sandy beaches with sand dunes. **47 B6**

Dunster Beach *Dunster* Quiet sandy beach. **45 B7**

Minehead Boasts a sandy beach and seafront. Varied choice of entertainments and shopping facilities nearby. **45 B6**

Torbay

Goodrington Sands *Goodrington* Long sandy beach. **15 D5**

Meadfoot *Torquay* Sandy beach to the east of Torquay in the middle of popular resort. **15 C6**

Oddicombe and Maidencombe Bay *Torquay* Known as 'the English Riviera', Torquay and its surrounding coast are popular because of mild climate and golden sands. **15 B6**

Shoalstone Beach *Brixham* Gently shelving shingle beach. Open-air swimming pool **15 D6**

Country and forest parks

Bath & NE Somerset

Avon Valley Adventure and Wildlife Park *Keynsham* Only 7.25 km (4½ miles) from the centres of both Bristol and Bath. Facilities include an outdoor adventure playground, junior assault course, pets' corner, soft-play area, boating and places for fishing. The riverside trail is way-marked with information about the plants and animals. The park itself is designed as a riverside trail, which is well marked with numbered signs providing information about the animals, birds and plants that can be seen along the way. Café.
🖥 www.avonvalleycountrypark.co.uk
📞0117 986 4929 **57 C5**

Cornwall

Kit Hill Country Park *Callington* A wild, rugged granite hilltop, at 333 m (1000 ft) Kit Hill dominates the landscape for miles. As well as heathland landscape and wildlife, there are lots of interesting archaeological features such as a Neolithic long barrow, several round barrows and evidence of human activity stretching back well over 5000 years. There are several old mine shafts, some of which have been colonised by bats. The views are stunning and there are explanatory boards at the summit. 📞01579 37 00 30
🖥 www.cornwall.gov.uk **10 A3**

Mount Edgcumbe Country Park *Cremyll, Torpoint* The earliest landscaped park and gardens in Cornwall, Mount Edgcumbe lies in an area that has been inhabited for over 3000 years and was an important early crossing point between Devon and Cornwall. Within the park are formal gardens, garden buildings and follies, two churches, two chapels, a coastguard station, a Bronze Age barrow, a grotto and deer. The South West Coastal Path runs through the park and the 'zig zag' paths criss-cross the steep cliffs. Restaurant. 🖥 www.mountedgcumbe.gov.uk
📞01752 822236 **10 E5**

Northam Burrows Country Park *Northam* This country park is on a coastal plain within an Area of Outstanding Natural Beauty and SSSI that forms part of a designated United Nations Biosphere Reserve. Habitats include unimproved coastal grassland, sand dunes and fragile salt marsh, providing refuge for a wide variety of wildlife. Access to Westward Ho! beach, visitor centre (summer).
🖥 www.torridge.gov.uk 📞01237 479708 **42 E3**

Tehidy Country Park *Camborne* Covering 100 ha (250 acres), the Tehidy estate was purchased by Cornwall County Council in 1983 and turned into a recreational country park. It has a mixture of old formal landscaped gardens, woodland with a spring carpet of bluebells, grassland near the cliffs (from where visitors can get spectacular views) and wilder areas. The remnants of the headgear of South Crofty mine, the last working tin mine in Cornwall, can be seen, as can a number of granite engine houses. The area near the lake is popular for picnics, while Oak Wood and the path beside the Tehidy river are good places for walking. The wildlife here includes badgers, weasels and bats, as well as birdlife on the lake and river. Visitor centre and café. 📞01872 322 257
🖥 www.cornwall.gov.uk **3 B8**

Devon

Stover Country Park *Heathfield* Stover Country Park's 46 ha (114 acres) include a variety of grassland, heathland, lake, marsh and woodland, giving it a wide range of wildlife including roe deer, otters, dormice, dragonflies, adders, wildfowl and breeding birds such as nightjar, spotted flycatcher and tawny owl. The history of the development of the area, particularly the industrialisation of the 18th century, is explained on the waymarked Heritage Trail that passes through the park. 📞01626 835236
🖥 www.devon.gov.uk/stover_country_park.htm **21 E6**

Dorset

Durlston Country Park *Swanage* Set in the beautiful Isle of Purbeck, a World Heritage Site, Durlston has 113 ha (280 acres) of spectacular countryside – limestone downland, hay meadows, sea cliffs for spectacular views and woodland. There is a huge variety of wildlife, including the colonies of breeding seabirds on the cliffs in summer, peregrines and ravens, bottlenose dolphins offshore, large numbers of migrating birds in spring and autumn and a wide variety of insect life, including 34 species of butterfly. The visitor centre has video links to the seabird colonies. The area's geology and history can be seen in the landscape, with two quarries, a visible Saxon field system, the folly of Durlston Castle and the Great Globe, a monument in Portland limestone showing the Victorian view of the world in the 1880s. Guided walks with rangers, boat trips and way-marked trails. Visitor centre, shop and café. 📞01929 424443
🖥 www.durlston.co.uk **27 E7**

Moors Valley Country Park *Ashley Heath* A 300-ha (750-acre) country park with a broad range of habitats and wildlife, as well as a wide variety of facilities including a woodland adventure play area for older children, a tree-top rope walk and a castle and sand area for toddlers. A narrow-gauge steam railway runs alongside the lake, and

▲ **Salcombe, Devon**
Southwest Tourism

▼ **Durdle Door, Dorset**
Andy Farrer / iStockphoto.com

Aquaria

Bournemouth

Oceanarium *Bournemouth* Ocean displays of climates and wildlife from around the world. 📞01202 311 993
🖥 www.oceanarium.co.uk **28 B1**

Cornwall

Blue Reef Aquarium *Newquay* Undersea safari. 📞01637 878134
🖥 www.bluereefaquarium.co.uk **7 C7**

Mevagissey Aquarium *Mevagissey* Displays of the fish found in local waters. 📞01726 843305 **5 B8**

Dorset

Lyme Regis Marine Aquarium & Cobb History *Lyme Regis* Dorset's waters.
www.lymeregismarineaquarium.co.uk
📞01297 444230 **24 B1**

Weymouth Sea Life Park *Weymouth* Seal sanctuary, tropical shark nursery, splash pool, stingrays and otter centre
🖥 www.visitsealife.com/weymouth
📞01305 761010 **25 D8**

North Somerset

Seaquarium *Weston-super-Mare*
📞01934 613361 🖥 www.seaquarium.co.uk **55 D6**

Plymouth

National Marine Aquarium *Plymouth* Sharks, seahorses, deep reef displays, etc. The aquarium has created an offshore reef for animals to colonise by sinking the frigate *Scylla*.
🖥 www.national-aquarium.co.uk
📞0844 893 7938 **11 E5**

Somerset

Tropiquaria *Washford Cross, Watchet* Indoor tropical rain forests. Exotic creatures, farm animals, pirate ship adventure playground, trampolines, etc.
🖥 www.tropiquaria.co.uk
📞01984 640688 **45 C8**

Torbay

Living Coasts, *Torquay* Local and exotic marine life. 📞0844 474 3366
🖥 www.livingcoasts.org.uk **15 C6**

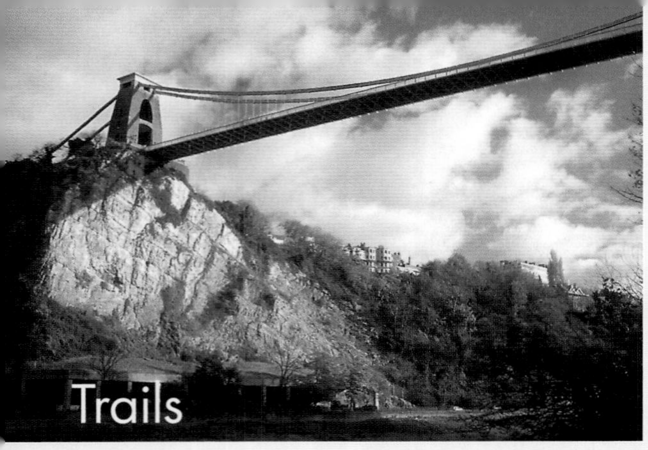

Trails

◀ **Clifton Suspension Bridge seen from the River Avon Trail, Bristol**
James Hughes / Alamy

Cornwall and Devon

Tamar Valley Discovery Trail *Cornwall and Devon* The Tamar river forms the historic boundary between Devon and Cornwall and this route follows the river valley for 48 km (30 miles) between Plymouth and Launceston. The landscape varies from the broad Tamar estuary to the quiet woodland higher up the valley. The route passes through a few quiet places, such as Bere Alston and Milton Abbot. Towards the end of the route, the river can be crossed by either the ferry or the train. 🖳www.devon.gov.uk

Two Castles Trail *Cornwall and Devon* This route runs 39 km (24 miles) west between Okehampton and Launceston. In the east it crosses open moorland while in the west it passes through peaceful valleys. There are a number of historic sites, including the Norman castles at Okehampton and Launceston, and several small villages. 🖳www.devon.gov.uk

West Devon Way *Devon* This 58-km (36-mile) trail runs along the western edge of Dartmoor between Okehampton and Plymouth. It passes across moorland and through river valleys, picturesque farmland, a number of small villages and Tavistock. 🖳www.devon.gov.uk

Cornwall, Devon, Dorset and Somerset

South West Coast Path *Cornwall, Devon, Dorset and Somerset* This is Britain's longest National Trail, which runs from Minehead in Somerset to South Haven Point near Poole in Dorset, via the spectacular Devon and Cornwall coastlines and the entire length of the Jurassic Coast World Heritage Site. ✆01392 383560. 🖳www.southwestcoastpath.com

Dorset

Castleman Trailway *Dorset* This gentle 27.9-km (16.5 mi) route follows the line of the former Southampton and Dorchester railway from Ringwood (Hampshire) to Poole. There is a connection with the Stour Valley Way at Wimborne Minster. 🖳www.dorsetforyou.com

Jubilee Trail *Dorset* This 145-km (90-mile) trail was created by local ramblers to celebrate the Ramblers' Association's 60th anniversary. It winds through wooded valleys and across rolling hillsides in the quietest areas of Dorset, from Forde Abbey in the west to Bokerley Dyke in the east. 🖳www.ramblers.org.uk/info/paths/name/j/jubileedorset

Stour Valley Way *Dorset* Route following most of the 100-km (64-mi) length of the River Stour, including sections between Tuckton Bridge and Mudeford Quay, Wimborne to Canford and Sturminster Newton to Fiddleford. A picturesque route, avoiding busier towns and passing such sights as Hengistbury Head. 🖳www.stourvalleyway.co.uk

Dorset, Gloucestershire, Somerset, Wiltshire

The Monarch's Way *Dorset, Gloucestershire, Somerset and Wiltshire* This 990-km (615-mile) walk from Worcester to Shoreham (West Sussex) closely follows the trail of Charles II after the Battle of Worcester in 1651. In the southwest, it passes south through or near Chipping Campden, Moreton-in-Marsh, Stow-on-the-Wold, Cirencester, Chipping Sodbury, Keynsham, Abbots Leigh, Compton Martin, Wells, Castle Cary, South Cadbury, Ham Hill, Crewkerne and Charmouth before heading back north towards Yeovil and and then east via Bridport, Winyard's Gap, Wincanton, Mere, Hindon, Great Wishford and Middle Winterslow, and from there to Shoreham. 🖳www.themonarchsway.com

Gloucestershire

Thames Path *Gloucestershire* The Thames Path in its entirety is 296 km (184 miles) long, but the western reaches are among the most pleasant landscape from the lower slopes of the Cotswolds at Thameshead near Kemble, it passes southeast through the Cotswold Water Park and then strikes east via Cricklade until it leaves the region at Lechlade. ✆01865 810224 🖳www.nationaltrail.co.uk

The Wysis Way *Gloucestershire* The Wysis Way runs for 88.5 km (55 miles) from Monmouth to Kemble through the Forest of Dean, the Leadon and Severn Vales, via Gloucester, and the Cotswolds. It links the Wye and the Thames and joins the Offa's Dyke and Thames paths. 🖳www.ldwa.org.uk

N Somerset, Bristol, Bath & NE Somerset

River Avon Trail *Pill to Bath* This 37-km (23-mile), mainly off-road, trail runs from Pill Harbour, via Clifton and Bristol to Pulteney Bridge in Bath. Sights along the way include the Avon Gorge, the Clifton Suspension Bridge, Leigh Woods and Hanham Weir. The trail is nearly all level and on good surfaces although it may be muddy in one or two places after wet weather. The path is off-road except for a couple of short sections in the centre of Bristol. You can quite easily link up with the Bristol and Bath Railway Path from the River Avon Trail at Hanham Weir to continue along the Avon Valley to Bath. ✆0117 922 4325 🖳www.riveravontrail.org.uk

Somerset

Coleridge Way *Somerset* A 58-km (36-mile) trail between Nether Stowey and Porlock. It crosses the Quantock Hills, then dips down before climbing up to cross the northen parts of Exmoor. 🖳www.coleridgeway.co.uk

Mendip Way *Somerset* An 80.5-km (50-mile) path that travels the entire length of the Mendips from the Roman port of Uphill near Weston-super-Mare to Frome, passing by Wookey Hole, Cheddar Gorge, Ebbor Gorge Nature Reserve and historic towns such as Wells and Shepton Mallet. including the broad vale of the Western Mendips, the high plateau of the central part and the wooded valleys of the eastern end. Includes some steep climbs. 🖳www.ldwa.org.uk

River Parrett Trail *Somerset* This 80.5-km (50-mile) walking route runs north from the Dorset/Somerset border near Crewkerne, roughly following the course of the River Parrett, which finally reaches the sea near Burnham on Sea. As well as the hills of the Dorset/Somerset border, it travels across the beautiful Somerset Levels and Moors and passes through several pretty villages. ✆01935 845946 🖳www.somerset.gov.uk

Wiltshire

The Ridgeway National Trail The whole of this ancient path is 140 km (87 miles) long, although only the very end lies within southwestern England. This section is on the Marlborough Downs and starts at the Sanctuary, runs close to Silbury Hill, Avebury and Barbury Castle, before heading off the downs and east through Oxfordshire and Berkshire. 🖳www.nationaltrail.co.uk

The White Horse Trail *Wiltshire* This 145-km (90-mile) walking route connects Wiltshire's eight white horses at Alton Barnes, Broad Town, Cherhill, Hackpen, Marlborough, Pewsey, Westbury and the new Millennium Horse at Devizes. The trail uses several of the ancient trackways that criss-cross the high downs. ✆01980 623255 🖳www.visitwiltshire.co.uk

there is an 18-hole golf course. Miles of footpaths, way-marked walks and cycle trails allow visitors to explore much of the valley. Visitor centre, restaurant, shop, wildlife events, cycle hire. ✆01425 470721 🖳www.moors-valley.co.uk **40 E5**

Gloucestershire

Cotswold Water Park *South Cerney* A vast complex of lakes created by gravel extraction. Activities on offer include walking, cycling, angling, sailing, canoeing, kayaking, horse riding, waterskiing and, wind surfing. Three of the lakes are designated nature reserves and have bird hides. The complex of parks includes Neigh Bridge Country Park and Cotswold Country Park and Beach ✆01285 861459 🖳www.waterpark.org **65 C5**

Forest of Dean Forest Park *near Cinderford* Formerly a royal hunting forest, this 90-km (35-mile) square area is a tranquil place. There are walking trails, way-marked cycling trails and a sculpture trail. There is a wide variety of wildlife and fallow deer can sometimes be seen. Visitor centre, café. 🖳www.forestry.gov.uk ✆01594 833057 **69 E6**

Robinswood Hill Country Park *Gloucester* Surprisingly close to the centre of Gloucester, this park has 100 ha (250 acres) of countryside with pleasant walks and views. There are way-marked geology, nature and riding trails. There is also a rare breeds farm. Gift shop. ✆01452 304779 🖳www.gloucestershire.gov.uk **70 E2**

Poole

Upton Country Park *Poole* This park consists of roughly 40 ha (100 acres) of parkland, gardens and woodland on the shores of Poole Harbour. The Italianate house was built in about 1818. Visitor centre, tearooms. ✆01202 672625 🖳www.boroughofpoole.com **27 B6**

Swindon

Barbury Castle Country Park *Chiseldon* The park, on the northern edge of the Marlborough Downs and within the Wessex Downs Area of Outstanding Natural Beauty, surrounds the Iron Age hillfort after which it is named. The hillfort lies next to the Ridgeway ancient track and the views over the downs from the top are breathtaking. The area is also a local nature reserve. The unimproved chalk grassland is rich in flowers, grasses and insects in summer. ✆01793 490150 🖳www.visitwiltshire.co.uk/swindon/what-to-do/places-to-visit-that-are-free/barbury-castle-country-park **59 A8**

Coate Water Country Park Two reservoirs, the smaller of which forms the heart of a nature reserve and SSSI with woodland and wildflower meadows. Facilities and activities on offer include pitch and putt, orienteering, fishing, cycle hire, mini golf, a paddling pool and birdwatching. Ranger centre, café. ✆01793 490150 🖳www.visitwiltshire.co.uk/swindon/what-to-do/places-to-visit-that-are-free/coate-water-country-park **65 F8**

Torbay

Berry Head Country Park *Brixham* See under 'Nature Reserves' **15 D6**

Wiltshire

Brokerswood Country Park *Westbury* Set in remnant ancient forest, this park has a strong emphasis on conservation with a Woodland Heritage Centre, as well as amusements including a woodland railway, fishing, an undercover play area for toddlers, and an adventure play area and play trails for older children. ✆01373 822238 🖳www.brokerswood.net **50 A1**

Nature reserves, national parks and conservation areas

Bath & NE Somerset

Chew Valley Lake (Avon Wildlife Trust) *Chew Magna* 83.5 ha (207 acres) of the extensive reed beds at the southern end of the large Chew Valley Reservoir, providing habitat for songbirds and wildfowl in summer, spring and autumn migrants and wintering wildfowl and waders.
Osprey may sometimes be seen on migration. There are bird hides (permit needed) and a visitor centre. ✆0117 9177270 🖳www.wildlifetrusts.org **56 D3**

Folly Farm (Avon Wildlife Trust) *Bishop Sutton* An unspoilt 17th-century farm of 101 ha (250 acres), with flower meadows and woodlands (meadows and Dowlings Wood are SSSI). In summer the meadows are full of traditional wild plants and butterflies. Much of Dowlings Wood is old coppiced hazel and the floor is carpeted with spring flowers. Buzzard, great spotted woodpecker and tawny owl may be seen (or heard). ✆0117 9177270 🖳www.wildlifetrusts.org **56 E3**

Cornwall

Golitha Falls NNR (NE) *Liskeard* The 18-ha (44½-acre) reserve is a relic of ancient oak and ash woodland occupying a steep-sided gorge on the southern edge of Bodmin Moor, with the River Fowey flowing through it in a series of spectacular cascades. The area is rich in mosses, lichens and liverworts as well as plants typical of valleys and meadow areas. Noctule, brown long-eared and lesser horseshoe bats roost in the old mine workings and some 30 species of birds breed here. There are more than 80 moth species and a good variety of butterflies. 🖳www.naturalengland.org.uk ✆01872 265710 **9 B7**

Goss Moor NNR (NE) *St Colomb* This 482-hectare reserve is situated in a broad, flat valley basin and has wetland habitats (resulting from tin mining and gravel extraction) and dry heathland, both with a wide variety of plant species. Insects found at the site include some rarities such as the double line moth and the small red damselfly. Nightjars, reed buntings and spotted flycatchers are among the less common birds that breed here, while great grey shrikes, hen harriers and hobbies may be present in winter. ✆01872 265710 🖳www.naturalengland.org.uk **8 C2**

Hayle Estuary (RSPB) *Hayle* The estuary is an important location for overwintering ducks and a good place to watch birds in autumn and winter. ✆01736 711682 🖳www.rspb.org.uk **3 C7**

Helman Tor A 217-ha wetland reserve on the slopes of Helman Tor, incorporating Breney Common and Red Moor Memorial Nature Reserve. The old tin streaming industry created channels that moulded the landscape into areas of wet and dry heathland, grassland, wet woodland and open water that support a rich variety of wildlife. 🖳www.wildlifetrusts.org ✆01872 273939

Marazion Marsh (RSPB) *Marazion* Cornwall's largest reedbed with rare breeding warblers, and a large variety of plants and insects. Rare summer migrants include the spotted crake and aquatic warbler, with birds bitterns overwinter. ✆01736 711682 🖳www.rspb.org.uk **3 D6**

North Predannack Downs (Cornwall Wildlife Trust) *Helston* Set within an SSSI among the beautiful landscape of the Lizard peninsula, this reserve has 40 ha (99 acres) of heathland, wet willow woodland and pools. As well as being home to important plants, there are often dragonflies near the pools and in April and May. Emperor moths can be seen on sunny days. ✆01872 273939 🖳www.wildlifetrusts.org **5 G1**

Tamar Estuary (Cornwall Wildlife Trust) *Saltash* An SSSI and nationally and internationally important area for wintering wildfowl and waders, including nearly 405 ha (1000 acres) of wetland. Birds that may be seen in winter include a large population of avocets, black-tailed godwit, curlew and whimbrel. Otters are known to be in the area. ✆01872 273939 🖳www.wildlifetrusts.org **10 C4**

▼ **The Forest of Dean**
fotoVoyager / iStockphoto.com

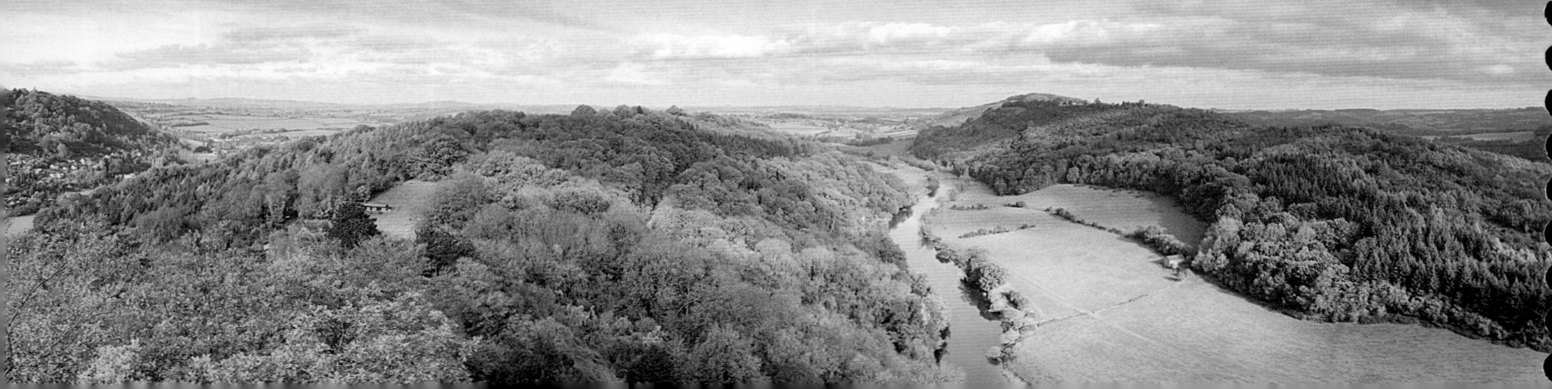

The Lizard NNR (NE) *Helston* The Lizard NNR is a complex of isolated coastal grasslands and heaths and inland heaths: Mullion and Predannack Cliffs are good for early summer flowers and birdlife; Caerthillian is an area of maritime grassland between Kynance and Lizard Point that holds rare clovers; Kynance cove itself has a wide range of rare plants; Goonhilly Down has expanses of heather and gorse as well as adders, buzzards, lizards, owls and many species of dragonfly; Gwendreath and Kennack Sands near Kuggar is a good place to look at the local geology and, sometimes in summer, basking sharks; Main Dale south of St Keverne has plentiful heathers and orchids. ☎01872 265710 🖥www.naturalengland.org.uk **5 G2**

Devon

Axmouth to Lyme Regis Undercliffs NNR (NE) *Axmouth/Lyme Regis* This whole area has been shaped by repeated landslides and cliff falls. The site is also part of Sidmouth to West Bay Special Area of Conservation and of the East Devon Area of Outstanding Natural Beauty. The site's importance lies in its geology, fossils and mosaic of different habitats. 🖥www.naturalengland.org.uk ☎01392 889770 **23 C7**

Aylesbeare Common (RSPB) *Aylesbeare* A small area of heathland in East Devon that provides good habitat for rare Dartford warblers, nightjars and stonechats. There are also good numbers of butterflies, damselflies and dragonflies. ☎01395 233655 🖥www.rspb.org.uk **22 B3**

Bystock Pools (Devon Wildlife Trust) *Budleigh Salterton* An area of heathland, grassland, woods, bogland and a small lake forming part of an SSSI. The heathland is gradually being reclaimed from scrub. It is home to a variety of heathland birds and flowers, damselflies and dragonflies as well as rare reptiles. ☎01392 279244 🖥www.wildlifetrusts.org **22 D2**

Chudleigh Knighton Heath (Devon Wildlife Trust) *Bovey Tracey* An SSSI and nature reserve of 42 ha (104 acres) of wet and dry heathland, scrub and small ponds. Insects include wood ants and narrow-headed ants, dragonflies, glow worms and some rare butterflies. There is a good variety of heathland birds and all 9 of Britain's reptile and amphibian species may also be found here. 🖥www.wildlifetrusts.org ☎01392 279244 **21 E6**

Dart Valley (Devon Wildlife Trust) *Ashburton* This reserve covers more than 290 ha (716 acres) of upland moor and wooded valley, and lies within an SSSI. It has a rich range of wildlife, including three species of woodpecker, dipper, several rare species of butterfly, the extremely rare blue ground beetle and otters. ☎01392 279244 🖥www.wildlifetrusts.org **14 A1/2**

Dartmoor National Park *Dartmoor* Designated a National Park in 1951, Dartmoor NP covers 954 sq km (368 sq miles) of primarily moorland, together with farmland, forest and woodland. There are over 720 km (nearly 450 miles) of accessible roads, tracks and paths. It is characterised by the granite of its tors and its high open moorland, dotted with more than 10,000 menhirs, tombs and other ancient monuments. There are several nature reserves and SSSIs within the park. It is home to a wide range of otherwise rare plants and animals. However, its best-known inhabitants are the ponies. 🖥www.dartmoor-npa.gov.uk ☎01822 890414 **20 D2**

Dawlish Warren NNR *Dawlish Warren* This important site is jointly owned and managed by the Teignbridge District Council and the Devon Wildlife Trust. It has a wide range of habitats, from mudflats where thousands of waders feed, to sand dunes. It is internationally important for its wintering bird populations. Its vast list of plant species includes the endemic Warren crocus. It is a Special Area of Conservation and a Ramsar site as part of the Exe Estuary. ☎01392 279244 🖥www.wildlifetrusts.org **22 E1**

Dunsdon (Devon Wildlife Trust) *Holsworthy* Dunsdon contains a type of pasture known locally as culm grassland, a marshy vegetation that grows well over the slates and shales of the area. There are nearly 200 species of flowering plant, liverworts and mosses, 26 butterfly species, a wide variety of moths, damselflies and dragonflies. More than 50 bird species have been recorded, including breeding herons, buzzards, rare songbirds, wintering snipe, owl, woodcock and curlew. Mammals include roe deer, badgers and dormice. ☎01392 279244 🖥www.wildlifetrusts.org **31 E5**

Dunsford (Devon Wildlife Trust) *Dunsford* Part of a larger SSSI and lying within the Dartmoor National Park, this reserve consists of 57 ha (140 acres) of river valley woodland, flood plain, scrub and heathy rocky slopes. This variety of habitats means that there is a huge number of different plants. In spring there is a spectacular display of wild daffodils on the floodplain. Animals that can be seen include many species of butterflies, dragonflies, wood ants and wood crickets, woodland birds, fallow deer, otters and dormice, as well as mink. ☎01392 279244 🖥www.wildlifetrusts.org **21 C6**

East Dartmoor NNR (NE) *Bovey Tracey* Yarner Wood, Trendlebere Down and the Bovey Valley Woodlands make up an internationally important western oakwood. The heathlands at Yarner Wood and Trendlebere Down add diversity. Birdlife at the latter includes nightjars, Dartford warblers and stonechats. The Bovey Valley Woodlands are home to a number of rare butterflies and the River Bovey has dippers, dragonflies and otters. ☎01392 889770 🖥www.naturalengland.org.uk **21 E5**

Haldson (Devon Wildlife Trust) *Dolton* A handsome reserve of 57 ha (140 acres) of valley woodlands, meadows and marsh and a stretch of the River Torridge. It is an SSSI. In spring the mixed woodland floors are carpeted with flowers. The real attraction, however, is the possibility of seeing otters. 🖥www.wildlifetrusts.org ☎01392 279244 **32 D4**

Hawkswood (Devon Wildlife Trust) *Honiton* Around 4 ha (10 acres) of north-facing mosaic of heath and grassland with areas of birch scrub. There are also small plantations of beech and rhododendron hedge. The lower areas have a good variety of bog plants and there is a particularly rich variety of fungi. In summer, there is a good population of butterflies. ☎01392 279244 🖥www.wildlifetrusts.org **23 A5**

Little Bradley Ponds (Devon Wildlife Trust) *Bovey Tracey* Two ponds in old clay workings, surrounded by 4 ha (10 acres) of mainly grassland. This reserve is particularly noted for its insects, including two species of water scorpion, 20 species of dragonfly, grasshoppers, bush crickets and rare butterflies. Keep to the rights of way. 🖥www.wildlifetrusts.org ☎01392 279244 **21 E6**

Lundy NNR (Landmark Trust) *Bristol Channel* Access is by boat from Bideford or Ilfracombe. The island boasts a wide variety of migratory seabirds, Lundy ponies and a spectacular landscape. Lundy Marine Nature Reserve (MNR) was the first designated Marine Nature Reserve. It encompasses the shores and sea around Lundy and contains spectacular marine plants and animals, including seals. ☎01271 863636 🖥www.lundyisland.co.uk **42 B2**

Marsland (Devon Wildlife Trust) *Welcombe* Marsland is a very large reserve on the northern border of Devon and Cornwall. Occupying two adjacent valleys and extending several miles inland from a dramatic coastline, this inspiring site offers something for everyone. Animals include dormice, butterflies in the sunnier areas and damselflies and dragonflies in the wet areas. Otters may be in the area. Keep to the public rights of way. 🖥www.wildlifetrusts.org ☎01392 279244 **30 C4**

North Devon Voluntary Marine Conservation Area (Devon Wildlife Trust) *Combe Martin* The area stretches from Hangman Point in the east to Down End in Croyde in the west, covering a 34-km (21-mile) long strip from the cliff base out to the 20m depth contour. Wildlife includes corals, rockpool species and in summer, occasional basking sharks. ☎01392 279244 🖥www.wildlifetrusts.org **42 D3/ 43 B6**

Rackenford and Knowstone (Devon Wildlife Trust) *Knowestone* An important area of culm grassland with a rich mix of bog, heath, wet grassland and scrub, which is particularly important for butterflies. It is common land and the grazing cattle should not be disturbed. Birds include curlew, stonechat and whinchat, and jack snipe, snipe and woodcock in winter. There are also red and roe deer. ☎01392 279244 🖥www.wildlifetrusts.org **34 B1**

Ruggadon Middlepark (Devon Wildlife Trust) *Trusham* This 3.1-ha (7½-acre) reserve consists of sloping wildflower meadow, wet grass-land and a copse of mainly oak, the floor of which is carpeted with flowers in spring. There are good numbers of butterflies and woodland birds, as well as badgers and deer. ☎01392 279244 🖥www.wildlifetrusts.org **21 D7**

Scanniclift Copse (Devon Wildlife Trust) *Christow* An ancient coppiced woodland of 8 ha (20 acres) that lies on a steep slope in the Teign valley. Keep to the circular path. Tree and shrub species include ash, blackthorn, beech, hazel, holly, hornbeam and coppiced oak The flowers that can be seen at various times include bluebells, wood anemones, wild garlic, sweet woodruff and enchanter's nightshade. Insects include fritillary butterflies and rare beetles. There is also a good range of breeding woodland birds, including, in some years, redstarts. ☎01392 279244 🖥www.wildlifetrusts.org **21 C6**

Slapton Ley NNR (Field Studies Council) *Slapton* This reserve is an important stopping-off point for migrating and wintering birds as it includes a large freshwater lake, which is separated from the sea by a shingle bar. Unusual plants here include strapwort and there is an enormous range of fungi, some of which appear to be unique to the area. Birds include the rare Cetti's warbler. This reserve is managed by the Field Studies Council on behalf of the Whitley Wildlife Conservation Trust. 🖥www.field-studies-council.org ☎01548 580685**13 D7**

Stapleton Mire (Devon Wildlife Trust) *Stibb Cross* A rich area of culm grassland and wet and dry woodland. There is a wide variety of butterflies, wintering woodcock and snipe may be seen and roe deer are present throughout the year. ☎01392 279244 🖥www.wildlifetrusts.org **32 D1**

Stowford Moor (Devon Wildlife Trust) *East Putford* Stowford Moor is an important area of 19 ha (47 acres) of culm grassland. It is a nationally important site for heath spotted orchids, as well a rich in other plants. In summer, there are plenty of butterflies, among other insects. Mammals include roe deer and several species of bats. ☎01392 279244 🖥www.wildlifetrusts.org **31 C7**

Venn Ottery (Devon Wildlife Trust) *Venn Ottery* This reserve is part of the East Devon Pebblebed Heaths, which are an SSSI and Special Area of Conservation. It has large areas of wet and dry heathland, some raised bog, patches of birch and willow scrub, sallow carr and wet woodland. There is a range of plant species, including butterwort and oblong-leaved sundew (both of which are insect-eaters) in the raised bog. There are several species of dragonflies and butterflies, the birdlife includes stonechat and Dartford warbler and mammals include muntjac deer and dormice. ☎01392 279244 🖥www.wildlifetrusts.org **22 B3**

Warleigh Point (Devon Wildlife Trust) *Plymouth* A beautiful area of coastal oak woodland overlooking the Tamar estuary, with a mixture of trees and shrubs and flowers. The short-winged conehead (a very uncommon species of cricket) is a speciality. Among the birds, little egret can sometimes be seen. ☎01392 279244 🖥www.wildlifetrusts.org **10 C4**

Wembury Voluntary Marine Conservation Area (Devon Wildlife Trust) *Wembury* A length of 6.4 km (4 miles) of shore and adjacent coastal waters with a variety of wildlife habitats. Specialities include the bloody-eyed velvet swimming crab and other rockpool species. There are interactive displays in the Wembury Marine Centre. ☎01752 862538 01392 279244 🖥www.wildlifetrusts.org **11 F6**

Dorset

Brownsea Island (Dorset Wildlife Trust) *near Poole* A 100-ha (250-acre) island reserve and SSSI, with Scots and maritime pine woodlands, lakes with reedbeds and some wetland carr with sallow and alder; and a brackish lagoon. It is particularly well known for its red squirrel population, but also has breeding colonies of common and sandwich terns, a large heronry and thousands of wintering wildfowl and waders. Access, which is limited by numbers, is by ferry, via the National Trust land, for guided or self-guided tours. 🖥www.wildlifetrusts.org ☎01305 264620 **27 C7**

Fontmell Down (Dorset Wildlife Trust) *Fontmell Magna* An SSSI and reserve consisting of 58 ha (145 acres) of chalk downland, scattered scrub and woodland. It is rich in typical downland flowers and butterflies. ☎01305 264620 🖥www.wildlifetrusts.org **39 C7**

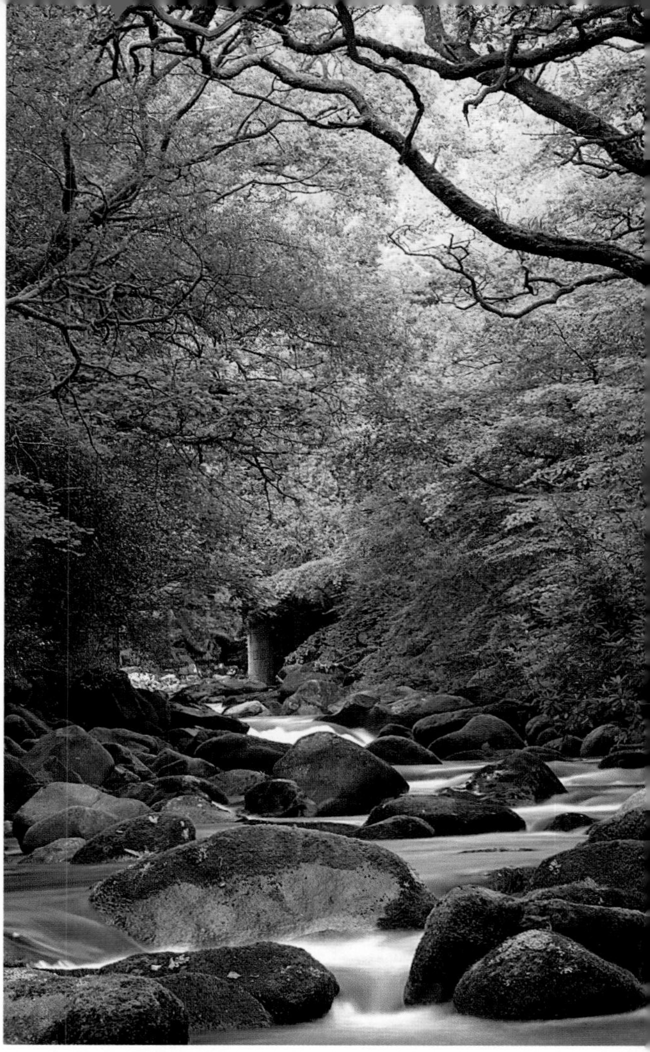

▲ **A woodland stream on Dartmoor**
Richard Loader /iStockphoto.com

Hambledon Hill NNR (NE) *Blandford Forum* The hilltop is encircled by an Iron Age earthwork and there are also several Neolithic features. The chalk grassland's thin infertile soils support a variety of typical grasses, sedges and flowers, particularly on the steep south and west facing slopes. Butterflies include the chalkhill blue and the even rarer adonis blue. ☎01929 557450 🖥www.naturalengland.org.uk **39 D6**

Hartland Moor NNR (NE) *Wareham* Hartland Moor NNR (243 ha/600 acres) is a superb example of an extensive heathland site. The NNR covers an entire drainage basin and is unique in having a Y-shaped bog system which includes both acid and alkaline drainage systems. Heathland is a rare and threatened habitat, and many of the species of plants and animals found on Hartland are equally rare. Typical plants found on site are ling, cross-leaved heath, bell heather, bog asphodel, white beak sedge, western gorse and rarities such as Dorset heath, marsh gentian and bog orchid. Heathland insects include rare heath and large marsh grasshoppers, and the site supports such birds as Dartford warbler, hobby, meadow pipit, stonechat, nightjar and hen harrier. ☎01929 557450 🖥www.naturalengland.org.uk **27 C6**

Higher Hide Heath (Dorset Wildlife Trust) *Wareham* An area of 40 ha (100 acres) of Dorset lowland heath and old sand and gravel workings. It is an SSSI. Plants include bog mosses, sundews and pale butterworts in the wet heath (the last two are carnivorous), and the dry heath is dominated by heathers and heaths. Insects include dragonflies, damselflies, emperor moths, butterflies and bog bush crickets. Sand lizards and smooth snakes are sometimes seen. Nightjars and Dartford warblers nest. ☎01305 264620 🖥www.wildlifetrusts.org **26 B4**

Hog Cliff NNR (NE) *Maiden Newton* A chalk downland reserve made up of three separate sites. The grassland supports a wide range of grasses, herbs and flowering plants as well as fungi, and butterflies. 🖥www.naturalengland.org.uk ☎01929 557450 **25 A7**

Holt Heath NNR (NE) *Ferndown* This is one of Dorset's largest remaining areas of lowland heathland. Holt Forest and Holt Wood are also part of the reserve. A mixture of habitats includes dry heath, wet heath and mire and sundews are among the rarer plants. It is a good area for Dartford warbler, nightjar, stonechat and breeding curlews. All six of Britain's reptile species are found here. 🖥www.naturalengland.org.uk ☎01929 557450 **40 F4**

Lodmoor (RSPB) *Weymouth* A grazing marsh with ditches, shallow pools and reedbeds. It is a prime site for watching autumn migrants, such as swallows, departing, in winter there are good numbers of wildfowl and waders, including bitterns. There is a large breeding colony of common terns and bearded tits and Cetti's warblers are present all year. ☎01305 778313 🖥www.rspb.org.uk **25 D8**

Morden Bog NNR (NE) *Wareham* A large valley bog that lies within the pine plantations of Wareham forest. The bog has rare plants, including sundews and bladderworts, which prey on the smaller insects, and many dragonflies. The dry heathland to the north has typical birds and reptiles such as sand lizard and smooth snake. 🖥www.naturalengland.org.uk ☎01929 557450 **27 B5**

Radipole Lake (RSPB) *Weymouth* In the centre of Weymouth, this reserve has reedbeds, open water and flood meadows. In autumn there are large numbers of migrant birds, wildfowl are around in winter and there is a variety of songbirds in summer. 🖥www.rspb.org.uk ☎01305 778313 **25 D8**

Stoborough Heath NNR (NE) *Wareham* The habitat is made up of dry heath, mire and acid grassland which management is helping to revert to heath. Plants found here include the rare bog orchid, while insects include the wartbiter cricket and a range of dragonflies. In spring and summer skylarks fill the air with song. ☎01929 557450 🖥www.naturalengland.org.uk **27 C5**

Studland Beach and Nature Reserve (NT) *Studland* The reserve includes 5 km (3 miles) of sandy beaches, as well as bogs, a freshwater lake (Little Sea), heathland, scrub, woodland and sand dunes. In

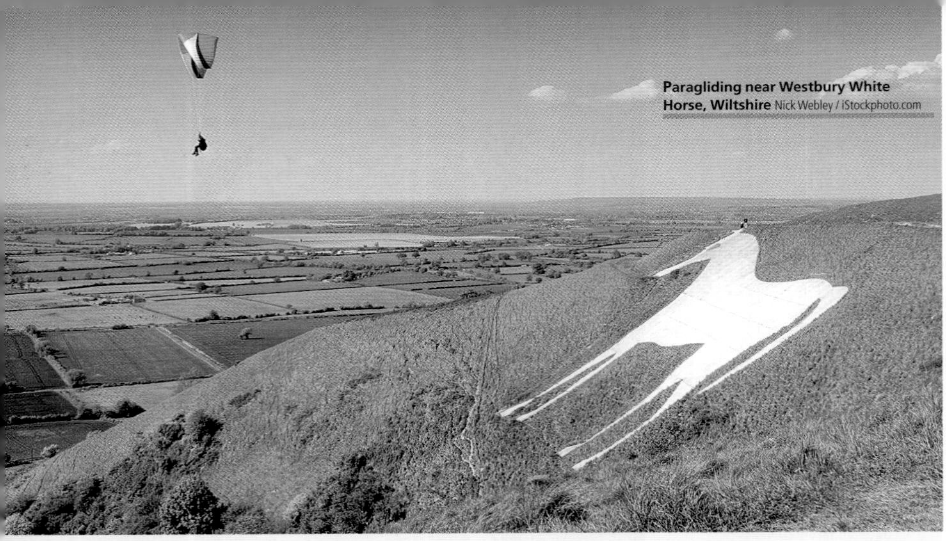

Paragliding near Westbury White Horse, Wiltshire Nick Webley / iStockphoto.com

Chalk carvings

Figures cut into chalk hillsides are a well-known feature of the south-western landscape.

Dorset

Cerne Abbas Giant (NT) *Just to the N of Cerne Abbas* 55-m (180-ft) chalk figure of a man, which some believe dates back to 1500 BC but is not mentioned in historical records until the late 17th century. **38 F3**

Wiltshire

Alton Barnes *On Walker's Hill, 1.2 km (¾ mile) N of Alton Barnes* Horse figure cut in 1812. **59 D7**

Broad Town *0.8 km (½ mile) NE of Broad Town* Horse figure thought to have been cut in 1864 but may be older. **59 A6**

Cherhill *Cherhill Down, nr Oldbury Castle hillfort* Horse cut in 1780. At various times the eye was formed from old glass bottles but is currently made of concrete. **59 C5**

Devizes *Nr Oliver's Castle hillfort, N of Devizes* Horse carved in 1999 as a mirror image of one cut in 1845 which is no longer visible. **58 D5**

Fovant Chalk Badges *On Fovant Down, 1.2 km (¾ mile) SE of Fovant* Regimental badges carved by solders camped in the area during WWI, 1914-1918. **50 F5**

Hackpen Hill *2.4 km (1½ miles) SE of Broad Hinton* Horse figure cut in 1838, probably to mark the coronation of Queen Victoria. **59 B7**

Marlborough *Off the A345 Granham Hill SW of Marlborough* Horse cut in 1804 by pupils from a local school. **59 C8**

Pewsey *On Pewsey Hill, 2 km (1¼ miles) S of the town* Horse figure cut 1937 to close to the site of an earlier one cut in 1785 which is no longer visible. **59 E8**

Westbury *On Westbury Hill, close to Bratton Camp hillfort* A horse carved in the late 17th-century, no longer truly a chalk figure as it has been concreted over. **50 A2**

summer all 6 British reptile species can be found here and in winter there are large wildfowl and wader populations. Godlingston Heath has large numbers of Dartford warblers, nightjars and all 6 British reptile species. Wintering waders feed at low tide and rest at the north end of Studland beach at high tide. Little egrets are present all winter. The heathland is also home to bees, dragonflies, grasshoppers and wasps. 01929 450259 www.nationaltrust.org.uk. **27 D7**

The Valley of Stones NNR (NE) *Littlebredy* The chalk grassland slopes are rich in butterflies such as adonis blue, and wild flowers such as autumn gentian. The stones after which the valley is named support many lichens, some of them very rare. www.naturalengland.org.uk 01929 557450 **25 C6**

Gloucestershire

Ashleworth Ham and Meerend Thicket (Gloucestershire Wildlife Trust) *Ashleworth* A good site for birdwatchers with 41 ha (101 acres) of meadow in the Severn's floodplain and a steep wooded bank. The meadow forms part of an SSSI. In winter thousands of mallard, teal and wigeon may be seen here, as can Bewick swans, fieldfares, goldeneye, great crested and little grebes, peregrines, pintail, pochard, shoveler and tufted ducks. Migrants include snipe, which also nest here, together with curlews, lapwings and redshank. 01452 383333 www.wildlifetrusts.org **70 B2**

Betty Daw's Wood (Gloucestershire Wildlife Trust) *Four Oaks* An ancient sessile oak wood, best known for its spectacular spring show of wild daffodils, wood anemone, bluebells and primroses. A box scheme has encouraged marsh tits, nuthatches and treecreepers and pied and spotted flycatchers to nest. Nightingales are sometimes heard. 01452 383333 www.wildlifetrusts.org **69 B7**

Chedworth (Gloucestershire Wildlife Trust) *Chedworth* A fragment of ancient Cotswold beechwood around a section of disused railway track, next to the Roman villa (see under 'Ancient Monuments'). Plants include autumn gentian, bluebell, primrose, wayfaring tree and wood spurge. There are also butterflies and moths typical of limestone grassland areas. Blackcap, woodcock and wood warblers are among the birds that can be seen, as can adders, bats, dormice, fallow deer, lizards and Roman snails. 01452 383333 www.wildlifetrusts.org **71 E7**

Chosen Hill (Gloucestershire Wildlife Trust) *Churchdown* The reserve lies on the edge of the Cotswold scarp and contains areas of ancient woodland with ash, field maple hazel and oak, conifers, grazed grassland and scrub. The woodland floor has a spectacular show of bluebells each spring. The grassland has a small colony of bee orchids. Birdlife includes linnets and little owls. 01452 383333 www.wildlifetrusts.org **70 D3**

Clarke's Pool Meadow (Gloucestershire Wildlife Trust) *Blakeney* An SSSI and reserve, this is one of the finest surviving traditional hay meadows in the county. There are thousands of green-winged orchids in May, together with adder's tongue, common twayblade, cowslip and pignut. In late summer the plants include fairy flax, field scabious, quaking-grass and yellow-rattle. Keep to the edge of the meadow. 01452 383333 www.wildlifetrusts.org **63 A5**

Cotswold Commons and Beechwoods NNR (NE) *Whiteway* The reserve contains some of Britain's finest beechwoods and comprises three main sites: Buckholt Woods, Cranham Common and Edge Common. There is also a variety of other broad-leaved trees and a range of under-storey species, as well as typical insects and bird species. 01531 638500 www.naturalengland.org.uk **70 E4**

Elliott (Swift's Hill) (Gloucestershire Wildlife Trust) *Stroud* A typical limestone grassland area which is renowned for its orchids and geology. Eleven orchid species regularly occur including autumn lady's-tresses, bee, fragrant and pyramidal, among many other flowers. Butterflies such as the dingy skipper and green hairstreak may be seen as can some rare grasshoppers. Reptiles include common lizards and slow worms. Breeding birds include green woodpeckers, meadow and tree pipits, skylarks and swifts. The old quarry is rich in fossils and is an SSSI for Middle Jurassic geology. 01452 383333 www.wildlifetrusts.org **64 A2**

Midger (Gloucestershire Wildlife Trust) *Lower Kilcott* An ancient woodland in a hidden valley, with typical plants such as bluebell, herb paris, spindle and wood anemone. Dormice are present, as are grey wagtails, nutches, treecreepers and great spotted woodpeckers. Good for fungi in autumn. 01452 383333 www.wildlifetrusts.org **63 E7**

Nagshead (RSPB) *Parkend* A small woodland reserve that is primarily known for its breeding pied flycatchers. Buzzards, hawfinches, ravens and wood warblers are among the other species that may also be seen. www.rspb.org.uk 01594 562852 **69 F6**

Slimbridge (Wildfowl and Wetlands Trust) *Slimbridge* On the shores of the Severn Estuary, this is a vital wintering area for thousands of geese and other wildfowl, such as Bewick's swans. It is also the headquarters of the Wildfowl and Wetlands Trust, and has a large visitor centre. 01453 890333 www.wwt.org.uk **63 B6**

Strawberry Banks (Gloucestershire Wildlife Trust) *Chalford* The limestone grassland reserve has been an SSSI since 1993 and includes plants such as bee, common spotted and greater butterfly orchids, as well as wild columbine, while in late summer , autumn gentians and pyramidal orchids can be seen. Butterflies include the small blue, green hairstreak, the rare chalkhill blue and silver-washed fritillary. 01452 383333 www.wildlifetrusts.org **64 B3**

Whelford Pools (Gloucestershire Wildlife Trust) *Fairford* A wetland site of 12.3 ha (31 acres) of old gravel pits. In winter the lakes are a haven for wildfowl, and in summer eleven species of dragonflies and damselflies breed here. 01452 383333 www.wildlifetrusts.org **65 B8**

North Somerset

Leigh Woods NNR (NT) *Bristol* The site comprises two main habitats – mixed, previously coppiced, broad-leaved woodland and dry limestone grassland. There are some rare trees in the woodland and a wealth of fungi. The grassland supports a wide variety of plant species, while ravens and peregrines nest in the gorge. www.nationaltrust.org.uk 0177 9731645 **56 B3**

Walborough (Avon Wildlife Trust) *Weston-super-Mare* A mixed reserve consisting of mudflats bordering the River Axe, which provides feeding and roosting habitats for wildfowl and waders. The saltmarsh area is rich in flowers and bird- and insectlife. The wet grassland and scrub are good hiding places for wintering birds and the limestone turf of Walborough Hill is rich in lime-loving wild flowers and butterflies, including the chalkhill blue. 0117 9177270 www.wildlifetrusts.org **55 E6**

Weston Big Wood (Avon Wildlife Trust) *Portishead* Avon's largest remnant of ancient woodland at 38 ha (94 acres); it is an SSSI. It has a broad range of trees and flowers. The open areas of ride are good for butter-flies in summer and there is a wide range of woodland birds. Bats and badgers are also found here. Keep to the ride or paths and avoid the quarry wall. www.wildlifetrusts.org 0117 9177270 **55 A9**

Somerset

Bridgwater Bay NNR (NE) *Cannington* This is a large (2559-ha/6323-acre) reserve on the north Somerset coast covering the river Parrett's lower reaches and estuary, as well as the coast between Burnham-on-Sea and Lilstock. It is also a Special Protection Area and Ramsar site and part of the area may be given Special Area of Conservation status. The reserve's intertidal mudflats, saltmash, sandflats and shingle provide feeding, nesting and roosting sites for nearly 200 species of birds. 01823 283211 www.naturalengland.org.uk **46 B5**

Catcott Complex (Somerset Wildlife Trust) *Burtle* The Lows, restored to wet grassland in 1991, flood in winter and harbour thousands of wildfowl and waders. Marsh harriers are often present. Catcott Heath has areas of carr woodland, bog myrtle scrub and tall fen and purple moor grass. There is an interesting range of flowers in the areas that are now managed. The pools have great crested newts and raft spiders. 01823 652400 www.wildlifetrusts.org **47 C8**

Dunkery and Horner Woods NNR (NT) *Porlock* Horner Woods is an ancient oakwood with a range of ferns, lichens, liverworts and mosses. 14 of the UK's 16 bat species occur, as well as a wide range of woodland birds. The upland area has rare plants; lots of insect life, including heath fritillaries, and its birdlife includes curlew, ring ouzel, stonechat and whinchat. 01643 862452 (Holnicote Estate office) www.nationaltrust.org.uk **44 C4**

Ebbor Gorge NNR (NE) *Wells* This reserve is part of the Mendip Woodlands Special Area of Conservation and sits on a scarp that is cut by two valleys: Hope Wood valley and the dry limestone gorge of Ebbor Gorge itself. Most of the reserve is ancient and secondary woodland but there are also areas of limestone grassland. Hope Wood Valley has large numbers of ferns, fungi, lichens, liverworts and mosses. The grasslands have a good range of wild flowers while the gorge provides roosting sites for greater and lesser horseshoe bats. www.naturalengland.org.uk 01823 283211 **48 B2**

Exmoor National Park Designated a National Park in 1954, Exmoor covers 693 sq km (267 sq miles). About a quarter of the land remains as open heath and moorland with much of the rest having been turned into arable or grazing land. It is home to more than 30 native mammals, including fallow, red and roe deer and Exmoor ponies. Nearly 250 species of birds have been recorded, of which more than 100 breed here, and there are more than 1000 types of flowers and grasses as well as more than 1750 insect species. The moor has been exploited by humans for some 10,000 years, and there are more than 4000 archaeological sites, including Neolithic standing stones and Iron Age hillforts. As well as moorland, there are some patches of ancient woodland, spectacular coastal cliffs and more than 480 km (300 miles) of rivers, which near the coast flow through deep wooded valleys known locally as combes. www.exmoor-nationalpark.gov.uk 07970 099111 **44 C2**

Ham Wall NNR (RSPB) *Meare* In the area known as the Avalon Marshes within Somerset Levels and Moors, this internationally important 190-ha (470-acre) wetland has been specially created from old peat diggings. Species that have colonised include marsh harrier, garganey, reed bunting and, in winter, bitterns. Water voles and otters may sometimes be seen. 01458 860494 www.rspb.org.uk **47 D9**

Shapwick Heath NNR (NE) *Shapwick* This reserve is a major wetland forming a large part of the Avalon Marshes. Its habitats include traditionally managed grassland, reedbeds in old peat-extraction sites, open water, ferny wet woodland, fen and scrub. The water levels are controlled and the grassland grazed to benefit the plant- and wildlife, which includes otters, bitterns, dragonflies. Remnants of a Neolithic track – the Sweet Track – survive. 01458 860120 www.naturalengland.org.uk **47 D8**

West Sedgemoor (RSPB) *Fivehead* This reserve is within the Somerset Levels and Moors. Large numbers of waders breed and in winter the area is populated by thousands of wildfowl and waders. 01458 252805 www.rspb.org.uk **36 B5**

Torbay

Berry Head to Sharkham Point NNR *Brixham* The two areas of the reserve are on the south side of Torbay and are separated by St Mary's Bay. Caves quarried in the limestone of Berry Head provide breeding roosts for both greater and lesser horseshoe bats, while the sea cliffs house a guillemot colony and scrubby areas behind the cliffs are home to breeding cirl buntings and whitethroat, among others. There are many rare plants here, including orchids. Common dolphin and harbour porpoise can sometimes be seen offshore. The reserve is owned by the Torbay Coast and Countryside Trust. www.countryside-trust.org.uk 01803 60603515 **D6**

Wiltshire

Coombe Bissett Down (Wiltshire Wildlife Trust) *Salisbury* This chalk grassland reserve of nearly 35 ha (90 acres) is tucked away in a quiet secluded valley on the downs south of Salisbury. It is basically a chalk downland reserve with species-rich chalk banks and flat areas caused by ancient ploughing. There are also small areas of scrub and a beech woodland. This is one of the best sites in Britain for the burnt orchid; other scarce plants include dwarf sedge. Adonis blue, chalkhill blue, small blue and brown argus butterflies are seen here. www.wildlifetrusts.org 01380 725670 **40 A5**

Fyfield Down NNR (NE) *Marlborough* Part of a World Heritage Site because of its archaeological links – particularly its sarsen stones, which were brought here by glaciers – Fyfield Down is on a high plateau of chalk grassland. Keep to the public rights of way. www.naturalengland.org.uk 01380 726344 **59 B7**

Langley Wood NNR (NE) *Redlynch* An extensive tract of ancient, mainly oak, forest with several very rare tree species. Dormice, and five species of deer may be seen and there is a good range of woodland birds. www.naturalengland.org.uk 01380 726344 **41 B7**

North Meadow Special Area of Conservation (part NE) *Cricklade* One of the finest traditionally managed lowland hay meadows in Europe, North Meadow has a great variety of wildflowers, including Britain's largest population of wild snake's head fritillaries. In spring and summer the meadow is alive with flowers, insects and birds. During winter, when the meadow usually floods, it is a haven for wildfowl. www.naturalengland.org.uk 01380 72634465 **D6**

Pewsey Downs NNR (NE) *Pewsey* On the southern edge of the Marlborough Downs overlooking the Vale of Pewsey, this reserve includes three hills: Milk, Walkers and Knap and it is also a Special Area of Conservation because it is on one of the best areas of chalk downland in England, with a wide range of typical chalkland plants and butterflies. 01380 726344 www.naturalengland.org.uk **59 D7**

Smallbrook Meadows (Wiltshire Wildlife Trust) *Warminster* These water meadows were created two or three centuries ago – using a system of sluices from the nearby streams they were flushed with warm, silty water to promote an early growth of spring grass for sheep grazing. The reserve has plants that are now generally rare, such as water avens and ragged robin. In spring there are marsh marigolds, yellow flag and then great willow herb. In summer, area is shoulder-high with meadowsweet, which attracts butterflies. There are many dragonflies and damselflies. The damp willow woodland is full of mosses, lichens and ferns. 01380 725670 www.wildlifetrusts.org **50 C2**

Other natural features

Cornwall

Land's End *Sennan* The westernmost point of England, this is an 18-m (60-ft) cliff with beautiful cliff-top walks to both north and south. On a clear day, the views extend almost 40 km (25 miles). Visitor attraction with interactive exhibits. **2 E2**

► **The Royal Crescent, Bath**
James Hughes / Alamy

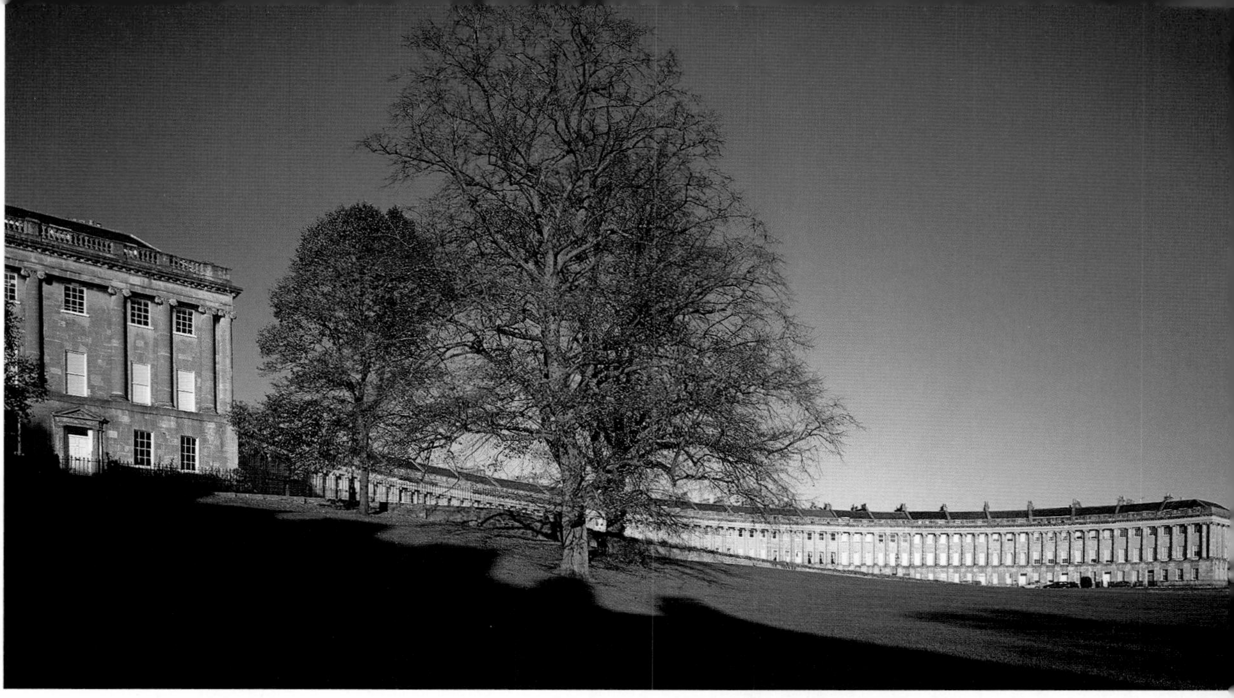

Lizard and Kynance Cove (NT) *Lizard* A dramatic stretch of south Cornwall's coast. As well as cliff-top walks, rare wildflowers, Looe Pool and the beautiful Kynance Bay, the area is home to Britain's rarest breeding bird, the chough. www.nationaltrust.org.uk 01326 561407 **5 H1**

Devon and Dorset

Jurassic Coast *Devon and Dorset* The Jurassic Coast World Heritage Site stretches from Orcombe Point in the west to Swanage in the east. It is an area rich in geology and wildlife and has some of the south coast's most spectacular scenery. Movements in the Earth's crust over millions of years mean that rock layers that originally formed on top of each other now lay side by side with the older rocks in the west and the younger rocks in the east, showing how the area's geology was formed and, in some places, how it is being destroyed. Highlights include fossil-spotting at Charmouth, Lyme Regis and Kimmeridge Bay, the stark grandeur of Portland Bill, beautiful Lulworth Cove and the dramatic coastal scenery of Ladram Bay, Durlston Head and Chesil Beach. There are also good beaches and walks. www.jurassiccoast.com **22–27**

Somerset

Brean Down (NT) *Brean* This coastal headland and cliffs form a dramatic landmark. A network of paths lead the visitor through the rich landscape. At the bottom of a steep walk down the cliffs is Palmerston Fort. Guided walks are sometimes available. 01934 844518 www.nationaltrust.org.uk **55 E5**

Cheddar Gorge *Cheddar* see under 'Family Attractions' **56 F1**

Glastonbury Tor (NT) *Glastonbury* A hill that dominates the Somerset levels and overlooks the Isle of Avalon and Glastonbury. The site is linked to many legends including King Arthur and the Glastonbury Thorn, which was reputed to have been brought here by Joseph of Arimithea. The views from the summit are stunning. 01985 843600 www.nationaltrust.org.uk **48 D2**

Wookey Hole *near Wells* see under 'Family Attractions' **48 B2**

Parks and gardens

Many houses and castles listed elsewhere on these pages also have fine and important gardens.

Bath & NE Somerset

Botanical Gardens *Bath* More than 5000 varieties of plants. Rock garden and pond. 01225 482624 www.cityofbath.co.uk/Parks_rec/body_botanicalgardens.html **57 C7**

Claverton Manor *Claverton* The grounds of the American Museum are a copy of George Washington's formal flower garden at Mount Vernon. 01225 460503 www.americanmuseum.org **57 D7**

Prior Park Landscape (NT) *Bath* Beautiful and intimate, partly restored, 18th-century landscaped garden. 01225 833422 www.nationaltrust.org.uk **57 C7**

Cornwall

Bosvigo *Truro* Enclosed and walled gardens surrounding Georgian house. 01872 275774 www.bosvigo.com **4 B4**

Burncoose Gardens and Nurseries *Gwennap* 12-ha (30-acre) woodland garden. 01209 860316 www.burncoose.co.uk **4 C2**

Caerhays Castle Gardens *St Austell* Informal woodland garden extending some 24 ha (60 acres). 01872 501310 www.caerhays.co.uk **5 B7**

Eden Project *St Austell* Specially created temperature and humidity controlled giant 'biomes' in an ex china-clay pit contain a wide range of plants and fauna from different world regions. This spectacular centre also has interactive displays celebrating the varied life on our planet and show the importance of conserving it for future generations. 01726 811911 www.edenproject.com **8 E3**

Glendurgan Garden (NT) *Mawnan Smith* One of best subtropical gardens in the South West. 01326 250906 www.nationaltrust.org.uk **4 E3**

Long Cross Victorian Gardens *Trelights* Victorian garden in 1 ha (2½ acres). Maze, pets' corner. 01208 880243 www.longcrosshotel.co.uk/gardens.php **16 E4**

Lost Gardens of Heligan *Pentewan* More than 80 acres including kitchen garden, fruit houses. 01726 845100 www.heligan.com **5 A7**

Pinetum Park & Pine Lodge Gardens *St Austell* 12 ha (30 acres) with more than 6000 plants. www.pinetumpark.com 01726 73500 **8 E3**

Prideaux Place *Padstow* Deer park and restored garden 01841 532411 www.prideauxplace.co.uk **16 E3**

Trebah Garden Trust *Mawnan Smith* 10-ha (25-acre) wooded ravine garden in grounds to private beach. 01326 250448 www.trebahgarden.co.uk **4 E3**

Trelissick Garden (NT) *nr Truro* Artistically planted garden and orchard. 01872 862090 www.nationaltrust.org.uk **4 C4**

Trengwainton Garden (NT) *Penzance* Shrub and woodland garden. 01736 363148 www.nationaltrust.org.uk **2 D4**

Trerice (NT) *Nr Newquay* Summer garden, orchard. 01637 875404 www.nationaltrust.org.uk **7 D7**

Devon

Bicton Park Gardens *East Budleigh* Historic gardens. Play areas, museum and train rides. www.bictongardens.co.uk 01395 568465 **22 C3**

Burrow Farm Gardens *Dalwood* 2.8-ha (7-acre) site, part of which was created from ancient Roman clay pit. 01404 831285 www.burrowfarmgardens.co.uk **23 A6**

Dartington Hall *Dartington* Large garden of trees and shrubs. 01803 847100 www.dartingtonhall.com **14 C3**

Escot Park *Ottery St Mary* Wild gardens in 101 ha (250 acres) of landscaped parkland. Currently has the only otters in East Devon. Wild boar enclosures and birds of prey. 3.2 ha (8 acres) of wetlands, maze, adventure playground. 01404 822188 www.escot-devon.co.uk **22 A3**

Lee Ford *Budleigh Salterton* 16 ha (40 acres) of parkland, formal and woodland gardens. 01395 445894 www.leeford.co.uk/id7.html **22 D3**

Marwood Hill Gardens *Marwood* 7.2-ha (18-acre) garden, bog garden. 01271 342528 www.marwoodhillgarden.co.uk **43 D5**

Rosemoor Garden (RHS) *Great Torrington* Rose garden as well as herbaceous borders and a potager 01805 624067 www.rhs.org.uk **32 C2**

Stone Lane Gardens *Chagford* 2-ha (5-acre) landscaped arboretum and water garden. 01647 231311 www.mythicgarden.eclipse.co.uk **20 C4**

Dorset

Abbotsbury Sub-Tropical Gardens *Abbotsbury* Victorian walled gardens in 8 ha (20 acres) of woodland valley. Children's play area. Nature trail. www.abbotsbury-tourism.co.uk 01305 871387 **25 C6**

Bennett's Water Gardens *Weymouth* 2.4 ha (6 acres) of ponds, including collection of more than 150 types of lilies. 01305 785150 www.waterlily.co.uk **25 E7**

Compton Acres Gardens *Canford Cliffs* Series of themed gardens over 6 ha (15 acres) of land. 01202 700778 www.comptonacres.co.uk **27 C8**

Corfe Castle Model Village and Gardens *Corfe Castle* Detailed model of the Corfe Castle and village. Old English country garden. 01929 481234 www.corfecastlemodelvillage.co.uk **27 D6**

Cranborne Manor Garden *Cranborne* 01725 517289 www.cranborne.co.uk **40 D4**

Knoll Gardens *Hampreston* A nationally acclaimed modern garden. 01202 873931 www.knollgardens.co.uk **2 7 A8**

Mapperton Gardens *Beaminster* Terraced hillside gardens with ancient fishponds and summerhouse. 01308 862645 www.mapperton.com **24 A5**

Minterne *Minterne Magna* Large shrub garden. Fine Japanese cherry-blossom display in spring. 01300 341370 www.minterne.co.uk/mjs/gardens.html **38 F3**

Stapehill Abbey Gardens *Stapehill* Award-winning gardens in grounds of restored monastery. 01202 861686 **40 F4**

Gloucestershire

Barnsley House Garden *Barnsley* Vegetable garden, herb garden and fruit trees. Telephone for availability 01285 740000 www.barnsleyhouse.com **65 B6**

Batsford Arboretum *Moreton-in-Marsh* Established 1880s. More than 20 ha (50 acres) with 1500 different species. Waterfall. 01386 701441 www.batsarb.co.uk **77 F6**

Hidcote Manor Garden (NT) *Hidcote Bartrim* Arts and Crafts garden on a hilltop. www.nationaltrust.org.uk 01386 438333 **77 D6**

Kiftsgate Court *Mickleton* Roses. 01386 438777 www.kiftsgate.co.uk **77 D6**

Lydney Park Gardens *Lydney* Extensive gardens. Roman temple site and museum. 01594 845497 www.lydneyparkestate.co.uk **62 B4**

Miserden Park *Miserden* Well established garden. Topiary and parterre. www.misardenpark.co.uk 01285 821303 **70 F4**

Painswick Rococo Garden *Painswick* Ponds, woodland walks, maze, kitchen garden. 01452 813204 www.rococogarden.co.uk **70 E3**

Westbury Court (NT) *Westbury-on-Severn* Formal water garden with canals and yew hedges. 01452 760461 www.nationaltrust.org.uk **69 E8**

Westonbirt – The National Arboretum *Westonbirt* 01666 880220 www.forestry.gov.uk/westonbirt **64 E2**

Scilly Isles

Tresco Abbey *Tresco* Sub-tropical gardens and remains of Benedictine priory. 01720 424108 www.tresco.co.uk **6 B2**

Somerset

Cothay *nr Wellington* Virtually untouched since Edward IV. Small individual gardens. 01823 672283 **35 B6**

East Lambrook Manor *South Petherton* Notable garden. Many unusual plants. 01460 240328 www.eastlambrook.co.uk **37 C6**

Hestercombe Gardens *nr Taunton* Formal garden. 01823 413923 www.hestercombegardens.com **46 F4**

Tintinhull Garden (NT) *nr Yeovil* 17th-century house. 1.6 ha (4 acres) with of formal gardens and an orchard. 01935 823289 www.nationaltrust.org.uk **37 C8**

Wiltshire

Broadleas *Devizes* 3.2 ha (8 acres) of beautiful garden and woodland. 01380 722035 **58 D5**

Heale House Garden *Middle Woodford* 01722 782504 www.healegarden.co.uk **51 D7**

Stourton House Flower Garden *Stourton* Over 1.6 ha (4 acres) of flower gardens. 01747 840417 **49 E7**

The Courts Garden (NT) *Holt* English garden style at its best. Garden includes topiary, water features. 01225 782875 www.nationaltrust.org.uk **58 D2**

The Peto Garden *Bradford-on-Avon* Italian-style manor garden. 01225 863146 www.ifordmanor.co.uk **57 E8**

River cruises and boat rides

Bath & NE Somerset

Bath Narrowboats *Bath* 01225 447276 www.bath-narrowboats.co.uk **57 C7**

Pulteney Cruisers *Bath* 01225 312900 www.bathboating.com **57 D7**

Devon

Dartmouth Boat Trips/Dartmouth River Cruises Dartmouth River, harbour and coastal wildlife cruises. Linked to Dartmouth Steam Railway (see under Family Attractions). 01803 555 872 www.dartmouthrailriver.co.uk **15 E5**

Exmoor Coast Boat Trips *Lynmouth* Along heritage coastline. 01598 753207 **44 B1**

Sound Cruising *Plymouth* www.soundcruising.com 01752 408590 **10 E5**

Stuart Line Cruises *Exmouth* www.stuartlinecruises.co.uk 01395 222144 **22 D2**

Tamar Cruising *Plymouth* 01752 822105 www.tamarcruising.com **10 E5**

Tarka Cruises *Appledore* Pleasure cruises on the Taw Estuary and sea fishing trips. 01237 476191 **42 E4**

Whitestrand Boat Hire *Salcombe* Cruises and self-drive boats available. www.whitestrandboathire.co.uk 01548 843818 **13 E5**

Gloucestershire

Kingfisher Ferries *Tewkesbury* 01684 294088 **70 A3**

Towns and villages

There are many charming and fascinating towns and villages in the regions covered by this atlas. What follows is a selection of some that are particularly worth visiting.

Bath & NE Somerset

Bath Bath became a fashionable spa town in the 18th century and is famous for the Palladian elegance of its squares, terraces and crescents, all built in the local stone. Attractions include the Roman and Regency baths, the abbey, No 1 Royal Crescent, the Assembly Rooms and Guildhall, Bath Postal Museum, Bath Royal Literary and Scientific Institution, the Building of Bath Museum, the Holburne Museum of Art, the Jane Austen Centre, the Fashion Museum, the Museum of East Asian Art, the Roman Baths Museum, the Victoria Art Gallery and The Herschel Museum of Astronomy. Green spaces within the city include the Botanical Gardens, Prior Park Landscape Garden (NT), the Royal Victoria Park and Sydney Gardens. **57 D7**

Bristol

Bristol An old cathedral city and port with historical architecture and a 19th-century university. The city is now a vibrant centre for the arts, with reminders of its mercantile and maritime heritage. Sights include Bristol Cathedral, the Lord Mayor's Chapel, St John's on the Wall, St Mary Redcliffe, the Temple Church (EH), the New Room, the Georgian House, Red Lodge, Thomas Chatterton's house and the SS *Great Britain*. Museums and galleries include the Arnolfini Arts Centre, Bristol Industrial Museum, the British Empire and Commonwealth Museum, the City Museum and Art Gallery, M Shed, and the Maritime Heritage Centre. **56 B4**

Cornwall

Altarnun This is a pretty village and the 15th-century church of St Nonna, known as the cathedral of the moors, is one of best churches in Cornwall. **18 D1**

Bodmin The traditional county town of Cornwall. St Petroc's is the largest medieval church in Cornwall. Other attractions in the town include the Duke of Cornwall's Light Infantry Regiment Museum and the old Bodmin Jail. Lanhydrock (NT), Pencarrow House and Restormel Castle are nearby,

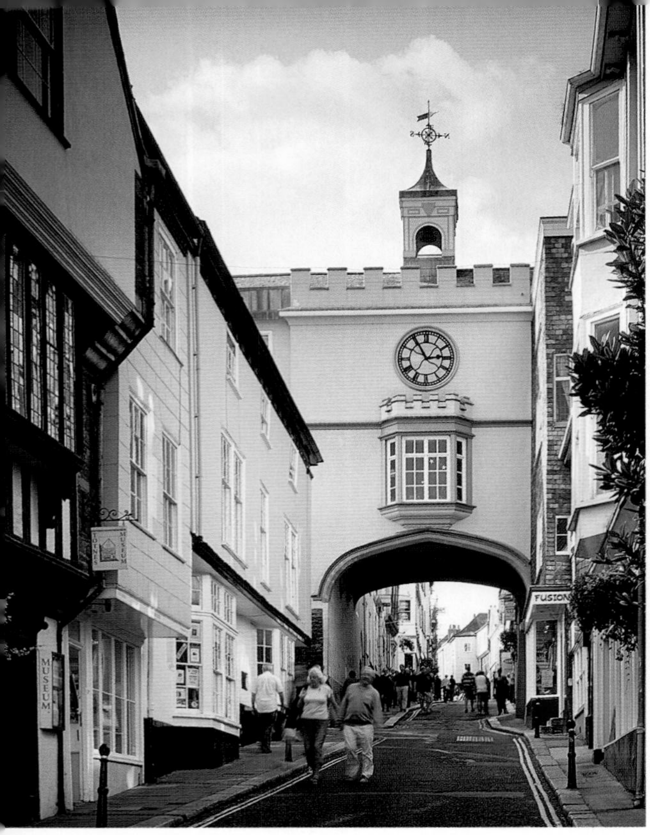

▲ **The Eastgate arch over Fore Street in Totnes, Devon** James Hughes / Alamy

while the mysterious Stripple Stones are on Bodmin moor to the north of the town. **8 B4**

Boscastle Has a small disused harbour (NT), flanked by steep cliffs which provide spectacular views. Within the village is the Museum of Witchcraft and Crackington Haven is a few miles to the north. **17 B6**

Charlestown A handsome harbour village, with a good Shipwreck and Heritage Centre. Nearby attractions include Tregrehan gardens, Wheal Martyn Museum and the Eden Project. **8 E3**

Coverack Charming place with sandy beaches and good windsurfing. **5 G3**

Fowey This former port has a charming square, medieval and Tudor cottages, cobbled streets, a Gothic church dedicated to St Finnbarus and the ruins of St Catherine's Castle (EH). **9 E5**

Launceston A pleasant town that was once capital of Cornwall and has plenty of historical architecture including the ruined Norman castle (EH), St Mary Magdalene's church and Lawrence House (NT), which houses the local museum. **18 D3**

Liskeard Picturesque ancient stannery (tin-mining) and market town on Bodmin Moor, with spacious town square, large Perpendicular church and the Southern Art Gallery. Nearby are St Clarus' church in St Cleer, Trethevy Quoit, King Doniert's Inscribed Stone and the Hurlers stone circles. **9 C8**

Looe Historic little port, now a popular resort and British centre for shark fishing. **9 E8**

Lostwithiel The 13th-century capital of Cornwall. Highlights include the medieval Restormel Castle (EH summer only), Fowey Bridge and Stannery Court and the Guildhall of 1740. **9 D5**

Mevagissey Attractive fishing village with cottages and fine harbour. There is a folk museum in the village and the Lost Gardens of Heligan are a few miles to the north. **5 A8**

Padstow A fishing port on the estuary of the river Camel with attractive medieval houses and a bustling harbour. On May Day the town's traditional celebrations include the 'Obby 'Orse parade. Prideaux Place has good gardens and a deer park and guided tours of the house are sometimes available. **16 E3**

Penzance One of Cornwall's most attractive towns in terms of both architecture and position, set within the curve of Mount's Bay. Nearby are St Michael's Mount, Trengwainton Garden and Lanyon Quoit (both NT) Chysauster and Carn Euny Ancient Villages (both EH) and Men-An-Toi. **3 D5**

Polperro Picturesque fishing village with colour-washed cottages. Like many places in the area, it was renowned in past for smuggling and this is reflected in the village's Smuggling Museum. **9 E7**

Polzeath Sandy resort with Pentire Point (NT) to the north and Trebetherick and Daymer Bay to the south. St Enodoc church is situated in the middle of the local golf course. **16 E3**

St Ives A popular resort town on one of the most charming bays in England. It has thriving artistic connections, reflected in the presence of the Barbara Hepworth Museum and Sculpture Garden and Tate St Ives. Other attractions include the Heritage Museum. The local church is dedicated to St Ia, while the Chapel of St Nicholas is the oldest in the area. **3 B6**

Tintagel One of the most famous places in Cornwall. Village connected with the romantic ruins of Tintagel castle and legend of King Arthur. The church is dedicated to St Materiana. The Old Post Office (NT) is actually a 14th-century manor house that served as a post office in the 19th century. **17 C6**

Truro Situated on the Fal river. Historically important as market centre and port, Truro became a cathedral city in the 19th century. The late 19th- early 20th-century cathedral incorporates some of the 16th-century parish church. There are good gardens at Bosvigo House and Trelissick (NT). Other attractions in the city include the Royal Cornwall Museum **4 B4**

Devon

Barnstaple An ancient port and old trading centre with handsome old buildings and the 15th-century Long Bridge across the River Taw. Within the town are the Museum of Barnstaple & North Devon and St Anne's Chapel and Museum, while Arlington Court (NT) and the gardens of Marwood Hill are within easy reach. **43 E6**

Chagford Quiet and charming old 'Stannary' (tin-mining) town right in the centre of Devon and set in the northern part of Dartmoor. Stone Lane Gardens and Castle Drogo are both northeast of the town. **20 C3**

Clovelly A picturesque fishing village with steep cobbled streets and pretty white cottages. The grounds of Clovelly Court provide views over the coast. **31 B6**

Combe Martin A popular north-coast resort situated at the head of a sheltered valley. Arlington Court (NT) is a few miles to the south. **43 B6**

Exeter Historic cathedral city with medieval walls and the remains of Roman roads. Other buildings include the cathedral, Killerton (NT), the Customs House, the Guildhall and Marker's Cottage (NT). Other things to see include the Bill Douglas Centre and the Royal Albert Memorial Museum and Art Gallery. **21 B8**

Sidmouth Regency style resort situated between reddish cliffs. York Terrace has balconied Georgian houses with wrought-iron railings. Attractions include the Norman Lockyer Observatory and James Lockyer Planetarium. **22 C4**

Totnes One of oldest and most handsome towns in England. It primarily consists of one main street with many Elizabethan houses. Totnes Castle (EH) is at the top of the High Street. The Guildhall is 16th–17th century and the Elizabethan House Museum was built in the 1570s and has a collection of furniture and other domestic objects. Outside the town, Berry Pomeroy Castle (EH) and Dartington Hall gardens are worth visiting. **14 C4**

Dorset

Beaminster Set within the beautiful countryside of northwest Dorset, this is a handsome place set below the extravagantly decorated Gothic St Mary's church, Georgian buildings and picturesque 17th-century cottages. Nearby attractions include Mapperton. **37 F7**

Blandford Forum A market town on the Stour with some fine buildings of 1735–40 by John and William Bastard and a near-contemporary Palladian church. Within the town are Blandford Museum and the The Blandford Fashion Museum, while Milton Abbey is to the southwest and Badbury Rings to the southeast. **39 E7**

Bridport Pleasant little maritime town with attractive main street and 18th-century Town Hall. Believed to have last thatched brewery in the country. **24 B4**

Cerne Abbas Pretty village with the 15th-century gatehouse from a long-gone Benedictine monastery and a small church with a 15th-century screen and wall paintings. The village is most famous for the chalk figure of the Cerne Abbas Giant (NT) on a nearby hill. **38 F3**

Corfe Castle A pretty village clustered around the foot of a hill. Its ruined Norman castle (NT) is spectacular and holds a local museum. The water of the Blue Pool west of the village changes colour and is set within an SSSI. **27 D6**

Cranborne Set in beautiful countryside as known as 'Chaseborough' in novels of Thomas Hardy. Cranborne Manor Gardens were originally laid out by John Tradescant, one of the earliest and greatest plant-hunters. Knowlton Church and Earthworks (NT) consists of a Norman ruin set within the remains of an ancient henge. **40 D4**

Dorchester Dorset's county town. Attractions in and around the town include Wolfeton House, the Dorset County Museum, The Keep Military Museum, Hardy's Cottage (NT), Cloud's Hill (NT) and Max Gate (NT). Evidence of the areas earlier human inhabitants can be seen at Maiden Castle (EH), Maumbury Rings and Poundbury hillfort. **25 B8**

Lyme Regis A charming old resort overlooking Lyme Bay with many Regency buildings remaining from the height of its popularity. Set within the World Heritage Coast, its attractions include the Cobb (with a Marine Aquarium and Cobb History Exhibition), the Town Mill, Dinosaurland, the Philpott Museum, and the Guildhall. The beaches west of the town are popular for fossil-hunting, Lambert's Castle hillfort (NT) is in the hills north of the town and Forde Abbey is on the Somerset border. **24 B1**

Shaftesbury Picturesque old town with abbey ruins, a castle, 12 churches and four market crosses. Shaftesbury's Gold Hill looks over the picturesque Blackmore Vale of North Dorset. There is a small museum and Wardour Castle, Old Wardour Castle and White Sheet Hill are nearby. **39 B7**

Sherborne Handsome stone-built town with a magnificent Abbey Church, the ruined Old Castle, Sherborne Castle, Sherborne Museum and nearby is Sandford Orcas House. **38 C2**

Studland A charming village 4.8 km (3 miles) north of Swanage. Tiny Norman church, pretty bay and Studland nature reserve (NT). West of the village, on the Black Down, is the Agglestone. **27 D7**

Swanage An attractive town at the southern end of beautiful Studland Bay. There is a museum and heritage centre, while at nearby Langton Matravers is the Coach House Museum of Stone crafts and local history. **27 E7**

Wareham An interesting little town, on the river Frome, which was built within Anglo-Saxon earthworks and still has some Saxon walls and St Martin's church (parts of which date to 1020). The Wareham Museum includes a local items dating right back to the Iron Age and a collection of Lawrence of Arabia memorabilia. The Royal Armoured Corps Tank Museum is at Bovington a few miles to the northwest. **27 C5**

Weymouth An old harbour town and popular resort with late Georgian buildings. Historic buildings include Nothe Fort and the Tudor House. Open spaces include the Nothe gardens, Bennett's Water Gardens and the nature reserves of Lodmoor and Radipole Lake. The Isle of Portland is joined to the mainland by the shingle strip of Chesil Beach. Portland Castle (EH, summer) was built by Henry VIII. At the southern end of the island is the spectacular rocky Portland Bill. **25 E8**

Wimborne Minster A historic market town on the Allen, where it meets the Stour. It has charming narrow Georgian streets and pretty squares. The parish church is dedicated to St Cuthburga. Near to Badbury Rings and Kingston Lacy (both NT). **27 A7**

Gloucestershire

Bibury One of the most popular Cotswold villages, with the beautiful Arlington Row group of stone-built cottages. St Mary's church is a mixture of Saxon, Norman and all phases of Gothic. Barnsley House Garden is to the southwest of the town. **65 A7**

Chipping Campden Once a rich centre of the wool trade, this town has plenty of handsome stone buildings (including St James' church, the Market Hall (NT) and Woolstaplers Hall) in a picturesque High Street with styles ranging from the 14th century to the 18th. Nearby are Kiftsgate Court and Hidcote Manor Garden (NT). **77 E6**

Fairford Small and attractive town on the Coln, with the late 15th-century St Mary's church and 17th- and 18th-century buildings around the market place. **65 B8**

Gloucester An interesting city with a beautiful medieval cathedral. The historic docks have been handsomely redeveloped. Other places of interest include Gloucestershire Folk Museum, Soldiers of Gloucestershire Museum, Gloucester Waterways Museum, Robert Raikes House, Gloucester City Museum and Art Gallery. **70 D2**

Tewkesbury Old riverside town in the Cotswolds with half-timbered houses, great scenery and one of the best English Abbey churches – St Mary's. There are two museums, the John Moore Countryside Museum and the Town Museum. **70 A3**

Plymouth

Plymouth A major historical seaport and garrison at the head of Plymouth Sound. It is rich in maritime history. Buildings include St Andrew's Church, the Guildhall, the Roman Catholic Cathedral, Prysten House and the Royal Citadel (EH, guided tours in summer). On The Hoe is Smeaton's Tower – part of the third Eddystone Lighthouse. Museums include the City Museum and Art Gallery, the Merchant's House Museum, the Mayflower Centre and Plymouth Dome. The National Marine Aquarium is a major attraction on the water front. Attractions nearby include Saltram House, Cotehele, Anthony House and Buckland Abbey (all NT), Mount Edgcumbe, The Garden House and Mary Newman's Cottage. **10 E5**

Poole

Poole A major port set by the biggest natural harbour in Europe, Poole is particularly popular with sailors. As well as old buildings and quaint narrow streets, it has good beaches, St Osmund's church, the Poole Museum, Poole History Centre and an arts centre in Poole Lighthouse. Brownsea Island (NT/Dorset Wildlife Trust) is reachable by Ferry from Poole Quay and Sandbanks. **27 B7**

Somerset

Dunster An attractive small town just inside Exmoor. Medieval buildings include the butter cross, Gallox Bridge (EH) and St George's church. Among later buildings are Dunster Working Watermill (NT), the Yarn Market (EH) and the heavily rebuilt Dunster Castle (NT) **45 C6**

Taunton A bustling county town dating back to Saxon times which lies in the pretty valley of Taunton Deane, known for its apples and cider. Attractions include St Mary Magdalene's church, Combe Sydenham Hall, Hestercombe Gardens (RHS), Somerset Cricket Museum and the Museum of Somerset, which is housed in the 12th-century castle. **36 A2**

Torbay

Brixham A resort and fishing port with beaches and attractive harbour. Attractions include the Brixham Heritage Museum. There is also a good fish market. Coleton

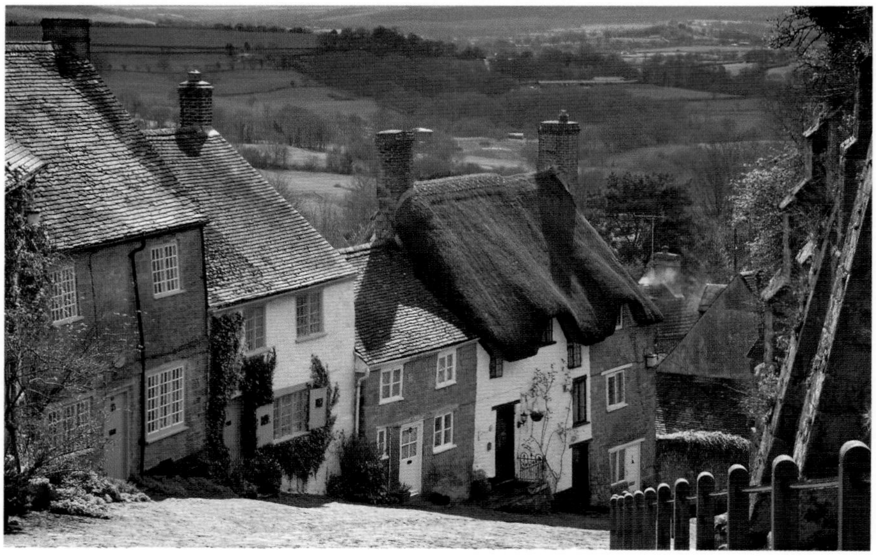

◀ **Gold Hill, Shaftesbury, Dorset** Southwest Tourism

Fishacre (NT) is nearby and there are good coastal walks to the south of the town. **15 D6**

Wiltshire

Bradford on Avon A pretty little town with one of the best Saxon churches in the country, a 17th-century town bridge with a lock-up at one end, a medieval tithe barn, pretty gardens at Westwood Manor (NT) and the Hall and pleasant walks along the banks of the Avon. Farleigh Hungerford Castle (EH) is to the southwest. **57 D8**

Devizes A busy market town with a pretty church and handsome 18th-century buildings, including the town hall and market cross. Other places to visit include the Kennet and Somerset Canal Museum and Broadleas Gardens. The ancient monuments of Avebury, Silbury Hill, Windmill Hill neolithic camp, the Sanctuary and West Kennet long barrow are a little to the east. **58 D5**

Lacock Pretty village with lots of picturesque cottages, very few of which date from after 1800. It is often used in films and television programmes. Nearby is Lacock Abbey (NT), which contains the Fox Talbot Museum of Photography. **58 C3**

Malmesbury Pleasant town above the Avon. Remains of Malmesbury Abbey, in which the historian William of Malmesbury (1090–1143) was a monk. Westonbirt Arboretum is nearby. **64 E3**

Salisbury Cathedral city with historic buildings in the surrounding close. On Salisbury Plain to the north are Old Sarum (EH), Stonehenge (EH) and the surrounding historic landscape including Durrington Walls (NT), Woodhenge (EH) and Earl's Farm Down Barrows. Museums include the Salisbury and South Wiltshire Museum and The Wardrobe. Nearby is Wilton House. **51 E8**

Buildings

The places listed here are a selection of the finest houses, castles and gardens in the counties covered by this atlas. Make sure you check opening times before visiting, as many of the places listed are open only at limited times or seasons.

Castles

Cornwall

Launceston Castle (EH) *Launceston* Set on the motte of a Norman castle. 🖳www.english-heritage.org.uk ☎01566 772365 **18 D3**

Pendennis Castle (EH) *Falmouth* End of chain of castles built by Henry VIII along coast. 🖳www.english-heritage.org.uk ☎01326 316594 **4 D4**

Restormel Castle (EH) *Lostwithiel* One of oldest and best Norman motte-and-bailey castles in Cornwall. Founded 1100. 🖳www.english-heritage.org.uk ☎01208 872687 **9 C5**

St Catherine's Castle (EH) *Fowey* Small fort built by Henry VIII. 🖳www.english-heritage.org.uk **9 E5**

St Mawes Castle (EH) *St Mawes* Built by Henry VIII. Stands in subtropical gardens. 🖳www.english-heritage.org.uk ☎01326 2705264 **D4**

St Michael's Mount (NT) *Marazion* Spectacular castle on rocky island, dating from 14th century. ☎01736 710507 🖳www.nationaltrust.org.uk **3 E6**

Tintagel Castle (EH) *Tintagel* Remains of medieval castle, thought to date from 13th century. Associated in popular legend with King Arthur. ☎01840 770328 🖳www.english-heritage.org.uk **17 C6**

Devon

Berry Pomeroy Castle (EH) *Totnes* Combines medieval castle with flamboyant courtier's mansion. ☎01803 866618 🖳www.english-heritage.org.uk **20 B4**

Castle Drogo (NT) *Nr Exeter* Last castle to be built in Britain, now 20th-century home. 🖳www.nationaltrust.org.uk ☎01647 43330621 **B8**

Dartmouth Castle (EH) *Dartmouth* Defensive castle. ☎01803 833588 🖳www.english-heritage.org.uk **15 E5**

► **Nunney Castle, near Frome, Somerset**
Southwest Tourism

Lydford Castle (EH) *Lydford* Late 12th-century keep with rectangular bailey. Earthworks of original Norman fort are to the south and the earlier Saxon defences to the north. 🖳www.english-heritage.org.uk **19 D7**

Okehampton Castle (EH) *Okehampton* Ruins of largest castle in Devon with Norman motte and keep's jagged remains. 🖳www.english-heritage.org.uk ☎01837 5284419 **B8**

Totnes Castle (EH) *Totnes* Superb Norman motte-and-bailey castle. ☎01803 864406 🖳www.english-heritage.org.uk **14 C4**

Dorset

Christchurch Castle and Norman House (EH) *Christchurch* Built late 11th century. 🖳www.english-heritage.org.uk **28 B3**

Corfe Castle (NT) *Wareham* Magnificent ruins of 1000-yr-old castle dominate Isle of Purbeck. ☎01929 481294 🖳www.nationaltrust.org.uk **27 D6**

Lulworth Castle *Wareham* Early 17th-century hunting lodge. 18th-century house in parkland. ☎0845 450 1054 🖳www.lulworth.com **26 D4**

Portland Castle (EH) *Portland* One of best preserved of Henry VIII's coastal forts. Open in summer only. ☎01305 820539 🖳www.english-heritage.org.uk **24 D2**

Sherborne Old Castle (EH) *Sherborne* Ruins of early 12th-century castle. 🖳www.english-heritage.org.uk ☎01935 812730 **38 C2**

Gloucestershire

Berkeley Castle *Berkeley* Completed 1153 at command of Henry II. Castle is now a stately home. Terraced Elizabethan gardens. 🖳www.berkeley-castle.com ☎01453 810332 **63 C5**

Sudeley Castle *Winchcombe* Tudor building once home of Katherine Parr. Royal relics. Fine gardens and wildlife reserve. 🖳www.sudeleycastle.co.uk ☎01242 604244 **71 B6**

Scilly Isles

Cromwell's Castle (EH) *Tresco* 17th-century round tower. 🖳www.english-heritage.org.uk **6 A2**

Harry's Walls (EH) *St Mary's* Incomplete 16th-century fort. 🖳www.english-heritage.org.uk **6 B3**

King Charles's Castle (EH) *Tresco* Castle remains. 🖳www.english-heritage.org.uk **6 A2**

Somerset

Daws Castle *Watchet* Site of Saxon refuge. **45 C8**

Farleigh Hungerford Castle (EH) *Farleigh Hungerford* 14th-century castle with chapel. ☎01225 754026 🖳www.english-heritage.org.uk **57 E8**

Nunney Castle (EH) *Nunney* Small 14th-century castle with moat. 🖳www.english-heritage.org.uk **49 B6**

Wiltshire

Ludgershall Castle and Cross (EH) *Ludgershall* Ruins of early 12th-century royal hunting palace with late medieval cross. 🖳www.english-heritage.org.uk **52 A2**

Old Wardour Castle (EH) *Tisbury* 🖳www.english-heritage.org.uk ☎01747 870487 **40 A1**

Houses

Bath & NE Somerset

No 1 Royal Crescent *Bath* First house to be built here. Fine example of Palladian architecture. ☎01225 428126 🖳www.bath-preservation-trust.org.uk **57 C6**

Bristol

Georgian House *Bristol* Georgian town house built 1790 for wealthy merchant. ☎0117 9211362 🖳www.bristol.gov.uk **56 B3**

Red Lodge *Bristol* Last surviving suite of 16th-century rooms in Bristol. Tudor-style garden. ☎0117 9211360 🖳www.bristol.gov.uk **56 B3**

Cornwall

Antony (NT) *Torpoint* Early 18th-century house in extensive grounds. ☎01752 812191 🖳www.nationaltrust.org.uk **10 D4**

Cotehele House (NT) *Saltash* Medieval house. Formal gardens and valley garden. 🖳www.nationaltrust.org.uk ☎01579 35134610 **B4**

Godolphin House and Garden (NT) *Helston* Tudor house. ☎01736 763194 🖳www.nationaltrust.org.uk **3 D8**

Lanhydrock (NT) *Bodmin* Fifty rooms open to view. Wooded parkland and garden. 🖳www.nationaltrust.org.uk ☎01208 265950 **8 C4**

Mount Edgcumbe *Torpoint* House and furniture restored. Colourful 18th-century gardens. Landscaped park, woodland and coastal walks. ☎01752 822236 🖳www.mountedgcumbe.gov.uk **10 E5**

Pencarrow House *Bodmin* Georgian mansion. ☎01208 841369 🖳www.pencarrow.co.uk **8 A3**

Trerice (NT) *Nr Newquay* Small Elizabethan manor house with gabled facade. Pleasant gardens. ☎01637 875404 🖳www.nationaltrust.org.uk **7 D7**

Devon

A La Ronde (NT) *Exmouth* c. 1796. ☎01395 265514 🖳www.nationaltrust.org.uk **22 D2**

Arlington Court (NT) *Barnstaple* Noted for extensive collection of model ships and other works of art. Large collection of horse drawn carriages. Gardens and woods (not NT). 🖳www.nationaltrust.org.uk ☎01271 850296 **43 C7**

Bradley (NT) *Newton Abbot* Small, 15th-century manor house. Ramparts of Berry Wood earthwork stand in the grounds. ☎01803 661907 **14 A4**

Buckland Abbey (NT) *nr Tavistock* Originally Cistercian monastery, then home of Sir Francis Drake. Exhibitions. Elizabethan garden. ☎01822 853607 🖳www.nationaltrust.org.uk **11 B5**

Chambercombe Manor *Ilfracombe* Late 14th and early 15th century. Herb, rose and water gardens. ☎01271 862624 🖳www.chambercombemanor.co.uk **43 B5**

▲ **Berry Pomeroy Castle, Devon**
James Hughes / Alamy

Coleton Fishacre (NT) *Kingswear* House reflects Arts and Crafts tradition but has modern interiors. Garden has large collection of plants. ☎01803 752466 🖳www.nationaltrust.org.uk **15 E6**

Compton Castle (NT) *nr Paignton* Fortified manor house. ☎01803 843235 🖳www.nationaltrust.org.uk **15 B5**

Greenway (NT) *Galmpton* Former holiday home and gardens of Agatha Christie on the bank of the River Dart. ☎01803 842382 🖳www.nationaltrust.org.uk **13 B8**

Killerton (NT) *Exeter* Built in 1778. Collection of costumes. Hillside gardens, extensive lawns. ☎01392 881345 **34 F4**

Knightshayes Court (NT) *Tiverton* Completed 1874. Small woodland and terraced gardens. ☎01884 254665 🖳www.nationaltrust.org.uk **34 D4**

Overbecks Museum and Garden (NT) *Salcombe* Edwardian house contains social photographs; inventions by Otto Overbeck. Secret room for children. Beautiful garden. 🖳www.nationaltrust.org.uk ☎01548 842893 **13 E5**

Powderham Castle *Powderham* Medieval castle built c. 1390. Georgian interiors. Gardens. ☎01626 890243 🖳www.powderham.co.uk **22 D1**

Shute Barton (NT) *Shute* Important surviving non-fortified manor house from Middle Ages. ☎01752 346585 🖳www.nationaltrust.org.uk **23 A7**

Tiverton Castle *Tiverton* Hexagonal castle built in 1392. Partly destroyed in Civil War. ☎01884 253200 🖳www.tivertoncastle.com **34 D4**

Ugbrooke House *Chudleigh* House and church built c. 1200. Capability Brown landscaped the park. ☎01626 852179 🖳www.ugbrooke.co.uk **21 E7**

Watersmeet House (NT) *Lynmouth* Fishing lodge. ☎01598 753348 🖳www.nationaltrust.org.uk **44 B1**

Dorset

Athelhampton *Puddletown* Medieval house. Walled gardens include famous topiary pyramids. ☎01305 848363 🖳www.athelhampton.co.uk **26 B2**

Clouds Hill (NT) *Wareham* T E Lawrence's (Lawrence of Arabia) retreat. ☎01929 405616 🖳www.nationaltrust.org.uk **26 B3**

Hardy's Cottage (NT) *Dorchester* Thomas Hardy born here in 1840. ☎01305 262366 🖳www.nationaltrust.org.uk **26 B1**

Highcliffe Castle *Highcliffe* Completed 1835, including stonework from Benedictine abbey in Normandy. ☎01425 278807 🖳www.highcliffecastle.co.uk **28 B4**

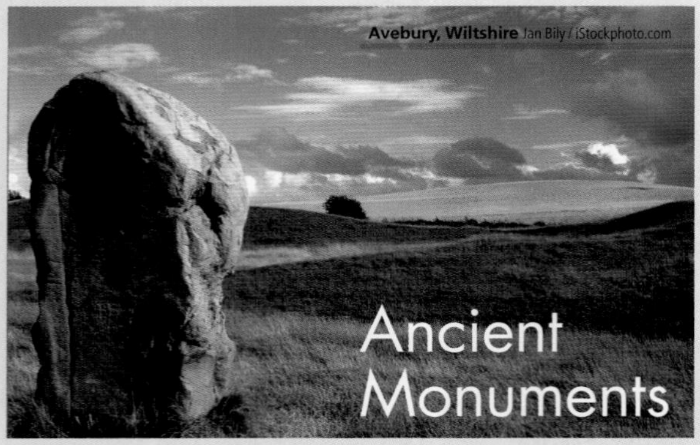

Avebury, Wiltshire Jan Bily / iStockphoto.com

Ancient Monuments

Bath & NE Somerset

Stanton Drew Circles and Cave (EH) *Stanton Drew* Three stone circles, two avenues and a burial chamber. One of finest Neolithic sites in the country. www.english-heritage.org.uk **56 D4**

Stoney Littleton Long Barrow (EH) *Wellow* Neolithic burial mound. **57 E6**

Bristol

Kings Weston Roman Villa *Lawrence Weston* Possibly 3rd century AD. Bath suite, living quarters, mosaic floors, court and east wing. Key obtainable from Bristol City Museum and Art Gallery. 0117 9223571 www.bristol-city.gov.uk **56 A2**

Cornwall

Ballowall Barrow (EH) *St Just* Unusual Bronze Age chambered tomb www.english-heritage.org.uk **2 D3**

Carn Brea *Redruth* Remains of Neolithic hillfort. **4 B1**

Carn Euny Ancient Village (EH) *Sancreed* Iron Age settlement, with foundations of huts and underground passage. www.english-heritage.org.uk **2 E4**

Castle An Dinas *St Columb* Iron Age Celtic hillfort, 300–200 BC. **8 C1**

Chysauster Ancient Village (EH) *Penzance* Site of Iron Age village dating from about 1 BC to the 3rd century AD. www.english-heritage.org.uk 07831 757934 **2 D5**

Halliggye Fogou *Garras* One of several underground tunnels, linked to Iron Age villages and unique to Cornwall. **4 F2**

King Doniert's Stone (EH) *St Cleer* Two decorated pieces of 9th-century cross believed to commemorate King of Cornwall, who drowned c. 875. www.english-heritage.org.uk **9 B7**

Lanyon Quoit *Penzance* Fine cromlech consisting of capstone supported on three granite slabs. c.1500 BC. **2 D4**

Men-An-Tol *Penzance* Holed Stone. **3 D5**

Merry Maidens *Lamorna* Circle of 19 standing stones. **2 F4**

St Breock Downs Monolith (EH) *nr Wadebridge* Prehistoric standing stone. www.english-heritage.org.uk **8 B2**

Stripple Stones *Nr Bodmin* Stone circle. **8 B4**

The Hurlers Stone Circles (EH) *Minions* Three Bronze Age stone circles in a line, some of best ceremonial standing stones in the southwest. www.english-heritage.org.uk **9 A8**

Tregiffian Burial Chamber (EH) *St Buryan* Neolithic or early Bronze Age chambered tomb. www.english-heritage.org.uk **2 F4**

Trencrom Hill *Penzance* 2nd-century BC rampart. Hut circles and well. **3 C6**

Trethevy Quoit (EH) *St Cleer* Cromlech or prehistoric burial place. www.english-heritage.org.uk **9 B8**

Zennor Cromlech *nr Zennor* Quoit, one of largest capstones in England **2 C5**

Devon

Blackbury Camp (EH) *Southleigh* Iron Age hillfort. www.english-heritage.org.uk **23 B5**

Hound Tor (EH) *Manaton* Remains of medieval village, first occupied in Bronze Age. www.english-heritage.org.uk **20 D5**

Merrivale Prehistoric Settlement (EH) *Dartmoor* Two rows of standing stones, remains of early Bronze Age village. www.english-heritage.org.uk **19 E8**

Upper Plym Valley *Nr Yelverton* Scores of prehistoric and medieval sites covering 15.5 sq km (6 sq miles). **11 B6**

Dorset

Badbury Rings *nr Shapwick* Iron Age hillfort with evidence of Bronze Age settlement. **40 F2**

Jordan Hill Roman Temple (EH) *Preston* Foundations of Romano-Celtic temple. www.english-heritage.org.uk **25 D8**

Kingston Russell Stone Circle (EH) *Abbotsbury* Bronze Age stone circle of 18 stones. www.english-heritage.org.uk **25 C6**

Knowlton Church and Earthworks (EH) *Cranborne* Ruins of Norman church in middle of Neolithic earthworks. www.english-heritage.org.uk **40 D3**

Lambert's Castle *Lyme Regis* Iron Age hillfort. **24 B1**

Maiden Castle (EH) *nr Dorchester* Largest Iron Age hillfort in Europe. www.english-heritage.org.uk **25 C8**

Maumbury Rings *Dorchester* Originally a sacred circle of the Stone Age, the Romans later turned Rings into 'Coliseum'. **25 C8**

Poundbury Hillfort *Dorchester* Ancient entrenchment. **25 B8**

Rawlsbury Camp *Milton Abbas* Iron Age hillfort **39 E5**

The Dorset Cursus *Pentridge* Two parallel banks stretching for 6 miles. Both banks flanked with barrows. **40 C3**

The Nine Stones (EH) *Winterbourne Abbas* Remains of nine standing stones constructed about 4000 years ago. www.english-heritage.org.uk **25 B7**

White Sheet Hill *Nr Shaftesbury* Neolithic long barrow and Bronze Age barrows. Remains of Neolithic Causeway camp and Iron Age hillfort. **40 B1**

Winterbourne Poor Lot Barrows (EH) *Winterbourne Abbas*, Part of 4000-year-old Bronze Age cemetery. www.english-heritage.org.uk **25 B6**

Gloucestershire

Belas Knap (EH) *nr Winchcombe* Good example of Neolithic long barrow. www.english-heritage.org.uk **71 B6**

Chedworth Roman Villa (NT) *Yanworth* One of largest Romano-British villas in country. Walls plus mosaics, bathhouses, hypocausts, water-shrine and latrine. Small museum. 01242 890256 www.nationaltrust.org.uk **71 E7**

Great Witcombe Roman Villa (EH) *Great Witcombe* Built around courtyard, luxurious bath-house. www.english-heritage.org.uk **70 E4**

Notgrove Long Barrow (EH) *Notgrove* A Neolithic burial mound. www.english-heritage.org.uk **71 C7**

Nympsfield Long Barrow (EH) *Nympsfield* Neolithic long barrow. www.english-heritage.org.uk **63 B7**

Uley Long Barrow (Hetty Pegler's Tump) (EH) *Uley* c. 3000 BC, Neolithic chambered burial mound www.english-heritage.org.uk **63 C7**

Scilly Isles

Bant's Carn (EH) *St Mary's* Bronze Age burial mound and Roman village. www.english-heritage.org.uk **6 B3**

Garrison Walls (EH) *St Mary's* Ramparts of walls and earthworks. www.english-heritage.org.uk **6 B2**

Innisidgen Lower and Upper Burial Chambers (EH) *St Mary's* Two Bronze Age cairns. www.english-heritage.org.uk **6 B3**

Porth Hellick Down Burial Chamber (EH) *St Mary's* Bronze Age. www.english-heritage.org.uk **6 B3**

Somerset

Cadbury Castle *South Cadbury* Iron Age hillfort (reputedly 'Camelot'). Impression of a great fortress lingers. **38 A2**

Swindon

Barbury Castle *Wroughton* Iron Age hillfort. **59 A8**

Wiltshire

Adam's Grave *Alton Barnes* Chambered long barrow. **59 D7**

Avebury Stone Circle (NT) *Avebury* Constructed 4000 years ago, originally using more than 180 stones. See also West Kennet Avenue. 01672 539250 www.nationaltrust.org.uk **59 C7**

Bratton Camp and Westbury White Horse (EH) *Bratton* Large Iron Age hillfort and chalk horse. **50 A3**

Cley Hill *Warminster* Iron Age hillfort c. 300 BC. Single banked hill with two Bronze Age round barrows. **50 C1**

Devil's Den *Fyfield* Chambered long barrow c. 4000 BC. **59 C8**

Ethandun Memorial *At Bratton Camp, Westbury,* Sarson stone commemorating 9th-century battle. **50 A3**

Everleigh Barrows *Everleigh* 2000 BC two bell barrows, two bowl barrows and a disc barrow **59 E8**

Fyfield and Overton Downs *Fyfield* Prehistoric landscape comprising an extensive field system of banks. **59 C7**

Giant's Grave *nr Pewsey* Unchambered long barrow c. 4000 BC **59 E8**

Gopher Wood *Huish* Small Bronze Age cemetery comprising seven bowl barrows and a disc barrow. **59 D7**

Hatfield Earthworks (Marden Henge) (EH) Marden Earthwork remains of part of a Neolithic enclosure complex and one of the largest henges in Britain. www.english-heritage.org.uk **59 E6**

Knap Hill *Alton Barnes* Neolithic causewayed enclosure. **59 D7**

Martinsell Hill *Pewsey* Iron Age hillfort enclosing 13 ha (32 acres). **59 D8**

Ogbourne Round Barrow *Ogbourne St Andrew* A round barrow in a Saxon churchyard. **59 B8**

Old Sarum (EH) *Salisbury* Great earthwork with huge banks and ditch built c. 500 BC. 01722 335398 www.english-heritage.org.uk **51 E7**

Oldbury Castle *Cherhill* Iron Age hillfort **59 B5**

Oliver's Castle *Bromham* Iron Age hillfort with single bank and ditch. **58 C4**

Overton Hill *West Kennett* Bronze Age burial mounds. **59 C7**

Rybury Camp *All Cannings* Causewayed Iron Age enclosure. **59 D6**

Silbury Hill (EH) *Avebury* Largest man-made mound in ancient Europe. www.english-heritage.org.uk **59 C6**

Stonehenge (EH) *nr Amesbury* Great ancient stone circle of Stonehenge stands at centre of extensive prehistoric landscape filled with remains of ceremonial and domestic structures and round barrows. 0870 333 1181 www.english-heritage.org.uk **51 C7**

The Sanctuary (EH) *West Kennett* Possibly 5000 years old. Consists of two concentric circles of stones and six timber uprights indicated by concrete posts. www.english-heritage.org.uk **59 C7**

West Kennett Avenue (EH) *Avebury* Avenue of standing stones which originally ran from Avebury Stone Circle to The Sanctuary, late Neolithic. www.english-heritage.org.uk **59 C7**

West Kennett Long Barrow (EH) *West Kennett* Neolithic chambered tomb. www.english-heritage.org.uk **59 C7**

Windmill Hill (EH) *Avebury* Neolithic remains of three concentric rings of ditches. **59 B6**

Woodhenge (EH) *Durrington* Neolithic ceremonial monument from 2300 BC. Entrance and long axis of the oval rings points to rising sun on Midsummer Day. www.english-heritage.org.uk **51 C7**

Kingston Lacy (NT) *Wimborne Minster* Completed 1665. Houses collection of Old Masters, celebrated 'Spanish Room'. www.nationaltrust.org.uk 01202 883402 **40 F2**

Sherborne Castle *Sherborne* 16th-century house built for Raleigh. Grounds by Capability Brown. www.sherbornecastle.com **38 C2**

Wolfeton House *Dorchester* Medieval and Elizabethan house. Cider house. 01305 263500 **25 B8**

Gloucestershire

Lodge Park (NT) *Aldsworth* 17th-century grandstand. Recently restored. 01451 844130 www.nationaltrust.org.uk **72 E1**

Newark Park (NT) *Ozleworth* Tudor hunting lodge, converted into house by Wyatt. 01793 817666 www.nationaltrust.org.uk **63 D7**

Snowshill Manor (NT) *Snowshill* Tudor manor house with early 18th-century facade. Famous for collection of musical instruments, clocks and toys. 01386 852410 www.nationaltrust.org.uk **76 F4**

Stanway House *Stanway* Jacobean manor house in 8 ha (20 acres) of landscaped grounds with 18th-century water garden and an important 14th-century tithe barn. www.stanwayfountain.co.uk 01386 584469 **71 A7**

North Somerset

Clevedon Court (NT) *nr Clevedon* Built c. 1320. One of the few complete houses of this time to have survived. www.nationaltrust.org.uk 01275 872257 **55 B8**

Tyntesfield (NT) *Wraxall* A hidden Gothic revival gem, with virtually intact Victorian decorative scheme, kitchens and family chapel. The grounds are extensive and include parkland, formal gardens and a walled kitchen garden. 0844 800 4966 www.nationaltrust.org.uk **56 B2**

Plymouth

Saltram (NT) *Plymouth* Former Tudor mansion. Tree and shrub garden. 01752 333500 www.nationaltrust.org.uk **11 D6**

Somerset

Coleridge Cottage (NT) *Nether Stowey* Samuel Taylor Coleridge lived here 1797 to 1800. 01278 732662 www.nationaltrust.org.uk **46 D3**

Dunster Castle (NT) *Dunster* House and medieval ruins framed with sub-tropical plants. 01643 823004 www.nationaltrust.org.uk **45 C6**

Forde Abbey *nr Chard* 12th-century Cistercian monastery converted into residence after Dissolution. Extensive grounds. 01460 220231 www.fordeabbey.co.uk **36 E5**

King John's Hunting Lodge (NT) *Axbridge* Early Tudor merchant's house now museum. 01934 732012 www.nationaltrust.org.uk **55 F8**

Lytes Cary Manor (NT) *Charlton Mackrell* Manor house and 14th-century chapel. Formal garden. 01458 224471 www.nationaltrust.org.uk **48 F2**

Montacute House (NT) *Montacute* Late Elizabethan house. Portraits from National Portrait Gallery. Beautiful gardens. www.nationaltrust.org.uk 01935 823289 **37 C7**

Priest's House (NT) *Muchelney* Late medieval house. Occupied and furnished by tenants. 01458 253771 www.nationaltrust.org.uk **37 A6**

The Bishop's Palace *Wells* 13th-century moated palace. State rooms and gallery. Relaxing gardens surrounding the springs that gave the city its name. www.bishopspalacewells.co.uk 01749 988111 **48 B2**

Treasurer's House (NT) *Martock* c.13th century. 01935 825815 www.nationaltrust.org.uk **37 C7**

South Gloucestershire

Dyrham Park (NT) *Dyrham* Built 1692–1702. Collection of Delft, paintings by Dutch masters. Formal garden, two lakes. Deer park has been here since Saxon times. www.nationaltrust.org.uk 0117 937 2501 **57 A6**

Horton Court (NT) *Nr Chipping Sodbury* Closed 2008 01179 372501 www.nationaltrust.org.uk **63 F7**

Swindon

Lydiard House *Swindon* Fine Georgian house in 107.6 ha (266 acres) of parkland. www.lydiardpark.org.uk 01793 770401 **65 F7**

Torbay

Kirkham House (EH) *Paignton* 14th-century stone house with modern furniture, pottery and fabrics. www.english-heritage.org.uk **15 C5**

Wiltshire

Avebury Manor and Garden (NT) *Avebury* Present buildings date from 16th century. Timed guided tours of house. Topiary and flower gardens. 01672 539250 www.nationaltrust.org.uk **59 C7**

Bowood House *Calne* 18th-century house designed by Adam. One of Capability Brown's most beautiful parks. Adventure playground. 01249 812102 www.bowood-house.co.uk **58 B4**

Corsham Court *Corsham* Elizabethan and Georgian house. Park and garden by Capability Brown. 01249 712214 www.corsham-court.co.uk **58 B2**

Great Chalfield Manor (NT) *Bradford on Avon* Restored 1480 moated manor house. www.nationaltrust.org.uk 01225 782239 **58 D2**

Lacock Abbey (NT) *Lacock* Originally an abbey, converted into house 1540. 01249 730459 www.nationaltrust.org.uk **58 C3**

Little Clarendon (NT) *Dinton* Tudor house, altered in the 17th century, with 20th-century Catholic chapel. 01985 843600 www.nationaltrust.org.uk **50 E5**

Longleat House *Warminster* Early Renaissance house. Extensive landscaped park. See 'Outdoors: Animal attractions'. www.longleat.co.uk 01985 844400 **49 C8**

Mompesson House (NT) *Salisbury* Turnbull collection of English 18th-century drinking glasses. Walled garden. 01722 420980 www.nationaltrust.org.uk **51 F7**

Philipps House and Dinton Park (NT) *Dinton* Neo-Grecian house completed in 1820. Landscaped park . 0172 716663 www.nationaltrust.org.uk **50 E5**

Sheldon Manor *nr Chippenham* Manor house. 15th-century detached chapel. Terraced gardens. 01249 653120 www.sheldonmanor.co.uk **58 B2**

Stourhead (NT) *nr Warminster* Wilts Built in 1722 and later enlarged. Grounds are famous example of early 18th-century landscape movement. 01747 841152 www.nationaltrust.org.uk **49 E7**

Westwood Manor (NT) *Bradford on Avon* 15th-century manor house. www.nationaltrust.org.uk 01225 863374 **57 E8**

Wilton House *Wilton* Acres of fine lawns. www.wiltonhouse.co.uk 01722 746714 **51 E6**

Other historic buildings

Bath & NE Somerset

Bath Assembly Rooms (NT) *Bath* Designed by John Wood the Younger in 1769. www.nationaltrust.org.uk 01225 477789 **57 C7**

Beckford's Tower *Bath* Built 1827, now a museum. Spiral staircase and panoramic view www.bath-preservation-trust.org.uk 01225 460705 **57 C7**

Guildhall *Bath* 18th century. 01225 477785 **57 C7**

Roman Baths and Pump Room *Bath* Baths fed by the only hot springs in Britain. The Pump Room is 18th-century. 01225 477785 www.romanbaths.co.uk **57 C7**

Bristol

Blaise Hamlet (NT) *Henbury* Picturesque cottages. ☎01225 461900
🖥www.nationaltrust.org.uk **56 A3**

Clifton Observatory *Clifton* Former snuff mill with camera obscura.
🖥www.cliftonobservatory.co.uk
☎0117 9741242 **56 B3**

Westbury College Gatehouse (NT) *Westbury on Trym* 15th-century gatehouse.
🖥www.nationaltrust.org.uk
☎01275 461900 **56 A3**

Cornwall

Dupath Holy Well (EH) *Callington* Built c.1500 and almost complete.
🖥www.english-heritage.org.uk **10 B3**

Tintagel Old Post Office (NT) *Tintagel* 14th-century stone house with thick slate roof. ☎01840 770024
🖥www.nationaltrust.org.uk **17 C6**

Wesley Cottage *Trewint* 18th-century cottage. Wesley stayed and preached here.
🖥www.wesleycottage.org.uk
☎01566 880265 **10 C1**

Devon

Bayard's Cove Fort (EH) *Dartmouth* A small artillery fort built c.1534.
🖥www.english-heritage.org.uk **15 E5**

Branscombe Old Bakery, Manor Mill and Forge (NT) *Seaton* ☎01752 346585
🖥www.nationaltrust.org.uk **10 E2**

Customs House *Exeter* Oldest (1680–81) surviving substantial brick building in Exeter.
☎01392 265700 **21 B8**

Exeter Guildhall *Exeter* 16th-century oak roof. 🖥www.exeter.gov.uk **21 B8**

Loughwood Meeting House (NT) *Dalwood* c. 1653. ☎01752 346585
🖥www.nationaltrust.org.uk **36 F2**

Marker's Cottage (NT) *Broadclyst* Medieval cob house. ☎01392 461546
🖥www.nationaltrust.org.uk **22 A1**

Totnes Guildhall *Totnes* Part of former Benedictine priory. ☎01803 862147 **14 C4**

Plymouth

Prysten House *Plymouth* 15th-century priest's house. ☎01752 661414 **10 E5**

Royal Citadel (EH) *Plymouth* 17th-century fortress. Guided tours only. Open in summer. ☎01752 775841 🖥www.english-heritage.org.uk **11 E5**

▶ **Barton Tithe Barn, Bradford on Avon**
James Hughes / Alamy

Dorset

Nothe Fort *Weymouth* Restored Victorian fort with ramparts and gun decks.
🖥www.nothefort.org.uk
☎01305 766626 **25 E8**

Gloucestershire

Ashleworth Tithe Barn (NT) *Ashleworth* Stone-tiled, 15th-century tithe barn.
🖥www.nationaltrust.org.uk
☎01452 814213 **70 B2**

Chipping Campden Market Hall *Chipping Campden* Built 1627. **77 E6**

Pittville Pump Room *Cheltenham* Built between 1825 and 1830. Spa waters still available. ☎01242 523852
🖥www.cheltenhamtownhall.org.uk **71 C5**

Woolstaplers Hall *Chipping Campden* Built in 1340. Now a museum. **77 E6**

Somerset

Abbot's Fish House (EH) *Meare* 14th-century stone building originally used to preserve and store fish for Glastonbury Abbey (Key available from Manor House Farm at reasonable hours.)
🖥www.english-heritage.org.uk **47 C9**

Gallox Bridge (EH) *Dunster* Stone packhorse bridge.
🖥www.english-heritage.org.uk **45 C6**

Glastonbury Tribunal (EH) *Glastonbury* Well-preserved medieval town house.
🖥www.english-heritage.org.uk
☎01458 832954 **48 D2**

Yarn Market (EH) *Dunster* 17th-century octagonal market hall.
🖥www.english-heritage.org.uk **45 C6**

Wiltshire

Barton Tithe Barn (EH) *Bradford on Avon* Medieval stone- and timber-built barn.
🖥www.english-heritage.org.uk **57 D8**

The North Canonry *Salisbury* Largest Tudor domestic building in city.
🖥www.salisburycathedral.org.uk
☎01722 55512151 **E8**

Religious buildings

Bath & NE Somerset

Bath Abbey *Abbey Churchyard* Site dates back to 7th century. Gothic church built in 1499. After the Dissolution, the church remained incomplete until 1864. Mostly a Victorian replica interior of a Tudor design with an 1860s fan vault. Bath Abbey Heritage Vaults contain finds relating to Christianity on the site, as well as items related to the building. ☎01225 422462
🖥www.bathabbey.org **57 D7**

Bournemouth

St Peter *Hinton Road and Parsonage Road* c.1854. Tall stone tower, south aisle from earlier building. Richly restored Gothic Revival chancel and south transept. Grave of Mary Shelley. **28 B1**

St Stephen *St Stephens Road* Founded 1880. High bell-tower. Serene interior, organ loft above a vaulted chapel. Restored altar triptych. **28 B1**

Bristol

Bristol Cathedral *Deanery Road, College Green* Unique among the English cathedrals as a 'Hall church' with aisles the same height as the nave. Norman Chapter House, early English Lady Chapel. ☎0117 9264879
🖥www.bristol-cathedral.co.uk **56 B3**

Lord Mayor's Chapel of St Mark *College Green* Founded c.1230 as hospital chapel; 16th-century roof; some rebuilding; European medieval glass. ☎0117 9294350 **56 B3**

St John's on the Wall *Broad Street* Gothic church standing above gateway of old city wall. **56 B3**

St Mary Redcliffe *Redcliffe Way* 12th- to 15th-century vaulted Gothic building with twin porches; Victorian stained glass and some medieval fragments. ☎0117 929 1487
🖥www.stmaryredcliffe.co.uk **56 B3**

Temple Church *Church Street, Temple Way* Walls and tower of 15th-century church bombed in World War II. Stands on site of 12th-century church. **56 B3**

◀ **Truro Cathedral, Cornwall**
James Hughes / Alamy

The New Room *Horsefair* Erected in 1739 as discussion room for elders of Methodism. Simple Georgian interior. Museum of Methodism. ☎0117 9264740
🖥www.newroombristol.org.uk **56 B3**

Cornwall

Holy Trinity *St Austell* Fine Gothic tower with carved statues; Norman font. **8 E3**

Quaker Meeting House *Come-to-Good* Early 18th-century thatched chapel. Bare interior and pine furnishings. **4 B4**

St Anthony *St Anthony-in-Roseland* Victorian restoration of a 12th-century monastic church; situated by the sea. **5 D5**

St Breaca *Breage* 15th-century Cornish granite church with 15th-century mural of St Christopher and Christ.
☎01326 573 449 **3 E8**

St Buriana *St Buryan* Tall granite tower and original painted rood screen. **2 E4**

St Endelienta *St Endellion* Carved Gothic altar tomb. **16 E4**

St Enodoc *St Enodoc* 13th-century church in the middle of golf course. Resting place of poet John Betjeman who lived nearby. **16 E3**

St Germanus *St Germans* Cornwall's cathedral until c.1409. Original church was seat of Saxon bishops, rebuilt as Norman outpost. 🖥www.stgermansparishes.com **10 D3**

St Ia *St Ives* Early 15th-century granite church; medieval choir stalls portray local scenes; local artist Barbara Hepworth's Madonna and Child. **3 B6**

St James *Kilkhampton* Norman south doorway and carved bench-ends. **31 D5**

St John the Baptist *Morwenstow* Church of eccentric poet Robert Hawker. Norman and early Gothic with Tudor pews. **30 C4**

St Just in Roseland *St Just in Roseland* Gothic church situated in sub-tropical garden on Fal estuary; palm trees, cedars.
🖥stjust.roselandchurches.co.uk **5 C5**

St Maddern *Madron* 'Mother church of Penzance'. Contains banner made to mourn Nelson's death at Battle of Trafalgar. **2 D5**

St Mary Magdalene *Launceston* Early 16th century. Carved granite facades, 20th-century woodwork. **18 D3**

St Materiana *Church Hill, Tintagel* Well-preserved Norman church on clifftop. Copy of National Gallery's Perugino altarpiece in Blessed Sacrament Chapel. **17 C6**

St Mellanus *Mullion* North door from 11th century, south door has dog flap for shepherd's dogs. Arts and Crafts screen. **5 G1**

St Mylor *Mylor Churchtown* Norman details, tallest Celtic cross in Cornwall. **4 C4**

St Neot *St Neot* Medieval windows depict lives of the saints. Panels depict medieval ship design. **9 B6**

St Nonna *Altarnun* 15th-century with tall west tower. Norman font with carvings of monsters; 16th-century benches. **18 D1**

St Petroc *Bodmin* Largest medieval church in Cornwall. Bodmin stone. Contains unique accounts listing contributors to building and St Petroc's casket (c.1170).
🖥www.st-petroc-bodmin.co.uk **8 B4**

St Probus *Probus* Cornwall's tallest tower. **7 F8**

St Protus and St Hyacinth *Blisland* Partly Norman, with 15th-century tower, porch, aisles and transepts.
🖥www.blisland.com **8 A4**

St Swithun *Launcells* 15th-century woodwork and tiles, Norman font and Gothic pulpit. Bench-ends depict Bible stories. **30 E4**

St Winwaloe *Gunwalloe* 15th-century 'Church of the Storms', built half on sea, half on land. Damaged by storm. **3 F9**

Truro Cathedral *St Mary's Street, Truro* A fairly modern cathedral consecrated in 1887. Cruciform building completed 1910 to the design of J.L. Pearson RA in Early English style with strong French influence. Largely on site of 16th-century parish church, south aisle incorporated into new building as additional choir aisle. Three powerful towers. The central tower rises to 76 m (250 ft) and is a Cornish memorial to Queen Victoria. ☎01872 276782
🖥www.trurocathedral.org.uk **4 B4**

Devon

Buckfast Abbey *Buckfastleigh* Built on site from the original plan of a Cistercian monastery in first half of 20th century. Remains an active monastery but welcomes visitors. ☎01364 645550
🖥www.buckfast.org.uk **14 B2**

Exeter Cathedral *Cathedral Yard and Cathedral Close* Built in Decorated style with three-storeyed west front and two great Norman transeptal towers. Famous for great west window with 14th-century tracery. Present building evolved from Norman building in middle of 13th century and displays much of the best in Gothic architecture. The north tower contains an ancient astronomical clock and Peter, one of the largest bells in England. The fine west front contains many niches filled with statues. Library contains a Exeter's copy of the Domesday Survey and other ancient documents. ☎01392 255573
🖥www.exeter-cathedral.org.uk **21 B8**

Holy Cross *Crediton* Founded 12th century, mainly 15th century. Contains 20th-century works of art. Carved sedilia.
🖥www.creditonparishchurch.org.uk
☎01363 77322634 **F1**

Ottery St Mary *Ottery St Mary* Copied from Exeter Cathedral by Bishop Grandisson from 1338–42. Painted roof, fan-vaulted aisle. Much original woodwork. Medieval weather vane. ☎01404-812062
🖥www.otterystmary.org.uk **22 A4**

St Andrew *Bere Ferrers* Slate tombs and granite interior. 14th-century stained glass features in east window. Ferrers monuments. **10 C5**

St Andrew *Cullompton* 15th century. Highly decorated tower with pinnacles and gargoyles. Richly carved, panelled ceiling. Complete, colourful screen.
🖥http://standrewscullompton.com **35 E5**

St John the Baptist *Ashton, Nr Chudleigh* 15th-century church in peaceful setting. Richly decorated north aisle chapel. South door scarred with bullet holes from Civil War. **21 D6**

St Mary *Molland* Georgian furnishings, medieval statues. **44 F3**

St Lawrence *Lechlade-on-Thames* church built in 1470 on earlier foundations. Additions in 16th century. Carvings and depictions of domestic and religious life. **66 C1**

St Mary *Berkeley* Sandstone church. Early Gothic west front. Berkeley memorials. East window memorial to Edward Jenner. **63 C5**

St Mary *Deerhurst* Former Anglo-Saxon monastery. Restored interior with much Saxon work still evident and in good condition. Wall of tower has 8th-century relief of Madonna and Child. **70 B3**

St Mary *Fairford* Late 15th-century church. England's only complete set of medieval narrative windows. ☎01285 712611 🖳stmaryschurchfairford.org.uk **65 B8**

St Mary's (EH) *Kempley*. Norman church. 12th to 14th-century frescoes. Roof timbers are oldest in England, c.1120–50. 🖳www.english-heritage.org.uk ☎01531 660214 **69 A7**

St Michael *Bishops Cleeve* Norman church, Jacobean musician's gallery. **71 B5**

St Peter and St Paul *Northleach* 15th-century wool church with brasses of local wool merchants. Decorated two-storey porch. ☎01451 869293 **71 E8**

Plymouth

Plymouth Cathedral *Cecil Street and Wyndham Street* Roman Catholic cathedral built mid-19th century in Early English style 🖳www.plymouthcathedral.co.uk **10 E5**

Poole

St Osmund *Poole* Built 1904–1927. Frankish turrets, Lombard arcading, Saxon patterning, Art Nouveau terracotta arch. Arts and Crafts grille. **27 B7**

Somerset

All Saints *Farley* Rare countryside example of 17th-century brick church. Built by one of Wren's master masons. **52 F1**

All Saints *Martock* 16th-century carved wooden 'quilted' ceiling. 🖳www.martockonline.co.uk **37 C7**

All Saints *Selworthy* Limewashed church on hilltop, rebuilt early 16th century. White and blue ceiling. **45 B5**

Cleeve Abbey (EH) *Washford* Rare 13th-century monastic site retaining a complete set of cloister buildings, including the refectory with its magnificent timber roof. 🖳www.english-heritage.org.uk ☎01984 640377 **45 C7**

Glastonbury Abbey *Glastonbury* Story of abbey is mix of fact and legend, some come for ancient Christian links, others to visit legendary burial site of King Arthur. Little remains of monastic buildings. 🖳www.glastonburyabbey.com ☎01458 832267 **48 D2**

Muchelney Abbey (EH) *Muchelney* Abbot's house is all that remains of former Benedictine monastery. Dating mainly from early 16th century, contains carved woodwork, fragments of wall paintings and stonework excavated from the ruined abbey. ☎01458 250664 🖳www.english-heritage.org.uk **37 B6**

Oare Church/St Mary's *Oare* Oare Church was the scene of Lorna Doone's wedding in the novel by R D Blackmore. Georgian box pews, pulpit and reading desk. 12th-century font, 15th-century chancel and nave. **44 B3**

St Andrew *Mells* Rebuilt 15th century. Highly decorated church porch. **49 B6**

St Andrew *Stogursey* Norman priory church built c.1100 and seized by Henry V 1414. Rare Somerset spire. **46 C4**

St Bartholomew *Crewkerne* Rebuilt at turn of 16th century. Window tracery among most complicated in England. 🖳www.stbartholomew-crewkerne.org **37 E6**

St Beuno *Culbone nr Porlock Weir* Allegedly the smallest church in England. Walls 12th-century or earlier. **44 B3**

St Cuthbert *St Cuthbert Street, Wells* Largest parish church in Somerset. Carved 17th-century pulpit. Ornate roof with angels, heralds, rosettes and shields. 🖳www.stcuthbertswells.co.uk ☎01749 673136 **48 B2**

St George *Dunster* 12th-century priory church, enlarged in the 13th and 15th centuries. Longest screen in England. **45 C6**

St John *Axbridge* Gothic building with 17th-century fittings. Blue and white nave ceiling. **55 F8**

St Mary *Croscombe* Tower with rare Somerset spire. Jacobean woodwork. Two-storey medieval treasury. **48 C3**

St Mary *Ilminster* Contains 17th-century tombs of founders of Wadham College, Oxford. Memorial brasses. **36 C5**

St Mary *Isle Abbotts* Ham stone and blue lias tower with 10 original statues. Norman font and original furnishings. **36 B5**

St Mary *Stogumber* Chancel decorated in style of William Morris. **46 D1**

St Mary *Westonzoyland* Good tie-beam roof decorated with rosettes and crowned with quatrefoils. **47 D7**

St Mary Magdalene *Hammet Street, Taunton* Tower has sculptures and is highest in Somerset. Oak roof and angels. 🖳www.stmarymagdalene.org.uk **36 A2**

St Michael *Brent Knoll* Norman with perpendicular additions. Satirical bench ends ridiculing church authorities. 17th-century memorial to John Somerset. **47 A6**

St Peter and St Paul *Shepton Mallet* Nave retains original Saxon walls. 14th-century tower. Panelled wagon roof. **48 C4**

Stoke sub Hamdon Priory (NT) *Stoke Sub Hamdon* Complex of buildings including dovecote. ☎01935 823289 🖳www.nationaltrust.org.uk **37 C7**

Wells Cathedral *Cathedral Green* Dates from late 12th to early 14th centuries and is renowned for majestic early English west front and great central tower. Noted features of the interior include massive but graceful scissor arches; capitals carved with moral tales, animals and people; 14th-century stained glass of the Lady Chapel; early clock with moving figures; choir stalls with misericords; and deeply worn steps to the Chapter House with a spectacular vaulted ceiling. Also Bishops Palace and Vicars Close. 🖳www.wellscathedral.org.uk ☎01749 674483 **48 B3**

Wiltshire

Malmesbury Abbey *Malmesbury* Abbey founded 7th century, only 12th-century nave survives. Porch with sculptured reliefs depicting scenes from Old Testament, Creation and Life of Christ. Norman stone carvings of apostles on interior walls of porch. Tomb of Saxon King Athelstan (died 939). 🖳http://malmesburyabbey.info **64 E3**

Salisbury Cathedral *The Close, Salisbury* Beautiful Early English building with later Decorated tower and tallest spire in Britain. Notable west front has many niches filled with figures representing the Te Deum. 🖳www.salisburycathedral.org.uk ☎01722 555118 **51 F7**

St John *Devizes* Mixture of Norman and Gothic styles. **58 D5**

St John the Baptist *Bishopstone* Many decorated features and interesting monuments. **40 A4**

St John the Baptist *Inglesham* 13th-century church saved by William Morris c. 1888-9. Late Saxon relief sculpture. **65 C9**

St Katharine and St Peter *Winterbourne Bassett* Mainly 14th-century Decorated style. Walls mainly of Sarsen stone, the stone from the Marlborough Downs used for Stonehenge. **59 A6**

St Laurence *Bradford on Avon* Built in 10th century, possibly on foundations of 8th-century church. Rediscovered 1871 after serving as barn. Simple interior with carved angels above the chancel. **57 D8**

St Mary *Bishops Cannings* Early Gothic. Vaulted porch with Decorated ballflower mouldings. 17th-century pew beneath huge hand intended to warn occupant of sin. **59 D5**

St Mary *Lydiard Tregoze* Mausoleum of St John family. Golden Cavalier monument. **65 F7**

St Mary, St Katherine and All Saints *Edington* Late Gothic completed at time of transition from Decorated to Perpendicular church styles. **50 A3**

St Thomas *High Street, Salisbury* Most complete Doom mural in Britain. ☎01722 322537 🖳www.stthomassalisbury.co.uk **51 E8**

St Nectan *Hartland* Site of Saxon abbey founded 1050. Second tallest tower in Devon, used to attract mariners at sea. **31 B5**

St Peter *Tawstock* 14th-century church with wooden gallery from local Tawstock Court. Collection of Bourchier and Wrey monuments. **43 F6**

St Saviour *Dartmouth* Nautical town church, medieval door and carved stone pulpit. gallery of 1633 with arms of merchant families. **15 E5**

Dorset

Abbey of St Mary *Sherborne* Cathedral until 1075. 11th-century doorway at west end and four pillars survive from last Saxon church on site. South porch, crossing arch and parts of north and south transepts survive from Norman church. Remainder is 15th century. Fan vaults cover virtually whole interior. 🖳www.sherborneabbey.com **38 C2**

Abbotsbury Abbey Buildings (EH) *Abbotsbury* Remains of cloister building of Benedictine abbey, founded c.1044. **25 C6**

Cerne Abbey *Cerne Abbas* Cerne Abbey, founded 987, consists of gatehouse, 987 onwards, Abbey House, the hospice or guesthouse, c.1450, and the abbot's porch, c.1509. **38 F3**

Christchurch Priory *Christchurch* Late 15th-century tower. North porch (1300) is largest in country; monument to Shelley. Norman nave and transepts. Decorated stone reredos representing

Jesse Tree. 🖳www.christchurchpriory.org ☎01202 488645 **28 B3**

Milton Abbey *Milton Abbas* 14th-century fragment of much bigger intended building. Decorated Gothic windows. Rich altar screen of 1492. **39 F5**

St Candida (St Wite) and Holy Cross *Whitchurch Canonicorum* Only parish church in England to retain relics and shrine of its saint. Norman font. **24 A2**

St Cuthburga *Wimborne Minster* Early 16th-century Flemish glass in east window. One Norman, one Gothic tower. Norman font on Purbeck marble shafts. Early 14th-century astronomical clock. **27 A7**

St Peter and St Paul *Blandford Forum* Rebuilt 1733–9. Palladian church with square tower. Pulpit from destroyed Wren church St Antholin in London. **39 E7**

Gloucestershire

Abbey of St Mary *Tewkesbury* Biggest Norman tower in Europe. Decorated chapels at east end contrast with Norman work. Carved roof bosses portray life of Christ. Brasses, monuments and 14th-century windows of the choir commemorate Lords of Tewkesbury. Vestry door covered with metal taken from armour of knights killed at Battle of Tewkesbury. ☎01684 850959 🖳www.tewkesburyabbey.org.uk **70 A3**

All Saints *Newland* Known as 'the Cathedral of the Forest'. Sandstone church with decorated spire. ☎01594 810036 **68 F5**

Gloucester Cathedral *Westgate Street, College Street* Romanesque building of 11th and 12th centuries with later 15th-century exterior. Beautiful Norman building with Perpendicular work on the exterior. Noted for fine 68.5 m (225 ft) high central tower and huge 14th-century east window. Choir stalls with fine misericords. Lady Chapel with rare Norman lead font. Interesting roof bosses, including several Green Men. 14th–15th-century cloisters with the first example of fan vaulting some medieval glass. 🖳www.gloucestercathedral.org.uk **70 D2**

Holy Innocents *Highnam* Founded 1849 Wall paintings cover the interior; iron screen and carved stone reredos. ☎01452 525567 **70 D1**

Odda's Chapel (EH) *Deerhurst* Rare Anglo-Saxon chapel attached to half-timbered farmhouse. 🖳www.english-heritage.org.uk **70 B3**

St James *Chipping Campden* Reputedly houses Britain's only complete set of medieval altar hangings. **77 E6**

St John *Elkstone* Norman church. West tower built c.1370; gargoyles. Fine woodwork. Priest's dovecote. **71 E5**

St John the Baptist *Cirencester* Largest and most complex south porch in Britain. Coats of arms of patrons. Garstang chapel surrounded by 15th-century screen. Second chapel with stone screen and timber roof. Anne Boleyn cup. **65 B5**

Museums and galleries

Arts and crafts

Bath & NE Somerset

American Museum in Britain *Claverton* In Claverton Manor. Development of North American decorative arts. Native American and folk art. See 'Gardens' ☎01225 460503 💻www.americanmuseum.org **57 D7**

Holburne Museum of Art *Bath* 17th–18th century fine and decorative art. Old Masters including Gainsborough, Stubbs, Turner. ☎01225 388588 💻www.holburne.org **57 C7**

Museum of East Asian Art *Bath* Five galleries and more than 500 art treasures from East Asia. ☎01225 464640 💻www.meaa.org.uk **57 C7**

Victoria Art Gallery *Bath* Paintings, drawings etc. Artists include Gainsborough, Turner and Sickert. ☎01225 477233 💻www.victoriagal.org.uk **57 C7**

Bournemouth

Russell-Cotes Art Gallery and Museum *Bournemouth* Victorian art collection, Japanese art and artefacts, contemporary art. ☎01202 451858 💻www.russell-cotes.bournemouth.gov.uk **28 B1**

Bristol

Arnolfini Arts Centre *Bristol* Visual arts centre. ☎0117 9172300 💻www.arnolfini.org.uk **56 B4**

Cornwall

Barbara Hepworth Museum and Sculpture Garden *St Ives* Sculptures in bronze, stone and wood, paintings and drawings. Studio and garden run by Tate Gallery. ☎01736 796226 💻www.tate.org.uk/stives/hepworth **3 B6**

Newlyn Art Gallery *Newlyn* Changing exhibitions of contemporary art by leading artists. ☎01736 363715 💻www.newlynartgallery.co.uk **2 E5**

Royal Cornwall Museum *Truro* Among the collections are a good number of Newlyn School paintings, some Old Master drawing, Egyptian antiquities including an unwrapped mummy, Greek and Roman objects and a world-famous collection of minerals. ☎01872 272205 💻www.royalcornwallmuseum.org.uk **4 B4**

Tate St Ives *St Ives* More than 200 works of modern art as well as special exhibitions from the other Tate galleries. ☎01736 796226 💻www.tate.org.uk/stives **3 B6**

Gloucestershire

Nature in Art *Twigworth* Located in Wallsworth Hall. Museum dedicated to art inspired by nature. ☎01452 731422 💻www.nature-in-art.org.uk **70 C2**

General museums

Bath & NE Somerset

Bath Royal Literary and Scientific Institution *Bath* Geology, natural history, ethnology, archaeology, art and historical artefacts. ☎01225 312084 💻www.brlsi.org **57 C7**

Fashion Museum *Bath* More than 150 complete outfits on display. ☎01225 477173 💻www.fashionmuseum.co.uk **57 C7**

Bristol

British Empire and Commonwealth Museum *Bristol* ☎0117 9254980 💻www.empiremuseum.co.uk **56 B3**

City Museum and Art Gallery *Bristol* Art and archaeology, geology and natural history, housed in a magnificent early 20th-century building. ☎0117 9223571 💻www.bristol.gov.uk **56 B3**

M Shed *Bristol* A new, interactive, museum exploring the story of Bristol from prehistoric times to the present day. ☎0117 352 6600 💻http://mshed.org **56 B3**

Cornwall

Museum of Smuggling *Jamaica Inn* Collection of smuggling artefacts ☎01566 86250 💻www.jamaicainn.co.uk **17 E8**

Museum of Witchcraft *Boscastle* The world's largest collection of items related to witchcraft. ☎01840 250111 💻www.museumofwitchcraft.com **17 B6**

Paul Corin's Magnificent Music Machines *St Keyne* Includes café organ, player pianos, American Wurlitzer theatre pipe organ. ☎01579 343108 💻www.paulcorinmusic.com **9 C8**

Devon

Bill Douglas Centre *Exeter* History of cinema. ☎01392 724321 💻www.billdouglas.org **21 B8**

Dorset

The Blandford Fashion Museum *Blandford Forum* Historical costumes covering a 250-year period. ☎01258 453006 💻www.theblandfordfashionmuseum.com **39 E7**

Priest's House Museum *Wimborne Minster* Varied collection including art and archaeology, costume, transport, photography, toys, warfare, medicine and music ☎01202 882533 💻www.priest-house.co.uk **27 A7**

Gloucestershire

Cheltenham Art Gallery and Museum *Cheltenham* Nationally important Arts and Crafts movement collection; furniture, paintings, ceramics, jewellery and local history. Closed until spring 2013. ☎01242 237431 💻www.cheltenhammuseum.org.uk **70 C4**

Holst Birthplace Museum *Cheltenham* Original piano and manuscripts. ☎01242 524846 💻www.holstmuseum.org.uk **71 C5**

Plymouth

City Museum and Art Gallery *Plymouth* Paintings, ceramics, archaeology, natural history. ☎01752 304774 💻www.plymouthmuseum.gov.uk **11 E5**

Local

Bath & NE Somerset

Bath Postal Museum *Bath* 4000 years of communication, from Sumerian clay tablets to the present day. ☎01225 460333 💻www.bathpostalmuseum.co.uk **57 C7**

Building of Bath Museum *Bath* History of transformation of Bath, from small provincial spa into Georgian splendour. ☎01225 333895 💻www.bath-preservation-trust.org.uk **57 C7**

Roman Baths Museum *Bath* Roman temple and bathing complex. ☎01225 477785 💻www.romanbaths.co.uk **57 C7**

Cornwall

Polperro Heritage Museum of Smuggling and Fishing *Polperro* Exhibits and photographs dating from the 18th century ☎01503 272423 💻www.polperro.org/museum.html **9 E7**

Shipwreck and Heritage Centre *Charlestown* Houses largest shipwreck artefact collection in UK. ☎01726 69897 💻www.shipwreckcharlestown.com **8 E3**

Devon

Dartmouth Museum *Dartmouth* Historic and maritime museum in former merchant's house from 1640. ☎01803 832923 💻http://dartmouthmuseum.org **15 E5**

Dorset

Blandford Museum *Blandford Forum* History of Blandford Forum and neighbouring villages. ☎http://blandfordtownmuseum.org ☎01258 450388 **39 E7**

Dorset County Museum *Dorchester* Local wildlife, rocks, fossils, archaeology and displays on Dorset writers.

💻www.dorsetcountymuseum.org ☎01305 262735 **25 B8**

The Philpot Museum *Lyme Regis* Winner of Museum of South-west prize and Gulbenkian Prize. ☎01297 443370 💻www.lymeregismuseum.co.uk **24 B1**

Tolpuddle Martyrs Museum *Tolpuddle* Story of the six workers transported to Australia in 1834 as punishment for forming a trade union. ☎01305 848237 💻www.tolpuddlemartyrs.org.uk **26 B2**

Gloucestershire

City Museum and Art Gallery *Gloucester* Local history and small collection of British paintings. ☎01452 396131 💻www.gloucester.gov.uk/citymuseum **70 D2**

Corinium Museum *Cirencester* Extensive collection of Romano-British antiquities from Corinium. ☎01285 655611 💻www.cirencester.co.uk/coriniummuseum **64 B5**

Gloucester Folk Museum *Gloucester* Local history exhibits, including what is claimed to be the stake at which Bishop Hooper was burned. ☎01452 396868 💻www.gloucester.gov.uk/Freetime/Museums/folkmuseum.aspx **70 D2**

Scilly Isles

Isles of Scilly Museum *St Mary's* Geology, archaeology, history and natural history. 💻www.iosmuseum.org ☎01720 422337 **6 B3**

Longstone Heritage Centre *St Mary's* History of Isles from prehistoric times. Also 'Papers Past at Longstone' – displays of original newspapers, c. 1793 onwards, including special birth-date papers to buy. 💻www.longstonecentre.co.uk ☎01720 423770 **6 B3**

Somerset

Somerset Cricket Museum *Taunton* Historic barn containing cricket memorabilia. 💻www.somersetcricketmuseum.co.uk **36 B2**

Wiltshire

Alexander Keiller Museum *Avebury* Collection of important local prehistoric material. ☎01672 529203 💻www.english-heritage.org.uk **59 C7**

Salisbury and South Wiltshire Museum *Salisbury* Includes Stonehenge, settlers from Stone Age to Saxons, Old Sarum and Salisbury, Wedgwood, pre-NHS surgery, costumes. ☎01722 332151 💻www.salisburymuseum.org.uk **51 E8**

Military history

Cornwall

Duke of Cornwall's Light Infantry Regiment Museum *Bodmin* History of Cornwall's county regiment from 1702–1959. ☎01208 72810 💻www.armymuseums.org.uk **8 B4**

Devon

Cobbaton Combat Collection *Cobbaton* World War II British and Canadian military equipment. ☎01769 540740 💻www.cobbatoncombat.co.uk **32 A5**

Dorset

Royal Signals Museum *Blandford Camp* Displays include ENIGMA, Special

◄ **Wheal Coates tin-mine near St Agnes, Cornwall** Jason Theaker / iStockphoto.com

▲ **The Fleet Air Arm Museum at Yeovilton** Fleet Air Arm Museum

Operations Executive, SAS. Many displays for children. ☎01258 482248 💻www.army.mod.uk/23500.aspx **39 E8**

The Keep Military Museum *Dorchester* History of infantry, cavalry and artillerymen of the counties of Devon and Dorset. 💻www.keepmilitarymuseum.org ☎01305 264066 **25 B8**

The Tank Museum *Bovington* WWI walk-through trench experience. Vehicle collection. ☎01929 405096 💻www.tankmuseum.org.uk **26 C3**

Gloucestershire

Soldiers of Gloucestershire Museum *Gloucester Docks* ☎01452 522682 💻www.glosters.org.uk **70 D2**

Wellington Aviation Museum *Moreton-in-Marsh* A small museum dedicated to the personnel and trainee pilots of the World War II flight training station ☎01608 650323 💻www.wellingtonaviation.org **72 A3**

Somerset

Fleet Air Arm Museum *RNAS Yeovilton* More than 90 aircraft and many models and equipment. ☎01935 840565 💻www.fleetairarm.com **37 B9**

Wiltshire

The Wardrobe *Salisbury* Collections include medals, uniforms and militaria. 💻www.thewardrobe.org.uk ☎01722 419419 **51 E8**

Mills, mines and factories

Cornwall

Cornish Mines and Engines (NT) *Pool* Two great beam engines. ☎01209 315027 💻www.nationaltrust.org.uk **4 B1**

Geevor Tin Mine Museum *Trewellard* Heritage centre. Tells story of production of tin and of miners. ☎01736 788662 💻www.geevor.com **2 D3**

Devon

Coldharbour Mill Museum *Uffculme* Displays of Victorian spinning, carding and weaving machines. ☎01884 840960 💻www.coldharbourmill.org.uk **35 D6**

Dartington Glass Centre *Great Torrington* Tours of the factory, displays of glass-making techniques. Exhibition on history of glass. ☎01805 626262 💻www.dartington.co.uk **32 C2**

Dorset

White Mill (NT) *Sturminster Marshall* Rebuilt in 1776. Guided tours only. Open in summer. ☎01258 858051 💻www.nationaltrust.org.uk **27 A6**

Somerset

Dunster Watermill (NT) *Dunster* 18th century ☎01643 821759 💻www.nationaltrust.org.uk **45 C6**

Stembridge Tower Mill (NT) *High Ham* Last thatched windmill in England. ☎01935 823289 💻www.nationaltrust.org.uk **47 E8**

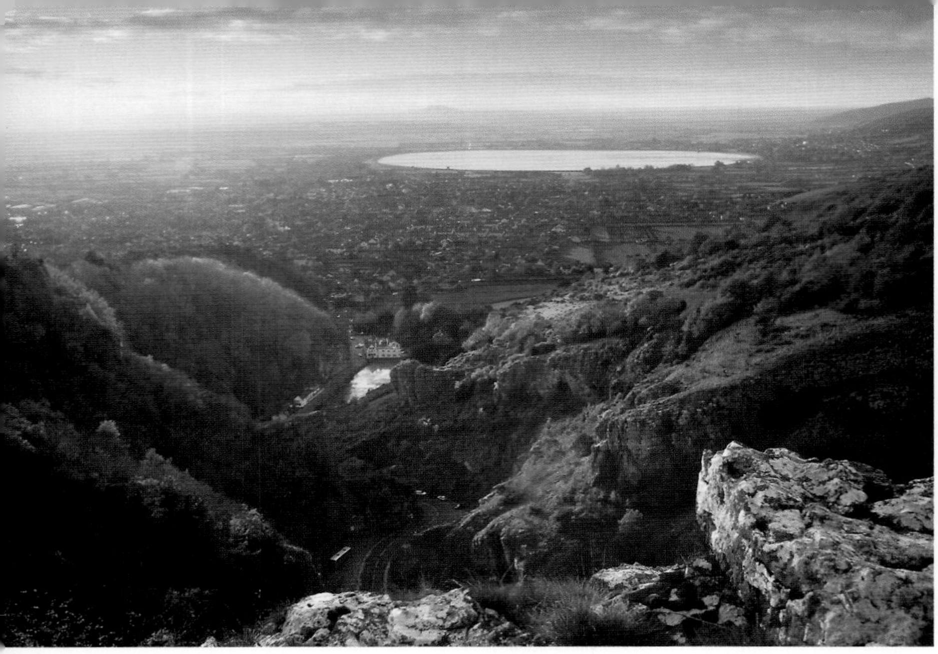

◄ **Cheddar Gorge, Somerset**
James Hughes / Alamy

Science and technology

Bath & NE Somerset

The Herschel Museum of Astronomy *Bath* Located in the house in which Herschel discovered the planet Uranus. 🖳www.bath-preservation-trust.org.uk ✆01225 446865 **57 C7**

Devon

British Photographic Museum, *Bowden House, Totnes* ✆01803 863664 **14 C4**

Dorset

Dinosaur Museum *Dorchester* Fossils, skeletons, reconstructions, interactive computer displays and videos. A World Heritage museum. ✆01305 269880 🖳www.thedinosaurmuseum.com **25 B8**

Gloucestershire

Dr Jenner's House *Berkeley* Georgian house and gardens. Home of Dr Edward Jenner, smallpox vaccination pioneer. ✆01453 810631 🖳www.jennermuseum.com **63 C5**

Somerset

Montacute Museum *Montacute* Vintage to modern day radios; film, TV and children's books and toys; televisions, household appliances; advertising signs and packaging. 🖳www.montacutemuseum.co.uk ✆01935 823024 **37 C7**

Wiltshire

Fox-Talbot Museum *Lacock* Commemorates the life and work of the inventor of modern photography ✆01249 730459 🖳www.nationaltrust.org.uk **58 C3**

Transport

Cornwall

Automobilia *St Stephen* More than 50 vehicles dating from 1904 to the 1960s. Automobilia. ✆01726 823092 **8 E1**

National Maritime Museum *Falmouth* National small boat collection, galleries, remote-controlled models and live demonstrations. ✆01326 313388 🖳www.nmmc.co.uk **4 D4**

Devon

North Devon Maritime Museum *Appledore* North Devon's maritime history illustrated by models, photographs, etc. ✆01237 422064 🖳www.devonmuseums.net **42 E4**

Gloucestershire

Cotswold Motoring Museum and Toy Collection *Bourton-on-the-Water* 30 cars and motorcycles on display with a selection of prams, toy and pedal cars. More than 800 vintage advertising signs. Also toy collection. ✆01451 821255 **72 C2**

Gloucester Waterways Museum *Gloucester Docks* Located in listed Victorian warehouse. ✆01452 318200 🖳www.gloucesterwaterwaysmuseum.org.uk **70 D2**

North Somerset

The Helicopter Museum *Weston-super-Mare* Examples from around the world with displays. ✆01934 635227 🖳http://helicoptermuseum.co.uk **55 D6**

Somerset

Haynes Motor Museum *Yeovil* Britain's largest collection of automobilia. 🖳www.haynesmotormuseum.com ✆01963 440804 **48 F4**

Swindon

Steam *Swindon* Museum of the Great Western Railway ✆01793 466646 🖳www.steam-museum.org.uk **65 E7**

Wiltshire

Atwell-Wilson Motor Museum Trust *Calne* Vintage and classic cars. Classic motorbikes. ✆01249 813119 🖳www.atwellwilson.org.uk **58 B5**

The Kennet and Avon Canal Museum *Devizes* ✆01380 721279 🖳www.katrust.org **58 D5**

Sports

Activity centres

Bath and North East Somerset

Bath Narrowboats *Bath* Narrowboat hire ✆01225 447276 🖳www.bath-narrowboats.co.uk **57 C7**

Cornwall

Hotrock Coasteer *Newquay* This centre offers abseiling, climbing, coasteering, hill-walking, navigating, scrambling and surfing. 🖳www.hotrockcoasteer.co.uk ✆01726 869162 **7 C6**

Penhale Adventure Centre *Newquay* A wide range of activities, including abseiling, archery, ballooning, buggying, climbing, flying, gliding, hang gliding, helicopter flights, karting, kayaking, kite surfing, landboarding, land yachting, microlighting, mountain biking, mountain boarding, off-road motor biking, orienteering, paintballing, parachuting, paragliding, powerkiting, rib rides, quad biking, rock climbing, sailing, scuba diving, shooting, surfing, survival training, tank driving, wakeboarding, waterskiing and 4 x 4 driving 🖳www.penhaleadventure.com ✆0800 781 6861 **7 C6**

Devon

Ashcombe Adventure Centre *Ashcombe, nr Dawlish* Among the activities are archery, clay pigeon shooting, fishing, karting, paintballing and quad biking. ✆01626 866766 🖳www.ashcombeadventure.co.uk **21 E8**

Mountain Water Experience *Kingsbridge* Activities include abseiling, assault course, body boarding, canyoning, caving, coasteering, gorge walking, high-wire walking, kayak training, open boat instruction, rock climbing and white water kayaking. ✆01548 550 675 🖳www.mountainwaterexperience.co.uk **13 D5**

Skern Lodge Outdoor Centre *Appledore* Offers abseiling, archery, assault course, canoeing, climbing, high ropes, orienteering, rafting, surf skiing and a zipwire. ✆01237 475992 🖳www.skernlodge.co.uk **42 E4**

North Somerset

Avon Ski and Action Centre *Churchill* Centre offering abseiling, archery, clay pigeon shooting, climbing, mountain boarding, power kiting, quad biking, shooting, skateboarding, skiing, snowblading, snowboarding, tobogganing and 4 x 4 driving. ✆01934 852 335 🖳www.highaction.co.uk **55 E8**

Somerset

Aardvark Endeavours *Cheddar* Aardvark Endeavours offer abseiling, archery, caving, climbing, kayaking, raft building, rifle shooting and a 100-m zip-wire. 🖳www.aardvarkendeavours.com ✆01934 844254 **56 F1**

Cycling

Cornwall

Bike Chain Bissoe Bike Hire *Truro* Sales, servicing, hire. ✆01872 870341 🖳www.cornwallcyclehire.com **4 B4**

Bridge Bike Hire *Wadebridge* ✆01208 813050 🖳www.cornwall-online.co.uk/bridgebikehire **8 A2**

Camel Trail Cycle Hire *Wadebridge* 🖳http://cameltrailcyclehire.co.uk ✆01208 814104 **8 A2**

Hayle Cycles *Hayle* ✆01736 753825 🖳http://haylecycles.com **3 C7**

North Coast Cycles *Bude* ✆01288 352974 **30 E4**

Padstow Cycle Hire *Padstow* 🖳http://padstowcyclehire.com ✆01841 533533 **16 E3**

Pedals Bike Hire *Penzance* ✆01736 360600 **3 D5**

Pentewan Valley Cycle Hire *St Austell* ✆01726 844242 🖳www.pentewanvalleycyclehire.co.uk **8 E3**

The Cycle Centre *Penzance* ✆01736 351671 🖳www.cornwallcyclecentre.co.uk **3 D5**

Trail Bike Hire *Padstow* ✆01841 532594 🖳www.trailbikehire.co.uk **16 E3**

Truro Cycles *Truro* ✆01872 271703 **4 B4**

Devon

Biketrail Cycle Hire *Barnstaple* ✆01271 7372586 🖳www.biketrail.co.uk **43 E6**

Hot Pursuit *Totnes* ✆01803 865174 🖳www.hotpursuit-cycles.co.uk **14 C4**

Knobblies *Exmouth* ✆01395 270182 🖳www.knobbliesbikes.co.uk **22 D2**

Otter Cycle Hire *Braunton* ✆01271 813339 **42 D4**

Saddles and Paddles *Exeter* Canoe and bike hire. ✆01392 424241 🖳www.saddlepaddle.co.uk **21 B8**

Tavistock Cycles *Tavistock* ✆01822 617630 🖳www.tavistockcycles.co.uk **19 F6**

Dorset

Bikeabout *Swanage* ✆01929 425050 **27 E7**

Dorchester Cycles *Dorchester* ✆01305 268787 🖳www.dorchestercycles.co.uk **25 B8**

Gloucestershire

Cotswold Country Cycles *Chipping Campden* ✆01386 438706 🖳www.cotswoldcountrycycles.com **77 E6**

Cotswold Water Park & Keynes Country Park *Cirencester* See under Country Parks **65 C5**

Forest Adventure *Coleford* ✆01594 835116 **69 E5**

Plymouth

Alltrax *nr Plymouth* ✆01752 863553 🖳www.alltraxcycles.co.uk **10 E5**

Poole

Cool Cats Leisure *Poole* ✆01202 701100 **27 B7**

Somerset

Blue Bell Cycle Hire *Bridgwater* ✆01278 722123 **47 D5**

Bow Bridge Cycles *Langport* Cycle hire and trails. ✆01458 250350 🖳www.bowbridgecycleslangport.co.uk **47 F8**

Ian's Cycle Centre *Taunton* 🖳www.ianscyclecentre.co.uk ✆01823 365917 **36 A2**

King's Cycles *Wellington* ✆01823 662260 🖳www.kingscycles.co.uk **35 B7**

King's Cycles *Taunton* ✆01823 352272 🖳www.kingscycles.co.uk **36 A2**

Torbay

Cyclehire *Torbay* ✆01803 521068 **15 C5**

Wiltshire

Towpath Trail *Bradford on Avon* 🖳www.towpathtrail.co.uk ✆01225 867187 **57 D8**

Football

Bournemouth

AFC Bournemouth *Bournemouth* ✆0844 5761910 🖳www.afcb.co.uk **26 B2**

Bristol

Bristol City FC *Bristol* ✆0871 2226666 🖳www.bcfc.co.uk **56 B3**

Bristol Rovers FC *Horfield* ✆0117 909648 🖳www.bristolrovers.co.uk **56 A3**

Devon

Exeter City FC *Exeter* ✆01392 411243 🖳www.exetercityfc.co.uk **21 B8**

Gloucestershire

Cheltenham Town FC *Cheltenham* 🖳www.ctfc.com ✆01242 573558 **71 C5**

Plymouth

Plymouth Argyll FC *Plymouth* ✆01752 562561 🖳www.pafc.co.uk **10 D5**

Somerset

Yeovil Town FC *Yeovil* ✆01935 706671 🖳www.ytfc.net **37 C8**

Swindon

Swindon Town FC *Swindon* ✆01793 513626 🖳www.swindontownfc.co.uk **65 E8**

Torbay

Torquay United FC *Torquay* ✆01803 388666 🖳www.torquayunited.com **15 B6**

Golf

The following is a selection of courses that welcome visitors at most times. Those marked* have restricted times for visitors or require a valid handicap certificate. Most clubs require prior booking for visitors, particularly groups. It is advisable always to contact the club/pro in advance before visiting to check for availability of tee times or in case of tournaments or restrictions such as times reserved for ladies or juniors.

Bristol

Shirehampton Park GC *Shirehampton* An 18-hole parkland course. ✆0117 982 2083 🖳www.shirehamptonparkgolfclub.co.uk **56 A2**

Cornwall

Bude & North Cornwall GC *Bude* An 18-hole, par-71 course in the centre of the coastal resort. ✆01288 352006 🖳www.budegolf.co.uk **30 E4**

Cape Cornwall G&CC *St Just* An 18-hole course overlooking the rugged west Cornish coast. ✆01726 814250 🖳www.capecornwall.com **2 D3**

Carlyon Bay GC *Carlyon Bay* An 18-hole course overlooking St Austell Bay. ✆01726 814250 🖳www.carlyongolf.com **8 E4**

China Fleet CC *Saltash* 18-hole course overlooking the Tamar. ✆01752 854665 🖳www.china-fleet.co.uk **10 D4**

Falmouth GC *Falmouth* 18-hole course near Swanpool Beach. ✆01326 311262/314296 🖳www.falmouthgolfclub.com **4 D3**

Killiow Golf Park *Kea* An 18-hole course south of Truro. ✆01872 270246 🖳www.killiowgolf.co.uk **4 B4**

Looe GC *Looe* An 18-hole course on the higher ground looking over Whitesands Bay. 🖳www.looegolfclub.co.uk ✆01503 240239 **9 D8**

Lostwithiel G&CC *Polscoe* An 18-hole course just outside Lostwithiel. ✆01208 873550 🖳www.golf-hotel.co.uk **9 C5**

Merlin GC *Mawgan Porth, Newquay* An 18-hole course inland from Cornwall's west coast and overlooking the Vale of Mawgan. 🖳www.merlingolfcourse.co.uk ✆01841 540222 **7 B8**

Newquay GC *Newquay* An 18-hole course, right next to the surfer paradise of Fistral Beach. ✆01637 872091 🖳www.newquaygolfclub.co.uk **7 C7**

Perranporth GC *Perranporth* An 18-hole links course right next to the south-west coast of Cornwall. ✆01872 572454 🖳www.perranporthgolfclub.com **7 E6**

Porthpean GC *St Austell* An 18-hole course overlooking St Austell Bay. ✆01726 64613 🖳www.porthpeangolfclub.co.uk **8 E3**

St Mellion Hotel G&CC *St Mellion* Two 18-hole courses, the Nicklaus Course and the Old Course set in East Cornish woodland ✆01579 351351 🖳www.st-mellion.co.uk **10 B3**

Tregenna Castle Hotel *St Ives* An 18-hole course overlooking St Ives Bay. ✆01736 795254 🖳www.tregenna-castle.co.uk **3 C6**

Whitsand Bay Hotel *Portwrinkle* 18-hole course on with views over Whitesand Bay. 🖳whitsandbayhotel.co.uk/golf-cornwall ✆01503 230276 **10 E3**

Devon

Ashbury GC *Okehampton* Four 18-hole courses set in woodland: Pines, Beeches, Oakwood and Willows (par 3) 🖳www.ashburygolfhotel.com ✆01837 55453 **19 B7**

Bigbury GC *Bigbury-on-Sea* 18-hole course overlooking the River Avon. ✆01548 810557 🖳www.bigburygolfclub.com **12 C4**

Dainton Park GC *Ipplepen* An 18-hole parkland course in East Devon. ✆01803 815000 🖳www.daintonparkgolf.co.uk **14 B4**

East Devon GC *Budleigh Salterton* 18-hole links course over looking the English Channel. ✆01395 443370 🖳www.edgc.co.uk **22 D2**

Exminster Golf Centre *Exminster* A 9-hole course and floodlit driving range overlooking the River Exe. ✆01392 833838 🖳www.exminstergolf.com **21 C8**

Fingle Glen GC *Tedburn St Mary* An 18-hole course near the northern edge of Dartmoor. ✆01647 61817 🖳www.fingleglen.com **21 B6**

High Bullen GC *Chittlehamholt* 18-hole course in wooded parkland ✆01769 540561, 🖳www.highbullen.co.uk **33 B6**

Holsworthy GC *Killatree, Holsworthy* An 18-hole course in northwest Devon. 🖳www.holsworthygolfclub.co.uk ✆01409 253177 **31 F6**

Honiton GC *Honiton* An 18-hole course in the East Devon hills ✆01404 44422 🖳www.honitongolfclub.co.uk **23 A5**

Hurdwick GC *Tavistock* An 18-hole course near the western edge of Dartmoor. ✆01822 612746 🖳http://hurdwickgolf.com **19 E6**

Ilfracombe GC *Ilfracombe* An 18-hole course in moorland above high cliffs over-looking the Bristol Channel.

www.ilfracombegolfclub.com
01271 862176 (option 1) **43 B5**

Newton Abbot (Stover) GC* *Stover* An 18-hole woodland course near the edge of Dartmoor. 01626 352460 www.stovergolfclub.co.uk **14 A4**

Okehampton GC* *Okehampton* An 18-hole course near the northern edge of Dartmoor. 01837 52113 www.okehamptongolfclub.co.uk **19 B8**

Royal North Devon GC* *Westward Ho!* An 18-hole links course in a popular resort. 01237 473817 www.royalnorthdevongolfclub.co.uk **42 E3**

Saunton GC* *Saunton* Two 18-hole links courses (East and West) by the sands of Braunton Burrows. 01271 812436 www.sauntongolf.co.uk **42 D4**

Sidmouth GC *Sidmouth* An 18-hole course on the edge of a popular resort. 01395 513451 www.sidmouthgolfclub.co.uk **22 C4**

Staddon Heights GC *Plymstock* An 18-hole course on high ground overlooking Plymouth Sound. 01752 402475 www.staddonheightsgolf.co.uk **11 E5**

Tavistock GC *Tavistock* An 18-hole course on the edge of Dartmoor. 01822 612344 www.tavistockgolfclub.org.uk **19 F6**

Teignmouth GC* *Teignmouth* An 18-hole course overlooking the Teign. 01626 777070 www.teignmouthgolfclub.co.uk **21 E8**

Thurlestone GC *Thurlestone* An 18-hole course next to Warren Point. 01548 560405 www.thurlestonegolfclub.co.uk **12 D4**

Tiverton GC *Tiverton* An 18-hole lowland course. 01884 252187 www.tivertongolfclub.co.uk **34 D4**

Warren GC *Dawlish Warren* An 18-hole links course on the promontary of Dawlish Warren 01626 862255 www.dwgc.co.uk **22 E1**

Waterbridge GC *Down St Mary* A 9-hole course in the heart of Devon. 01363 85111 www.waterbridgegc.co.uk **33 F8**

Woodbury Park GC* *Woodbury* Two courses: the 18-hole Oaks and the 9-hole Acorn. 01395 233500 www.woodburypark.co.uk **22 C2**

Wrangaton GC *Wrangaton* An 18-hole course on the southern edge of Dartmoor. 01364 73229 www.wrangatongolfclub.co.uk **14 D1**

Yelverton GC *Yelverton* An 18-hole course on the heights of Roborough Down. www.yelvertongolf.co.uk 01822 852824 **11 B6**

Dorset

Bridport & West Dorset GC* *Bridport* An 18-hole course with a 9-hole pitch and putt. 01308 421095 www.bridportgolfclub.org.uk **24 B4**

Broadstone GC *Broadstone* An 18-hole course on the on the hills behind Poole Harbour. 01202 692595 www.broadstonegolfclub.com **27 A7**

Bulbury Woods GC *Lytchett Matravers* 18-hole course on the edge of Wareham Forest. 01929 459574 www.bulbury-woods.co.uk **27 B5**

Canford Magna GC *Canford Magna* Three courses: the 18-hole Parkland and Riverside and the 9-hole Knighton. 01202 592505 www.canfordmagnagc.co.uk **27 A7**

Chedington Court GC *South Perrott* An 18-hole course in the north Dorset hills. 01935 891747 **37 E7**

Crane Valley GC *Verwood* Two courses: the 18-hole Valley and the 9-hole Woodland. 01202 814088 www.crane-valley.co.uk **40 E4**

Dudsbury GC *Ferndown* Tel 01202 593499 www.dudsburygolfclub.co.uk **27 A8**

Ferndown Forest GC *Ferndown* An 18-hole links course on the edge of Ferndown Forest. 01202 876096 www.ferndownforestgolf.co.uk **40 F4**

Ferndown GC *Ferndown* A heathland links with the 18-hole Championship course and the 9-hole Presidents course. www.ferndown-golf-club.co.uk 01202 653950 **27 A8**

Halstock GC *Halstock* An 18-hole woodland course in the hills of north Dorset. 01935 891689 **37 E8**

Highcliffe Castle GC *Highcliffe-on-Sea* An 18-hole course overlooking Christchurch Bay. 01425 272210/272953 www.highcliffecastlegc.co.uk **28 B3**

Isle of Purbeck *Studland* Two courses: the 18-hole Purbeck course and the 9-hole Dene course. 01929 450361 www.purbeckgolf.co.uk **27 D7**

Lyme Regis GC* *Lyme Regis* An 18-hole course at one end of Lyme Bay. www.lymeregisgolfclub.co.uk 01297 44296**324 B1**

Sherborne GC* *Sherborne* An 18-hole course on the hills north of Sherborne. www.sherbornegolfclub.co.uk 01935 814431 **38 C2**

The Ashley Wood GC *Blandford Forum* An 18-hole course set on the Dorset Downs. 08442484026 www.ashleywoodgolfclub.com **39 E8**

Wareham GC *Wareham* An 18-hole heathland course. 01929 554147 www.warehamgolfclub.com **27 C5**

Weymouth GC* *Weymouth* An 18-hole links course in the hills between Weymouth and Dorchester. 01305 750831 www.weymouthgolfclub.co.uk **25 E8**

Gloucestershire

Cleeve Hill GC* *Cheltenham* An 18-hole course on the edge of the Cotswolds. www.cleevehillgolfcourse.co.uk 01242 672025 **71 B5**

Cotswold Edge GC *Wotton-under-Edge* 18- hole course in the Cotwolds. www.cotswoldedgegolfclub.org.uk 01453 844167 **63 C7**

Cotswold Hills GC *Ullenwood* An 18-hole woodland course. 01242 515264 www.cotswoldhills-golfclub.com **70 D4**

Forest Hills GC *Coleford* An 18-hole parkland course. 01594 810620 www.foresthillsgolfandleisure.co.uk **69 E5**

Forest of Dean GC *Coleford* An 18-hole course on the edge of the Forest of Dean. 01594 832583 www.bells-hotel.co.uk **69 E5**

Lilley Brook GC *Cheltenham* An 18-hole course on the edge of the Cotswolds overlooking Cheltenham. 01242 526785 www.lilleybrook.co.uk **71 D5**

Snowshill/iStockphoto.com

Family attractions

Cornwall

Bodmin and Wenford Railway *Bodmin* Restored steam engines and rides. 0845 1259678 www.bodminandwenfordrailway.co.uk **9 B5**

Bodmin Jail *Bodmin* Former county prison dating back to 1776. Dungeons, plus displays. 01208 76292 www.bodminjail.org **8 B4**

Crealy Great Adventure Park *Wadebridge* Outdoor adventures, aerial walkways, slides, log flume, horses, farm animals and parkland 01841 540 276 www.crealy.co.uk **8 B1**

Hidden Valley *Launceston* Treasure hunt centre. Also 9-hole golf course, nature reserve, farm animals, miniature railway and play area. 01566 86463 www.hidden-valley.co.uk **18 D2**

Holywell Bay Fun Park *Newquay* Pitch and putt, kid's go-karting, rides, bumper boats, maze, indoor adventure area. 01637 830095 www.holywellbay.co.uk **7 D6**

Kidzworld *St Austell* Adventure centre. 01726 815553 www.kidzworldcornwall.co.uk **8 E3**

Land's End Landmark *Sennan* Visitor attraction with interactive exhibits. 0871 720 0044 *http://www.landsend-landmark.co.uk/index.php* **2 E2** See also Land's End in the *Other natural features* section

Lappa Valley Steam Railway *Newquay* 01872 510317 www.lappavalley.co.uk **7 D7**

Launceston Steam Railway *Launceston* 01566 775665 www.launcestonsr.co.uk **18 C3**

Poldark Mine *Wendron* Underground workings with guided tour. Children's play area. 01326 573173 www.poldark-mine.co.uk **4 D1**

Tamarisk Miniature Railway *Nr Padstow* 01841 540829 **16 E3**

The Flambards Experience *Helston* Recreation of Victorian and war-time street. Cornwall Aero Park and Exploratorium. Rides include log flume and rollercoasters. 01326 573404 www.flambards.co.uk **4 E1**

Devon

Beer Quarry Caves *Beer* Caverns dating from Roman times. Tours and exhibits. 01297 680282 www.beerquarrycaves.fsnet.co.uk **23 C6**

Bicton Woodland Railways *East Budleigh* 01395 658465 www.bictongardens.co.uk **22 C3**

Crealy Adventure Park *Clyst St Mary* Rides including log flume and rollercoaster, go-karts, indoor adventure play centre, farm animals and parkland 01395 233200 www.crealy.co.uk **22 B2**

Dartmoor Railway *Okehampton* Operates on the route of the old Southern Railway line from Crediton to Okehampton and Meldon Quarry. www.dartmoor-railway.co.uk 01837 55637 **19 B8**

Devon Railway Centre *Bickleigh* Operating 2-ft narrow-gauge railway, as well as short section of standard-gauge. 01884 855671. www.devonrailwaycentre.co.uk **34 E3**

Diggerland *Verbeer Manor, Cullompton* Adventure park with JCBs and dumper trucks. 0871 2277007 www.diggerland.com **35 E5**

Finch Foundry (NT) *Sticklepath* 19th-century water-powered forge. 01837 840046 www.nationaltrust.org.uk **20 B2**

Lynton and Barnstaple Railway *Martinhoe Cross* 01598 763487 www.lynton-rail.co.uk **43 B8**

Lynton and Lynmouth Cliff Railway *Lynton* Oldest working water operated cliff railway. 01598 753908 http://cliffrailwaylynton.co.uk **44 B1**

Morwellham Quay *Tavistock* World Heritage site with underground railway, working Victorian farm, historic port, costume museum, mining museum, rope making, nature and farm trail and child labour. 01822 832766 www.morwellham-quay.co.uk **19 F6**

Norman Lockyer Observatory and James Lockyer Planetarium *Sidmouth* Victorian telescopes, planetarium and displays. Visits by arrangement. Limited open evenings; check in advance. 01395 579941 http://projects.exeter.ac.uk/nlo **22 C4**

Pecorama Pleasure Gardens *Beer* Miniature train. Aviary, crazy golf, children's activity area. 01297 21542 www.peco-uk.com **23 C6**

Seaton and District Electric Tramway *Seaton* Miniature tramway system. 01297 20375 www.tram.co.uk **10 E2**

South Devon Railway *Totnes* Historic line following the scenic River Dart. 08453 451420 www.southdevonrailway.org **14 C3**

The Gnomes Reserve and Pixie Kiln *Princetown* 01409 241435 www.gnomereserve.co.uk **20 F1**

The Milky Way Adventure Park *Clovelly* Rides, adventure play area, archery, golf driving,railway, bird and sheep dog displays, etc. 01237 431255 www.themilkyway.co.uk **31 B6**

Underground passages *Exeter* Vaulted medieval passageways built to house the lead water pipes that supplied the city. 01392 265206 www.exeter.gov.uk **21 B8**

Watermouth Castle and Family Theme Park *nr Ilfracombe* Rides, adventure playground, mini golf, mazes, model railway, tube slides, crazy snooker, Gnomeland and swing boats. 01271 867474 www.watermouthcastle.com **43 B6**

Dorset

Adventure Wonderland *Hurn* 2.8 ha (7 acres) of landscaped park with variety of activities. 01202 483444 www.adventurewonderland.co.uk **28 A2**

Charmouth Heritage Coast Centre *Charmouth* Discover fossils with guided walks, theatre and displays. 01297 560772 www.charmouth.org **24 B2**

Moors Valley Railway *Ashley Heath* 01425 471415 www.moorsvalleyrailway.co.uk **40 E5**

Swanage Railway *Swanage* Line currently operates between Swanage and Norden. 01929 425800 www.swanagerailway.co.uk **27 E6**

Weymouth Bay Miniature Railway, *Lodmoor Country Park, Weymouth* 01305 785747 **25 D8**

Gloucestershire

Bourton Model Railway *Bourton-on-the-Water* 01451 820686 www.bourtonmodelrailway.co.uk **72 C2**

Cattle Country Adventure Park *Berkeley* Large outdoor park and indoor slides. 01453 810510 www.cattlecountry.co.uk **63 C5**

Dean Forest Railway *Lydney* Steam railway running between Lydney and Parkend. 01594 845840 www.deanforestrailway.co.uk **62 B4**

Gloucestershire Warwickshire Steam Railway *Toddington* 01242 621405 www.gwsr.com **71 A7**

Model Village *Bourton-on-the-Water* Copy of village. www.theoldnewinn.co.uk/village.htm 01451 820467**72 C2**

Perrygrove Railway *Coleford* 01594 834991 www.perrygrove.co.uk **69 E5**

The Merchant's House *Tewkesbury* One of row of restored cottages built around 1450. Restored to show medieval merchant's shop and house. 01684 297174 **70 A3**

North Somerset

Weston Miniature Railway *Weston-super-Mare* 01934 643510 www.westonminiaturerailway.co.uk **55 D6**

Plymouth

Plym Valley Railway *Plympton* Steam and diesel locomotives. www.plymrail.co.uk **11 D6**

Plymouth Miniature Steam Locomotive Society *Southway* www.plymouthminiaturesteam.co.uk **11 C5**

Poole

Gus Gorilla's Jungle Playground *Poole* Adventure playground for children up to 12 years. Spiral slides, aerial walkways, tube slides, tarzan ropes, roller challenge, ball pool. 01202 717197 www.gusgorillas.co.uk **27 B7**

Tower Park *Poole* Indoor playworld. UCI cinema, Megabowl, Quasar, waterpark and amusement arcade. 01202 723671 www.towerparkentertainment.co.uk **27 B7**

South Gloucestershire

Avon Valley Railway *Bitton* Along former branch of old Midland Railway. Wide variety of main-line, industrial steam and diesel locomotives. 0117 932 5538 www.avonvalleyrailway.org **57 B5**

Somerset

Brean Leisure Park *Brean* Pool complex with four water shutes. Funfair. 01278 751595 www.brean.com **55 F5**

Cheddar Caves and Gorge *Cheddar* Caves carved out by rivers over a million years. The show caves have massive stalactites and stalacmites, the Cheddar cannibal and a Crystal Quest adventure. 01934 742343 www.cheddargorge.co.uk **56 F1**

East Somerset Railway *Cranmore* Strawberry Line through the Mendip Hills. Loco shed, museum, art gallery, and play area. 01749 880417 www.eastsomersetrailway.com **49 C5**

Jungle Jungle *Yeovil* Jungle playground. 01935 433833 **37 C8**

Rug Ratz *Yeovil* Children's play centre 01935 476989 www.rug-ratz.co.uk **37 C8**

West Somerset Railway *Minehead* Britain's longest steam railway. 01643 704996 www.west-somerset-railway.co.uk **45 C7**

Wookey Hole *Wookey* Spectacular caves and legendary home of Witch of Wookey. 01749 672243 www.wookey.co.uk **48 B2**

Swindon

The Jolly Roger Adventure *Swindon* Children's indoor play area. 01793 522044 www.jollyrogerplay.com **65 E8**

Torbay

Babbacombe Model Village *Torquay* 01803 315315 www.babbacombemodelvillage.co.uk **15 B6**

Bygones *Torquay* Victorian street, giant model railway, World War I trench, Anderson shelter. 01803 326108 www.bygones.co.uk **15 B6**

Dartmouth Steam Railway *Paignton* 01803 555872 www.dartmouthrailriver.co.uk **15 E5**

Kents Cavern *Torquay* Prehistoric remains and the life of the Cave clan. Guided tours. 01803 215136 www.kents-cavern.co.uk **15 C6**

Rainbow Fun House *Torquay* 01803 296926 www.rainbowfunhouse.co.uk **15 C6**

Wiltshire

Swindon and Cricklade Railway *Near Swindon* 01793 771615 www.swindon-cricklade-railway.org **65 E7**

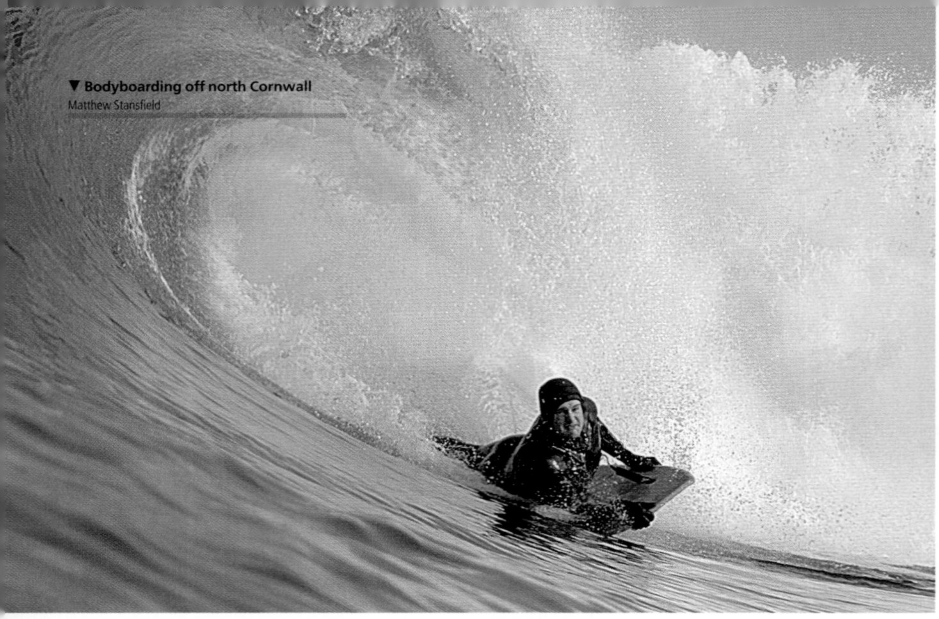

▼ **Bodyboarding off north Cornwall**
Matthew Stansfield

Minchinhampton GC* *Minchinhampton* Three courses: the Old, the Avening and the Cherington (all 18 holes) 01453 833840 http://minchinhamptongolfclub.co.uk **64 B2**

Painswick GC *Painswick* An 18-hole course at the foot of Painswick Hill. 01452 812615 www.painswickgolf.com **70 E3**

Rodway Hill GC *Highnam* 18-hole Championship-length course set between woodland and the Vale of Gloucester. http://rodway-hill-golf-course.co.uk 01452 384222 **70 C1**

Stinchcombe Hill GC *Dursley* An 18-hole course on the edge of the Cotswolds 01453 542015 www.stinchcombehillgolfclub.com **63 C6**

Thornbury Golf Centre *Thornbury* Two courses: High and Low (both 18 holes), and a driving range. 01454 281144 www.thornburygc.co.uk **62 E4**

Tracy Park GC (The Gloucestershire) *Tracy Park Estate, Wick* Two courses: the Crown and the Cromwell (both 18 holes) 0117 937 2251 **57 B6**

Woodlands G&CC *Almondsbury* Two 18-hole courses. www.woodlands-golf.com 01454 619319 **62 F4**

Somerset

Bath GC *Bath* 18-hole downland course on hills east of the city. 01225 463834 www.bathgolfclub.org.uk **57 C7**

Burnham & Berrow GC *Burnham-on-Sea* Two courses: 18-hole Championship course and 9-hole Channel course 01278 785760 www.burnhamandberrowgolfclub.co.uk **47 A5**

Clevedon GC *Clevedon* 18-hole course overlooking the Severn Estuary. http://clevedongolfclub.co.uk 01275 874057 **55 B8**

Enmore Park GC* *Enmore* 18-hole course www.enmorepark.co.ukon the edge of the Quantock Hills. 01278 672100 www.enmorepark.co.uk **46 D4**

Frome GC *Frome* 18-hole course in rolling countryside. 01373 453410 www.fromegolfclub.co.uk **49 B7**

Isle of Wedmore GC *Wedmore* 18-hole course set in the Somerset levels with panoramic views of the levels and the surrounding hills. 01934 712452 www.wedmoregolfclub.com **47 B8**

Lansdown GC *Bath* An 18-hole course on the heights above Bath. 01225 422138 www.lansdowngolfclub.co.uk **57 C6**

Long Ashton GC* *Long Ashton* An 18-hole course in open, hilly country. www.longashtongolfclub.co.uk 01275 392229 **56 B2**

Long Sutton GC *Long Load* An 18-hole parkland course set in rolling countryside. www.longsuttongolf.com 01458 241017 **37 B7**

Mendip Spring GC* *Congresbury* Two courses: the 18-hole Brinsea and the 9-hole Lakeside. 01934 852322 www.mendipspringgolfclub.com **55 D8**

Minehead & West Somerset GC *Minehead* An 18-hole course close to the seafront and town centre. 01643 702057 www.mineheadgolf.co.uk **45 B6**

Orchardleigh GC *Frome* An 18-hole parkland course. 01373 454200 www.orchardleighgolf.co.uk **49 A7**

Stockwood Vale GC *Keynsham* An 18-hole undulating parkland course. 0117 986 6505 www.stockwoodvale.com **56 C4**

Taunton Vale GC *Creech Heathfield* Two courses: the 18-hole Charlton course and the 9-hole Durston course. 01823 412220 www.tauntonvalegolf.co.uk **47 F5**

Vivary GC *Taunton* 18-hole course in Vivary Park www.toneleisure.co.uk/golf 01823 333875 **36 B2**

Wells GC *Wells* 18-hole course on the eastern edge of the town, overlooking the Somerset Levels. 01749 675005 www.wellsgolfclub.webs.com **48 B3**

Wheathill GC *Wheathill* An 18-hole course on the edge of the Somerset Levels. www.wheathillgc.co.uk 01963 240667 **48 E3**

Windwhistle GC *Cricket St Thomas* An 18-hole course on a ridge with amazing panoramic views. 01460 30231 www.windwhistlegolfclub.co.uk **36 E5**

Yeovil GC *Yeovil* Two courses: the 18-hole Old course and the 9-hole Newton course. 01935 422965 www.yeovilgolfclub.com **38 C1**

Torbay

Torquay GC* *St Marychurch* An 18-hole course on the northern edge of Torbay with views over Babbacombe Bay. www.torquaygolfclub.org.uk 01803 314591 **15 B6**

Wiltshire

Bowood Golf Resort *Derry Hill* An 18-hole course set in undulating parkland. 01249 822228 www.bowood-golf.co.uk **58 B4**

Erlestoke GC *Erlestoke* 18-hole course set in a blend of lakes and woodland 01380 831069 www.erlestokegolfclub.co.uk **58 F4**

High Post GC *Salisbury* An 18-hole course in the downland north of Salisbury. www.highpostgolfclub.co.uk 01722 782356 **51 D8**

Marlborough GC *Marlborough* An 18-hole club set in the rolling countryside of the Marlborough Downs. 01672 512147 www.marlboroughgolfclub.co.uk **59 B8**

North Wilts GC *Bishops Cannings* An 18-hole course set on the western edge of the Wessex Downs. 01380 860627 www.northwiltsgolf.com **58 C5**

Ogbourne Downs GC *Ogbourne St George* An 18-hole course in the Wessex Downs. 01672 841327 www.ogdgc.co.uk **59 B9**

Rushmore Golf Club GC *Tollard Royal* An 18-hole Championship course set in parkland surrounded by Cranborne Chase. www.rushmoregolfclub.co.uk 01725 516391 **40 C2**

Salisbury & South Wilts GC *Netherhampton* Two courses: the 18-hole main and the 9-hole Bibury. 01722 742645 www.salisburygolf.co.uk **51 F7**

Upavon GC *Upavon* An 18-hole course on the south edge of the Wiltshire downs. www.upavongolfclub.co.uk 01980 630787 **59 F7**

West Wilts GC* *Warminster* An 18-hole course on the edge of Salisbury Plain. www.westwiltsgolfclub.co.uk 01985 213133 **50 B2**

Horse Racing

Bath & NE Somerset

Bath Racecourse *Bath* Several flat meetings during spring, summer and autumn www.bath-racecourse.co.uk 01225 424609 **57 C6**

Devon

Exeter Racecourse *Exeter* National Hunt racing takes place throughout the autumn, winter, spring and early summer. www.exeter-racecourse.co.uk 01392 832599 **21 D7**

Newton Abbot Racecourse *Newton Abbot* National Hunt racing throughout the year. www.newtonabbotracing.com 01626 353235 **15 A5**

Gloucestershire

Cheltenham Racecourse *Cheltenham* There are 16 National Hunt meetings throughout the year, including the world-famous Festival in spring. 01242 513 014 www.cheltenham.co.uk **71 C5**

Somerset

Taunton Racecourse *Taunton* National Hunt meetings are held here during autumn, winter and spring. 01823 325035 www.tauntonracecourse.co.uk **36 B2**

Wiltshire

Salisbury Racecourse *Netherhampton* Flat meetings take place during spring, summer and autumn. 01722 326461 www.salisburyracecourse.co.uk **51 F7**

Motor Sports

Bristol

The Raceway *Bristol* A 450-m (1475-ft) indoor karting circuit. 0844 998 0000 www.theraceway.co.uk **56 A2**

Cornwall

St Eval Kart Circuit *St Eval* A 1-km (½ mile) outdoor circuit. 01637 860160 www.cornwallkarting.com **7 B8**

Devon

Raceworld *Woodbury Salterton* A 280-m (918-ft) indoor circuit. 01395 233397 www.raceworld-karting.co.uk **22 C2**

Gloucestershire

JDR Karting *Gloucester* An indoor circuit, 280 m (918 ft) in length. 01452 311211 www.jdrkarting.co.uk **70 D2**

West Country Karting *Bradley Stoke* An outdoor circuit, 350 m (1148 ft) in length. 01454 202666 www.westcountrykarting.co.uk **62 F4**

Wiltshire

Castle Combe Motor Racing Circuit *Chippenham* 1.85-mile championship circuit, car and bike race meeting, karting, track days, driving experiences, gift experience days. 01249 782417 www.castlecombecircuit.co.uk **58 A2**

Wessex Raceway Indoor Karting *Coombe Bisset* An indoor circuit, 750 m (2297 ft) in length. 0844 576 2420 www.wessexraceway.co.uk **40 A5**

Riding

There are numerous stables and riding schools located throughout the southwest. Consult local directories or information centres.

Rugby clubs

Bath & NE Somerset

Bath Rugby *Bath* 01225 325200 www.bathrugby.co.uk **57 D7**

Bristol

Bristol Rugby *Horfield* 01179 581630 www.bristolrugby.co.uk **56 A3**

Devon

Exeter Chiefs *Exeter* 01329 890890 www.exeterchiefs.co.uk **21 B9**

Cornwall

Cornish Pirates *Penzance* 01736 331961 www.cornish-pirates.com **2 E5**

Gloucester

Gloucester Rugby *Gloucester* www.gloucesterrugby.co.uk 0871 8718781 **70 D2**

Plymouth

Plymouth Albion *Plymouth* www.plymouthalbion.com 01752 565064 **10 E5**

Water sports

Bath & NE Somerset

Bath and Dundas Canal Co. *Bath* Day boat hire, canoe hire, bike hire. 01225 722292 www.bathcanal.com **57 C7**

Bath Boating Station *Bath* Hire a rowing boat, punt or canoe. 01225 312900 www.bathboating.co.uk **57 C7**

Cornwall

Cornish Cruising *Falmouth* Yachts available. 01386 211800 www.cornishcruising.com **4 D4**

Coverack Windsurfing Centre *Coverack* Holidays and windsurfing courses to all standards. 01326 280939 www.coverack.co.uk **5 G3**

Dolphin Surf School *Newquay* BSA-approved surfing school 01637 873707 www.surfschool.co.uk **7 C7**

ESF Surf School *Newquay* Surfing GB-approved surfing school www.englishsurfschool.com 01637 879571 **7 C7**

Eves of St Mawes & Bluebell Classic Sailing Ltd *Portscatho* Traditional sailing boats. www.classic-sailing.co.uk 01872 58 00 22 **5 C5**

Falmouth School of Sailing *Falmouth* www.falmouth-school-of-sailing.co.uk 01326 211311 **4 D4**

Fistral Beach Surf School *Newquay* School sited on one of the best surfing beaches in Britain. 01637 850737 http://fistralbeachsurfschool.co.uk **7 C6**

Harlyn Bay Surf School *Padstow* BSA-approved surfing school 01841 533076 www.harlynsurf.co.uk **16 E3**

Outdoor + Active Roadford *Nr Launceston* Canoeing, sailing, windsurfing and archery. Rowing boats to hire. Visitor centre. 01409 211507 www.swlakestrust.org.uk **18 D3**

Outdoor + Active Siblyback *Nr Liskeard* Play area, sailing, trout fishing, wind surfing, sailing, canoeing, rowing boats for hire. 01579 346522 www.swlakestrust.org.uk **9 C8**

Outdoor + Active Stithians *Redruth* Windsurfing, canoeing, trout fishing, boat hire, sailing. 01209 860301 www.swlakestrust.org.uk **4 C2**

Outdoor + Active Tamar *Kilkhampton* Sailing, windsurfing and canoeing. 01288 321712 www.swlakestrust.org.uk **31 D5**

Trysail *Falmouth* 01326 212320 www.trysail.net **4 D4**

Devon

Canoe Adventures *Totnes* www.canoeadventures.co.uk 01803 365301 **14 C4**

Saddles and Paddles *Exeter* Canoeing. See 'Cycling'. **21 B8**

Salcombe Boat Hire *Salcombe* www.salcombeboathire.co.uk 01548 844475 **13 E5**

Salcombe Powerboat School *Salcombe* Sailing, powerboating and canoeing. www.salcombepowerboats.co.uk 01548 842727 **13 E5**

Start Point Sailing *Ringmore* 01548 810917 www.sail-west.co.uk **12 C4**

Surf South West *Croyde Bay* Surfing GB-approved surfing school 01271 890400 www.surfsouthwest.com **42 D3**

Whitestrand Boat Hire *Salcombe* See River Cruises and Boat Rides **13 E5**

Gloucestershire

Cotswold Water Park, Keynes Country Park *Cirencester* See Country Parks **65 C5**

Dartmouth Yacht Cruise School *Bussage* Yacht hire. 01803 863162 www.dycs.net **64 B2**

Plymouth

Dittisham Boats *Totnes* Sailing tuition. Daily and weekly hire of boats and dingies. http://dittishamboats.co.uk 01803 722365 **14 C4**

Mount Batten Centre *Plymouth* Sailing and watersports 01752 404567 www.mount-batten-centre.com **10 E5**

Plymouth Sailing School *Plymouth* www.plymsail.demon.co.uk 01752 493377 **10 E5**

Somerset

Outdoor + Active Wimbleball *Dulverton* Sailing, fishing, camping. 01398 371460 www.swlakestrust.org.uk **45 F6**

Torbay

Plain Sailing *Brixham* Channel crossings, weekend breaks. 01803 853843 www.plainsailing.co.uk **15 D6**

▼ **Windsurfing in Poole harbour**
Joe Gough / iStockphoto.com

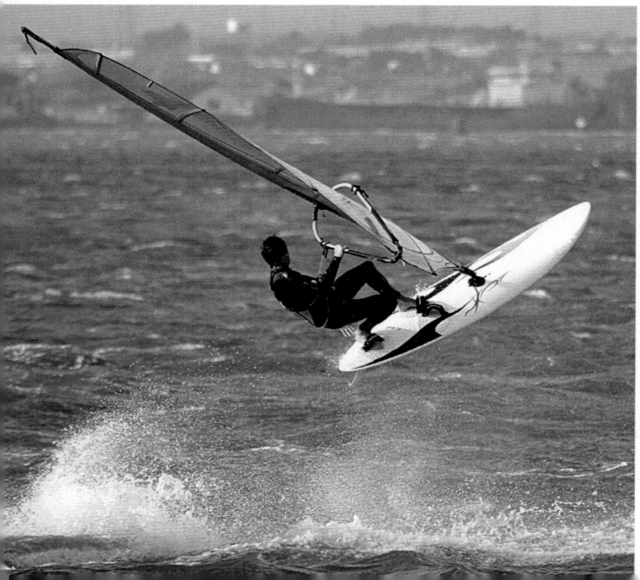

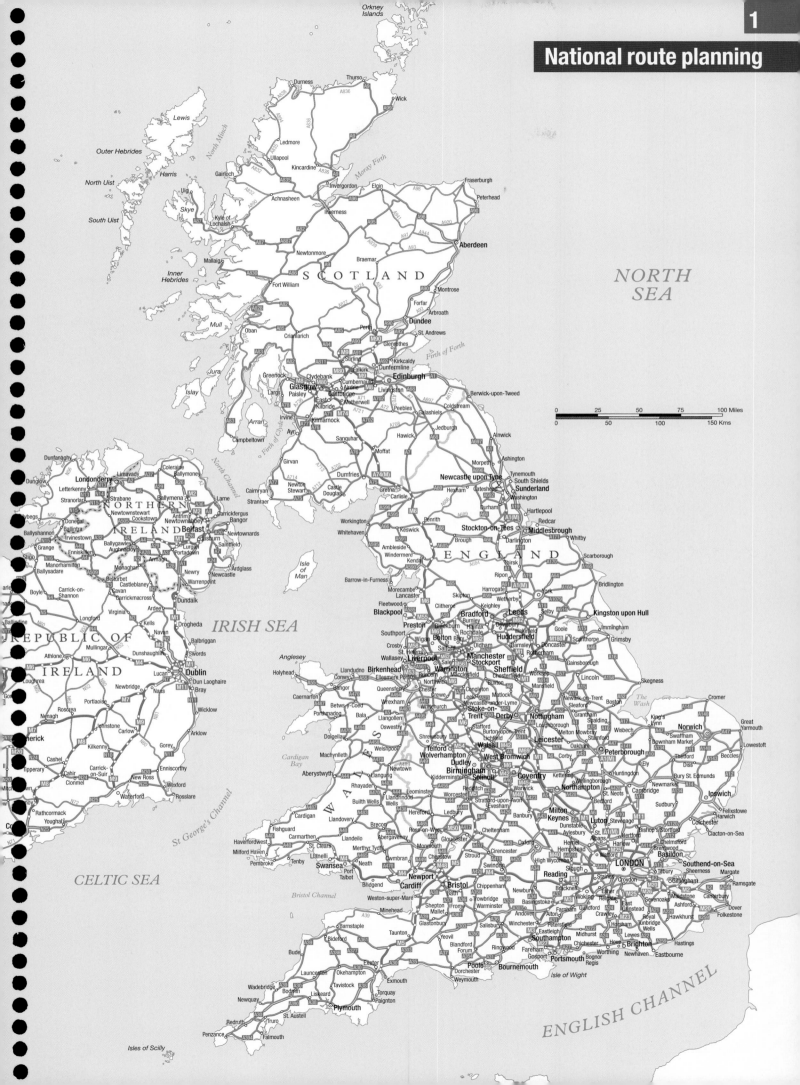

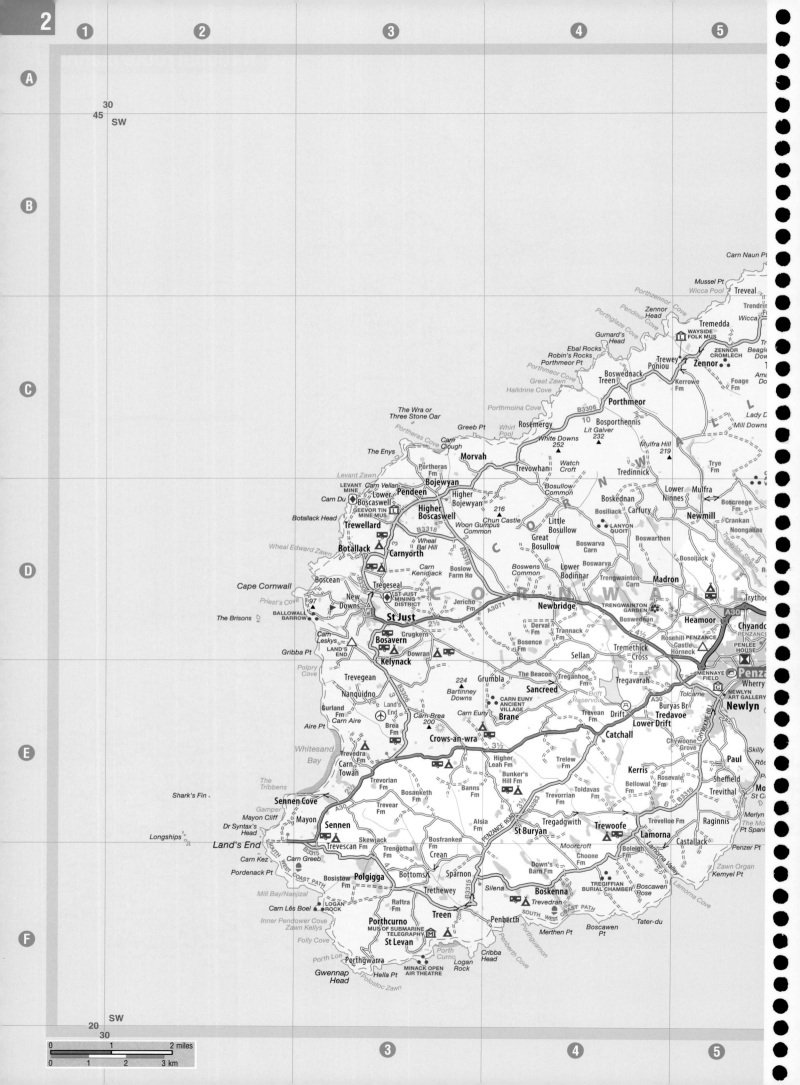

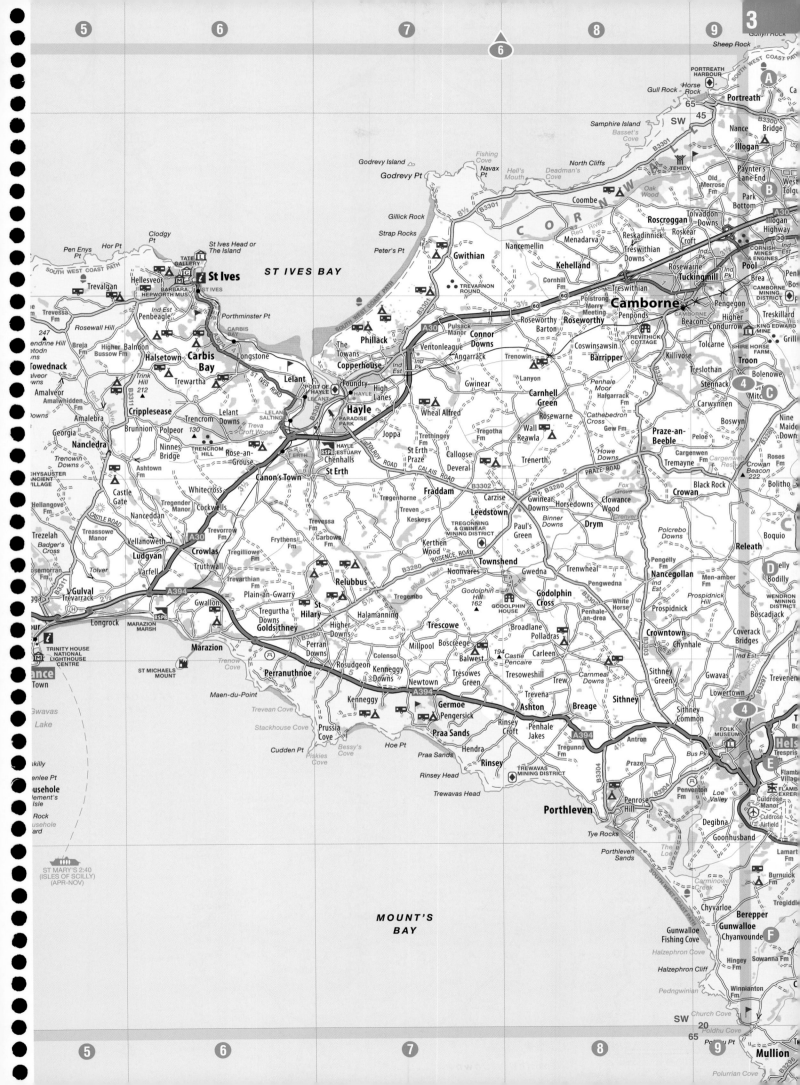

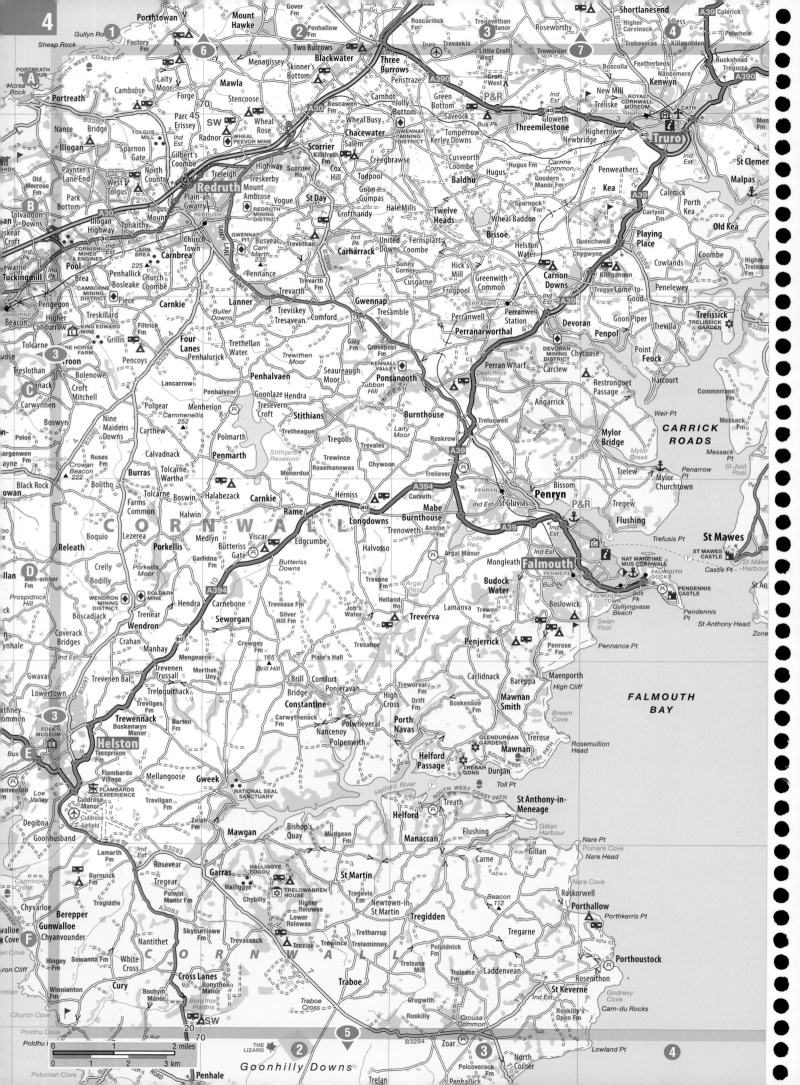

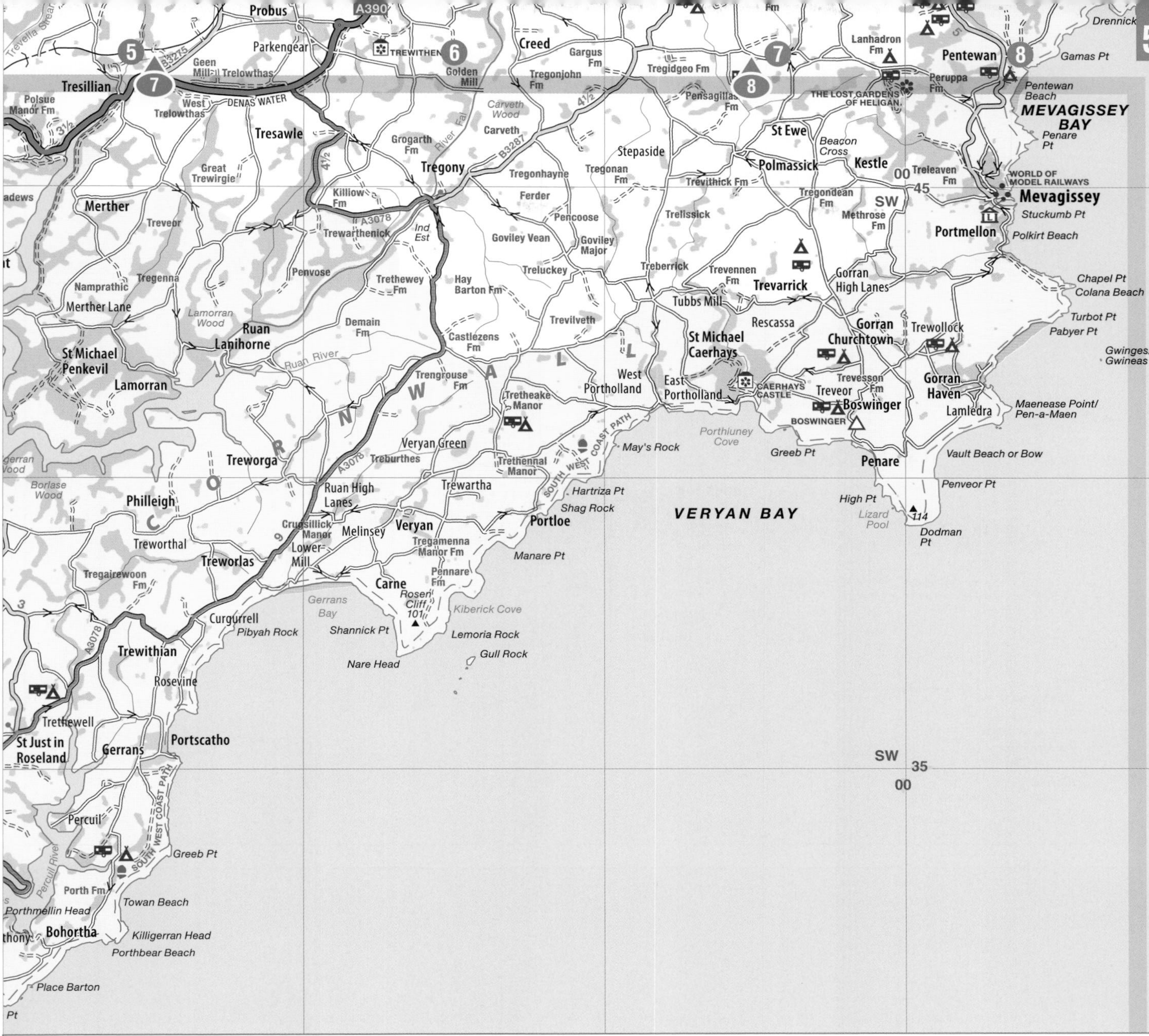
Probus
A390
Parkengear
TREWITHEN
Creed
Gargus Fm
Lanhadron Fm
Pentewan
Gamas Pt
Drennick
Tresillian
Geen Mill
Trelowthas
Golden Mill
Tregonjohn Fm
Tregidgeo Fm
Pensagillas Fm
THE LOST GARDENS OF HELIGAN
Peruppa Fm
Pentewan Beach
MEVAGISSEY BAY
Polsue Manor Fm
West Trelowthas
DENAS WATER
Carveth Wood
Carveth
Penare Pt
Tresawle
Grogarth Fm
River Fal
B3287
Stepaside
St Ewe
Beacon Cross
Polmassick
Kestle
Treleaven Fm
WORLD OF MODEL RAILWAYS
Mevagissey
Stuckumb Pt
Portmellon
Polkirt Beach
Great Trewirgie
Tregony
Tregonhayne
Tregonan Fm
Trevithick Fm
Tregondean Fm
Methrose Fm
Merther
Killiow Fm
A3078
Ferder
Pencoose
Trelissick
Treveor
Trewarthenick
Ind Est
Goviley Vean
Goviley Major
Namprathic
Tregenna
Penvose
Treluckey
Treberrick
Trevennen Fm
Trevarrick
Gorran High Lanes
Chapel Pt
Colana Beach
Merther Lane
Lamorran Wood
Trethewey Fm
Hay Barton Fm
Tubbs Mill
Rescassa
Turbot Pt
Pabyer Pt
Ruan Lanihorne
Demain Fm
Trevilveth
St Michael Caerhays
Gorran Churchtown
Trewollock
Gwinges/Gwineas
St Michael Penkevil
Ruan River
Castlezens Fm
Lamorran
Trengrouse Fm
West Portholland
East Portholland
CAERHAYS CASTLE
Treveor
Trevesson Fm
Boswinger
BOSWINGER
Gorran Haven
Lamledra
Maenease Point/ Pen-a-Maen
Tretheake Manor
Porthluney Cove
May's Rock
Greeb Pt
Vault Beach or Bow
Treworga
Veryan Green
Treburthes
Trethennal Manor
SOUTH WEST COAST PATH
Penare
Borlase Wood
Ruan High Lanes
Trewartha
Hartriza Pt
Shag Rock
VERYAN BAY
Penveor Pt
Philleigh
Crugsillick Manor
High Pt
Lizard Pool
114
Dodman Pt
Treworthal
Melinsey
Veryan
Portloe
Lower Mill
Tregamenna Manor Fm
Manare Pt
Treworlas
Tregairewoon Fm
Pennare Fm
Carne
Gerrans Bay
Rosen Cliff 101
Kiberick Cove
Curgurrell
Pibyah Rock
Shannick Pt
Lemoria Rock
Gull Rock
Trewithian
Nare Head
Rosevine
Trethewell
St Just in Roseland
Gerrans
Portscatho
SW
35
00
Percuil
Percuil River
Greeb Pt
Porth Fm
Towan Beach
Porthmellin Head
Bohortha
Killigerran Head
Porthbear Beach
Place Barton
A
B
C
D

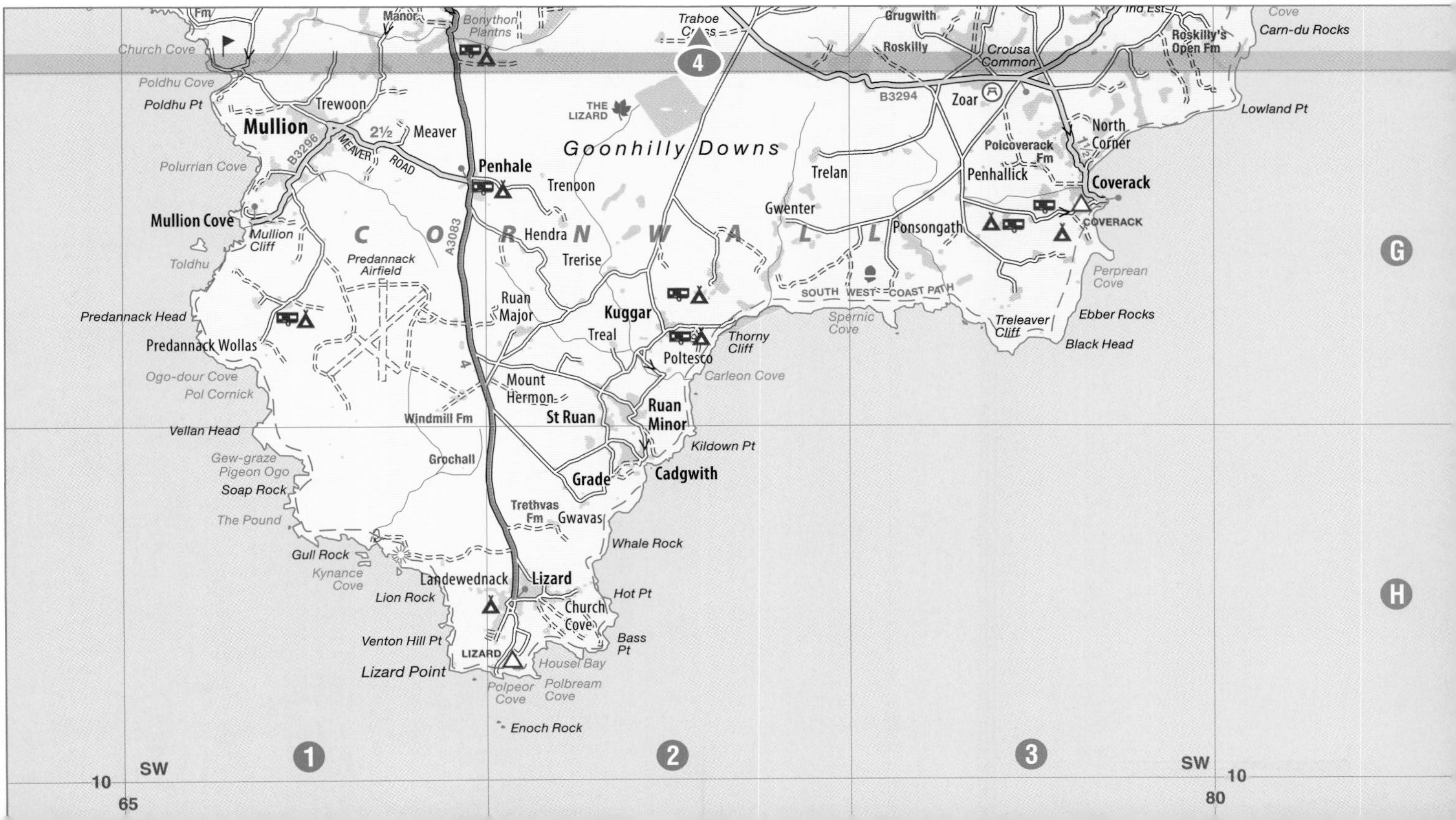
Manor
Bonython Plantns
Traboe Cross
Grugwith
Roskilly
Crousa Common
Ind Est
Roskilly's Open Fm
Carn-du Rocks
Church Cove
Poldhu Cove
Poldhu Pt
Trewoon
THE LIZARD
B3294
Zoar
Lowland Pt
Mullion
B3296
Meaver
MEAVER ROAD
Goonhilly Downs
North Corner
Polurrian Cove
Penhale
Trenoon
Trelan
Polcoverack Fm
Penhallick
Coverack
Gwenter
COVERACK
Mullion Cove
Mullion Cliff
A3083
Hendra
Ponsongath
CORNWALL
Toldhu
Predannack Airfield
Trerise
Perprean Cove
SOUTH WEST COAST PATH
Predannack Head
Ruan Major
Kuggar
Ebber Rocks
Predannack Wollas
Treal
Thorny Cliff
Spernic Cove
Treleaver Cliff
Black Head
Ogo-dour Cove
Poltesco
Carleon Cove
Pol Cornick
Mount Hermon
Ruan Minor
Windmill Fm
St Ruan
Vellan Head
Kildown Pt
Gew-graze
Pigeon Ogo
Grochall
Grade
Cadgwith
Soap Rock
The Pound
Trethvas Fm
Gwavas
Whale Rock
Gull Rock
Kynance Cove
Landewednack
Lizard
Lion Rock
Hot Pt
Church Cove
Venton Hill Pt
Bass Pt
LIZARD
Housel Bay
Lizard Point
Polpeor Cove
Polbream Cove
Enoch Rock
G
H
1
2
3
SW
10
65
80

1 **2** **3** **4**

A
B
C
D
E
F

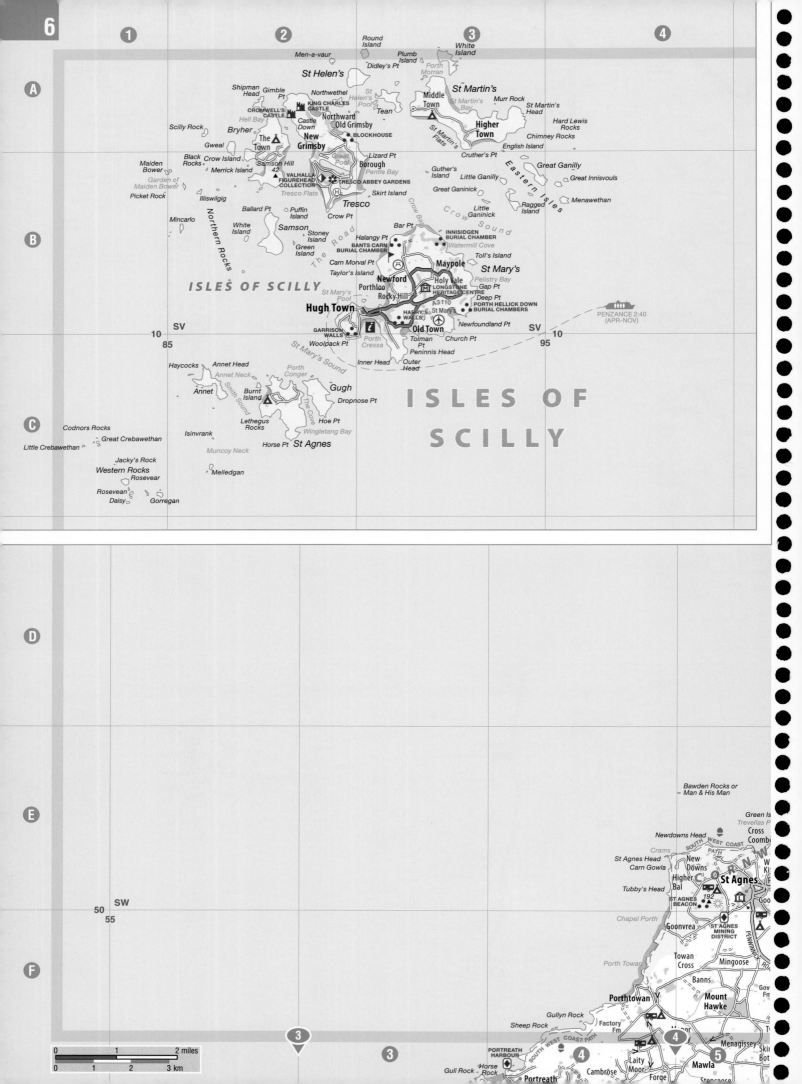

Round Island
Men-a-vaur
Plumb Island
White Island
Porth Morran
Didley's Pt
St Helen's
Shipman Head
Gimble Pt
Northwethel
St Martin's
St Martin's Bay
Murr Rock
St Martin's Head
Middle Town
KING CHARLES CASTLE
CROMWELL'S CASTLE
Hell Bay
Castle Down
Northward
Old Grimsby
St Helen's Pool
Tean
St Martin's Flats
Higher Town
Hard Lewis Rocks
Chimney Rocks
English Island
Scilly Rock
Bryher
Gweal
Black Rocks
Crow Island
New Grimsby
BLOCKHOUSE
Lizard Pt
Borough
Pentle Bay
Cruther's Pt
Maiden Bower
Merrick Island
Samson Hill
42
VALHALLA FIGUREHEAD COLLECTION
Tresco Flats
TRESCO ABBEY GARDENS
Skirt Island
Great Ganilly
Great Innisvouls
Guther's Island
Little Ganilly
Great Ganinick
Little Ganinick
Menawethan
Ragged Island
Eastern Isles
Garden of Maiden Bower
Picket Rock
Illiswilgig
Ballard Pt
Puffin Island
Crow Pt
Tresco
Mincarlo
Northern Rocks
White Island
Samson
Stoney Island
Green Island
The Road
Crow Bar
Crow Sound
Halangy Pt
Bar Pt
INNISIDGEN BURIAL CHAMBER
Watermill Cove
Toll's Island
ISLES OF SCILLY
BANTS CARN BURIAL CHAMBER
Carn Morval Pt
Taylor's Island
St Mary's Pool
Newford
Porthloo
Rocky Hill
Maypole
Holy Vale
LONGSTONE HERITAGE CENTRE
Pelistry Bay
Gap Pt
Deep Pt
PORTH HELLICK DOWN BURIAL CHAMBERS
St Mary's
Hugh Town
HARRY'S WALLS
A3110
St Mary's
Newfoundland Pt
GARRISON WALLS
Woolpack Pt
Porth Cressa
Old Town
Tolman Pt
Peninnis Head
Church Pt
PENZANCE 2:40 (APR-NOV)
SV 10
85
SV 10
95
Inner Head
St Mary's Sound
Outer Head
Haycocks
Annet Head
Annet Neck
Porth Conger
Burnt Island
Gugh
Dropnose Pt
Annet
Smith Sound
Lethegus Rocks
Hoe Pt
The Cove
Isinvrank
Wingletang Bay
ISLES OF SCILLY
Codnors Rocks
Great Crebawethan
Muncoy Neck
Little Crebawethan
Horse Pt
St Agnes
Jacky's Rock
Melledgan
Western Rocks
Rosevear
Rosevean
Daisy
Gorregan

Bawden Rocks or Man & His Man
Green Is
Trevellas P
Cross Coombe
Newdowns Head
SOUTH WEST COAST PATH
St Agnes Head
Carn Gowla
Crams
New Downs
Higher Bal
St Agnes
Tubby's Head
ST AGNES BEACON
192
CORNW
Ki
Goo
Chapel Porth
Goonvrea
ST AGNES MINING DISTRICT
Porth Towan
Towan Cross
Mingoose
Banns
Mount Hawke
Gov
Fm
Porthtowan
Gullyn Rock
SOUTH WEST COAST PATH
Sheep Rock
Factory Fm
Menagissey
Skir
Bot
PORTREATH HARBOUR
Gull Rock
Horse Rock
Portreath
Cambrose
Laity Moor
Forge
Mawla
Trevance

3 ▽   **3**   **4**   **4** ▽   **5**

0   1   2 miles
0   1   2   3 km

SW 50
55

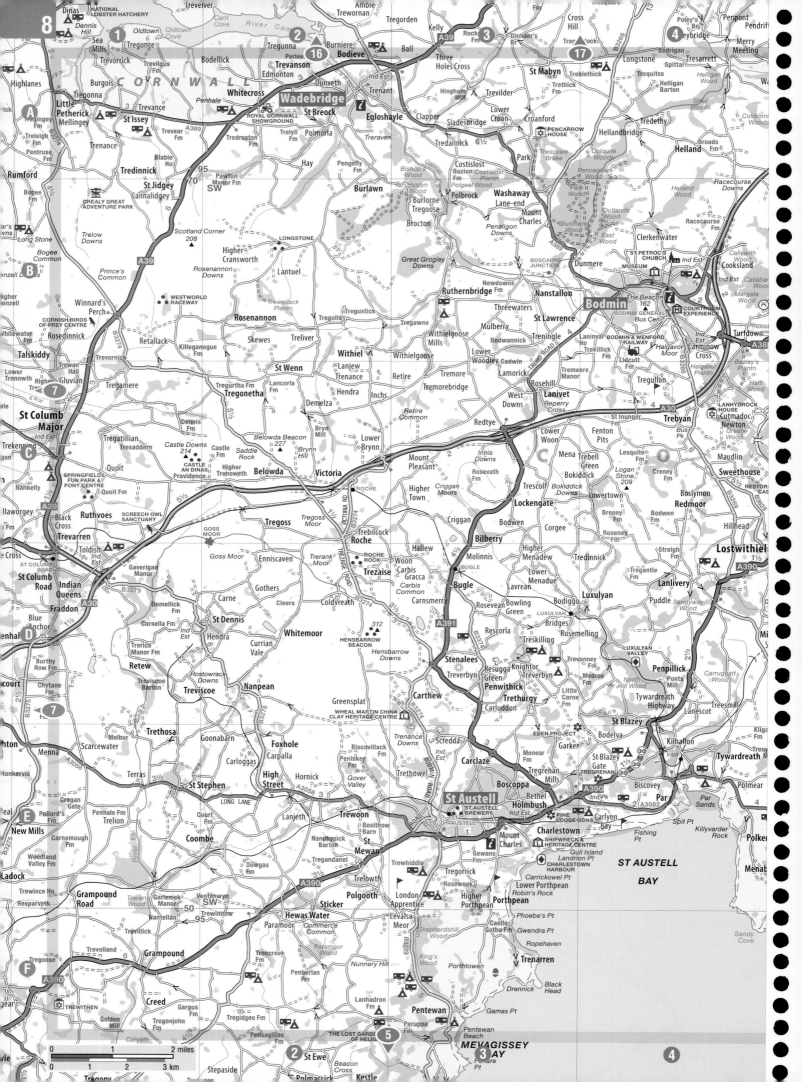

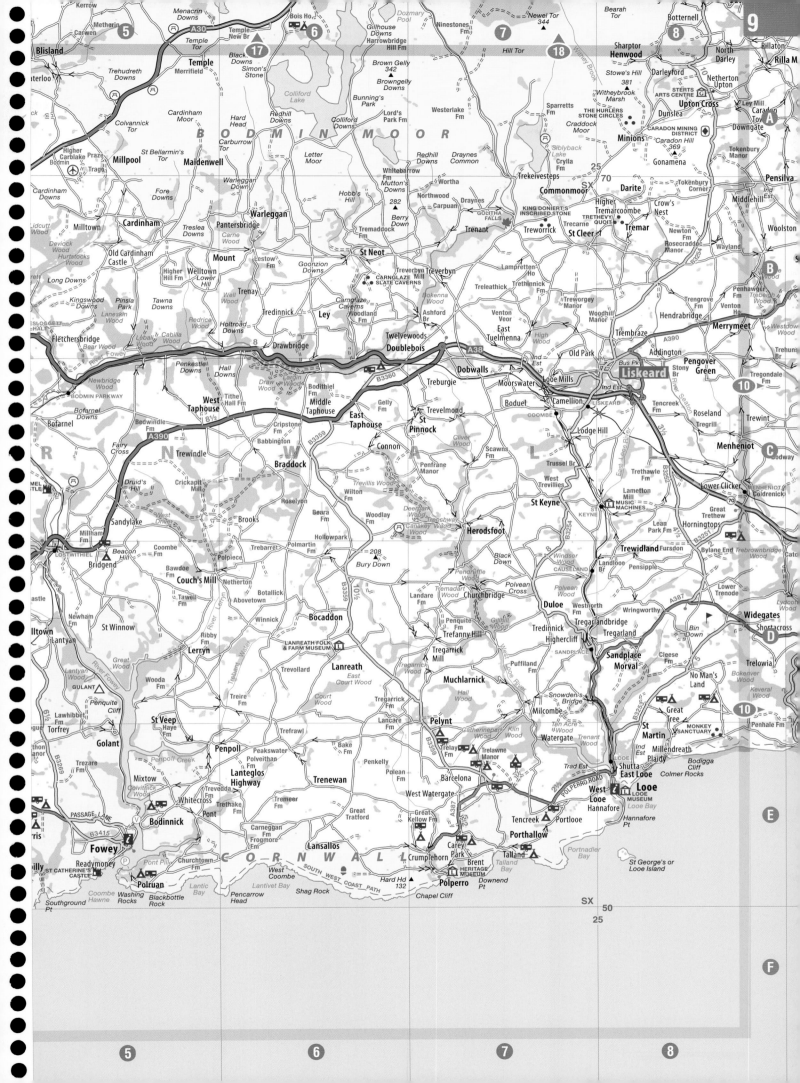

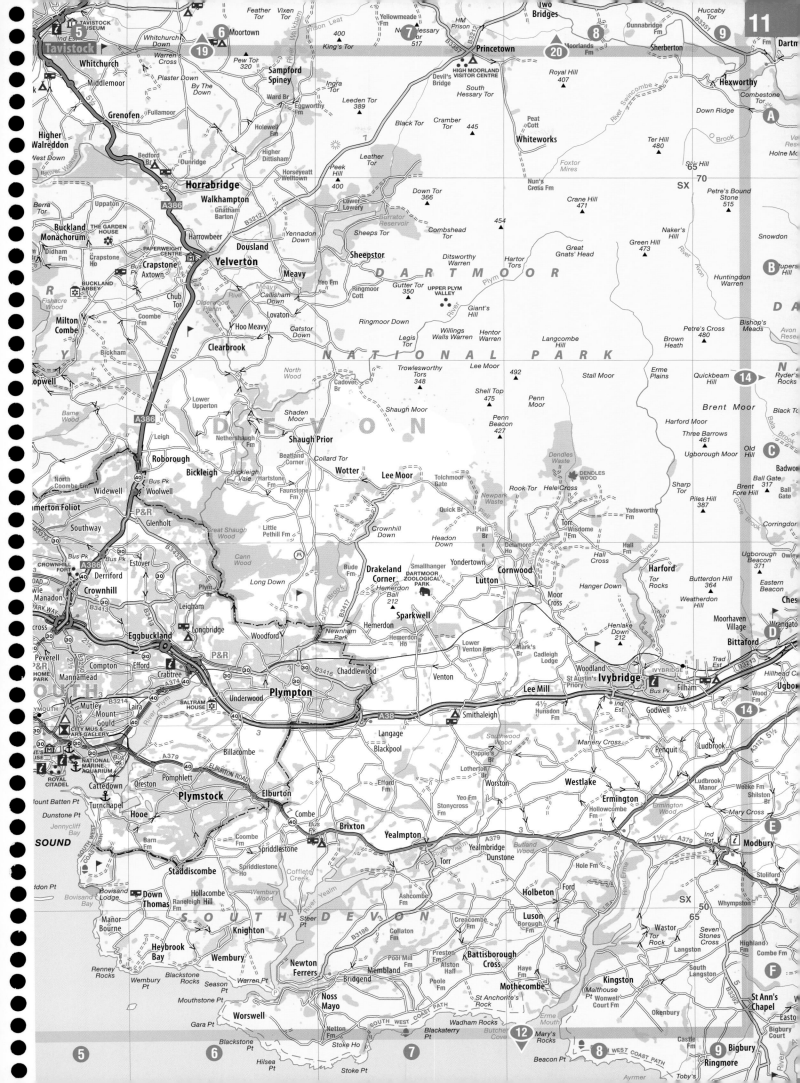

Longbridge
Woodford
Newnham Park
Sparkwell
Hemerdon
Heme
Lower Venton Fm
Mark's Br
Cadleigh Lodge
Henlake Down 212
Moorhaven Village
Wrangaton
Cannam Fm
Bittaford

Efford
P&R
Chaddlewood
Venton
Woodland
St Austin's Priory
Ivybridge
IVYBRIDGE
Trad Est
Hillhead Cross
Kitterford Cross
Venn Ho

Crabtree
Plympton
Underwood
Lee Mill
Bus Pk
Filham
Ugborough
Wood Fm
Well Cross

A38
Smithaleigh
Hunsdon Fm
Ind Est
Godwell
Ludbrook
Fowlescombe Gate

Laira
SX
Langage
Blackpool
Southwood Wood
Marjery Cross
Penquit
Ludbrook Manor
Higher Spriddlescombe

Billacombe
Popple's Br
Westlake
Weeke Fm
Shilston Br
Yarnacombe
California Cross

Pomphlett
Oreston
Lotherton Br
Worston
Ermington
Ermington Wood
Mary Cross
Brownston

Plymstock
Elburton
Efford Fm
Yeo Fm
Stonycross Fm
Hollowcombe
East Leigh

Barn Fm
Combe
Brixton
Yealmpton
Yealmbridge
Dunstone
Butland Wood
Modbury
Babland Fm
Polston Parks

Coombe Fm
Bus Pk
Torr
River Yealm
Hole Fm
Ind Est
Stoliford
Heathfield Manor

Spriddlestone
Spriddlestone Ho
Ashcombe
Holbeton
Ford
Whympston

Cofflete Creek
Creacombe Fm
Luson Borough Fm
Wastor Tor Rock
Seven Stones Cross
Langston
Highland Fm
Combe Fm
Wakeham

Down Thomas
Hollacombe
Raneleigh Hill
Wembury Wood
Steer Pt
Collaton Fm
Preston Fm
Alston Hall
Haye Fm
Kingston
Malthouse Fm
Wonwell Court Fm
South Langston
Tetwell
Ashford

SOUTH DEVON
Knighton
B3186
Pool Mill Fm
Membland
Poole
Mothecombe
Okenbury
Icy Park

Heybrook Bay
Wembury
Newton Ferrers
Bridgend
St Anchorite's Rock
Castle Fm
St Ann's Chapel
Waterhead
Aveto Giffo

Blackstone Rocks
Season Pt
Warren Pt
Noss Mayo
Wadham Rocks
Butcher's Cove
Mary's Rocks
Erme Mouth
Bigbury Court
Easton
Bridg End

Wembury Pt
Mouthstone Pt
Worswell
Netton Fm
Blackaterry
Beacon Pt
SOUTH WEST COAST PATH
Bigbury
Stadbury Fm

Gara Pt
Blackstone Pt
Stoke Ho
SOUTH WEST COAST PATH
Ringmore

Hilsea Pt
Stoke Pt
Ayrmer Cove
Toby's Pt

Challaborough
Warren Pt
FOLLY HILL
Bigbury-on-Sea
Butter Cove
Bantham
Buckland
Kerse Fm

Burgh Island
Murray's Rock
Thurlestone

BIGBURY BAY
Warren Pt
Horswell Ho
South Huish

Thurlestone Rock
Beacon Pt
Woolman Pt
Outer Hope

Hope Cove
Galmpton
Bolt Tail
Inner Hope
Bolb

Redrot Cove
Hope
Southdown Fm

Fernyhole Pt
West Cliff
Slippery Pt

Cathole Cliff
Lantern Rock

0 1 2 miles
0 1 2 3 km
30
SX
55

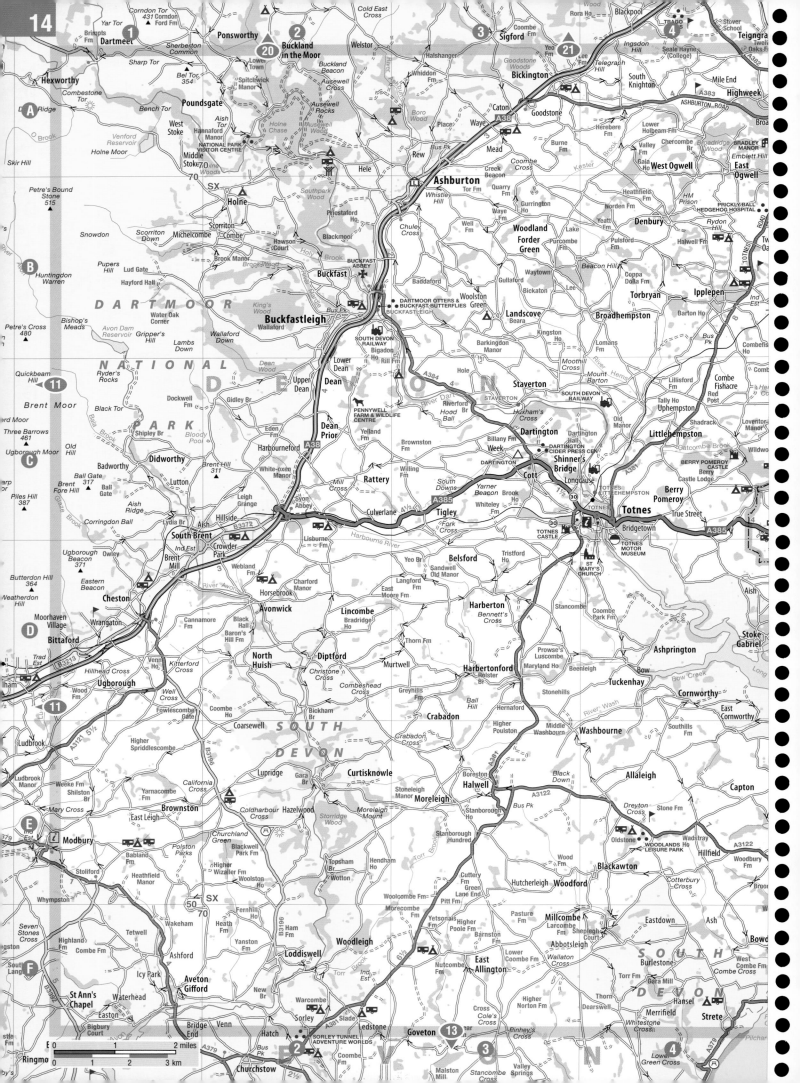

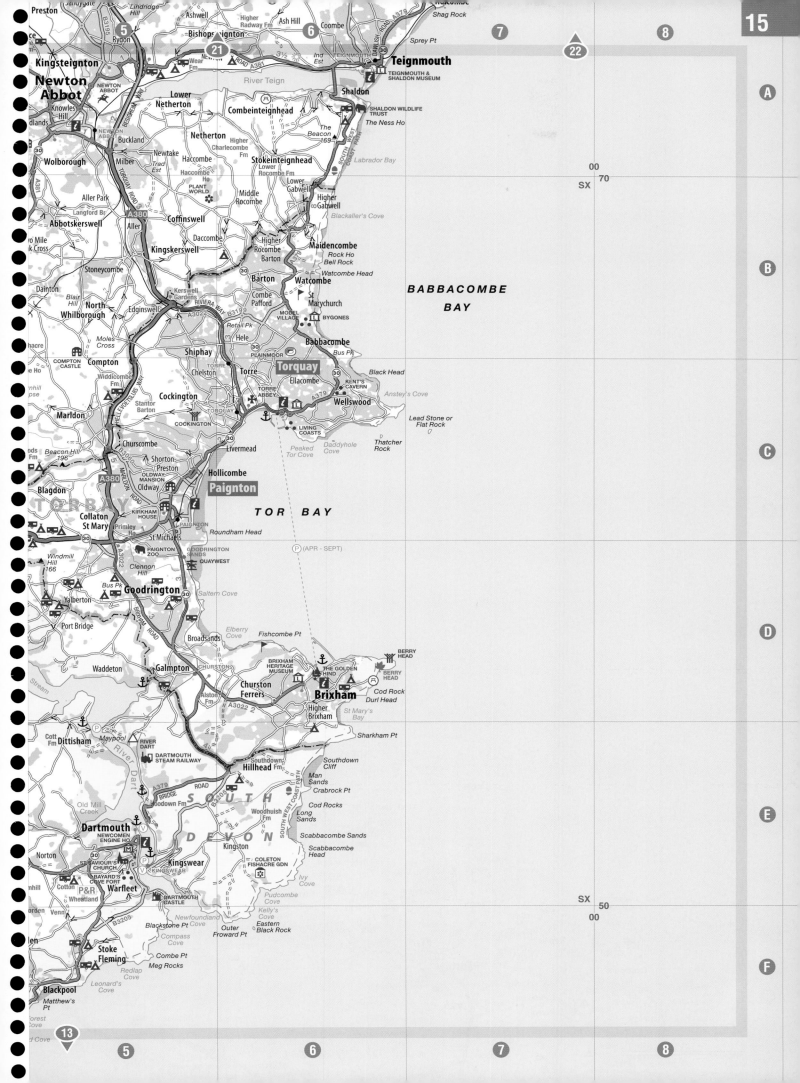

5 **6** **7** **8**

Preston
Sandygate
Lindridge
Hill
Ashwell
Ash Hill
Coombe
Shag Rock
A
ce
B3195
5
Rydon
Bishopsteignton
Higher
Radway Fm
Sprey Pt
A379
Kingsteignton
21
Wear
Fm
NEWTON
ROAD
3½
Ind
Est
Teignmouth
30
Teignmouth
22
Newton
Abbot
NEWTON
ABBOT
A381
TEIGNMOUTH & SHALDON MUSEUM
River Teign
Shaldon
Knowles
Hill
lands
NEWTON
ABBOT
Buckland
Lower
Netherton
Combeinteignhead
SHALDON WILDLIFE TRUST
The Ness Ho
30
Wolborough
Milber
Netherton
Newtake
Haccombe
Higher
Charlecombe
Stokeinteignhead
The Beacon 169
Labrador Bay
SOUTH WEST COAST PATH

A381
Aller Park
Langford Br
TORQUAY ROAD
Trad Est
Haccombe Ho
Lower
Rocombe Ho
Lower
Gabwell
B
Abbotskerswell
A380
Coffinswell
Daccombe
Middle
Rocombe
Higher
Gabwell
Blackaller's Cove
o Mile
k Cross
Aller
PLANT WORLD
Higher
Rocombe
Barton
Maidencombe
Rock Ho
Bell Rock
Stoneycombe
Kingskerswell
RIVIERA WAY
A3022
Barton
Watcombe Head
Dainton
Kerswell
Gardens
B3199
Combe
Pafford
Watcombe
BABBACOMBE
Blair
Hill
North
Whilborough
Edginswell
A3022
Retail Pk
MODEL VILLAGE
St
Marychurch
BAY
hacre
Moles
Cross
Shiphay
Hele
BYGONES
COMPTON CASTLE
Compton
Chelston
Torre
PLAINMOOR
Babbacombe
Bus Pk
o Ho
Widdicombe Fm
HELE
Torre
Torquay
30
Black Head
hill
se
Marldon
Stantor
Barton
Cockington
TORQUAY
Ellacombe
KENT'S CAVERN
Wellswood
Anstey's Cove
COCKINGTON
A379
Lead Stone or
Flat Rock
Churscombe
B3060
Shorton
Preston
Livermead
Peaked
Tor Cove
Daddyhole
Cove
Thatcher
Rock
C
ods
Fm
Beacon Hill
196
A380
OLDWAY
MANSION
Oldway
Paignton
Hollicombe
LIVING COASTS
Blagdon
MARLDON ROAD
KIRKHAM HOUSE
TOR BAY
Collaton
St Mary
Primley
Ho
St Michaels
PAIGNTON
Roundham Head
30
PAIGNTON
ZOO
GOODRINGTON
SANDS
(APR - SEPT)
Windmill
Hill 166
A3022
Clennon
Hill
QUAYWEST
Saltern Cove
Bus Pk
30
Goodrington
Yalberton
D
BRIXHAM
ROAD
Elberry
Cove
Fishcombe Pt
BERRY
HEAD
Port Bridge
Broadsands
Galmpton
CHURSTON
BRIXHAM HERITAGE MUSEUM
THE GOLDEN HIND
BERRY
HEAD
Waddeton
Churston
Ferrers
Alston
Fm
Brixham
Cod Rock
Durl Head
Stream
A3022
Higher
Brixham
St Mary's
Bay
Cott
Fm
Dittisham
Maypool
RIVER
DART
Sharkham Pt
River Dart
DARTMOUTH
STEAM RAILWAY
Hillhead
Southdown
Cliff
E
Old Mill
Creek
oodown Fm
A379
SOUTH
Man
Sands
Crabrock Pt
Dartmouth
NEWCOMEN
ENGINE HO
BRIDGE
ROAD
DEVON
Woodhuish
Fm
Cod Rocks
Long
Sands
SOUTH WEST COAST PATH
Norton
Kingston
Scabbacombe Sands
ST SAVIOUR'S CHURCH
A379
Kingswear
COLETON
FISHACRE GDN
Scabbacombe
Head
hill
Cotton
BAYARD'S
COVE FORT
Warfleet
KINGSWEAR
Ivy
Cove
P&R
Wheatland
DARTMOUTH
CASTLE
Pudcombe
Cove
orden
Venn
Blackstone Pt
Newfoundland
Cove
Outer
Froward Pt
Kelly's
Cove
Eastern
Black Rock
F
en
Compass
Cove
Combe Pt
Meg Rocks
Stoke
Fleming
Redlap Cove
Blackpool
Leonard's Cove
Matthew's
Pt
rest
Cove
13
d Cove

5 **6** **7** **8**

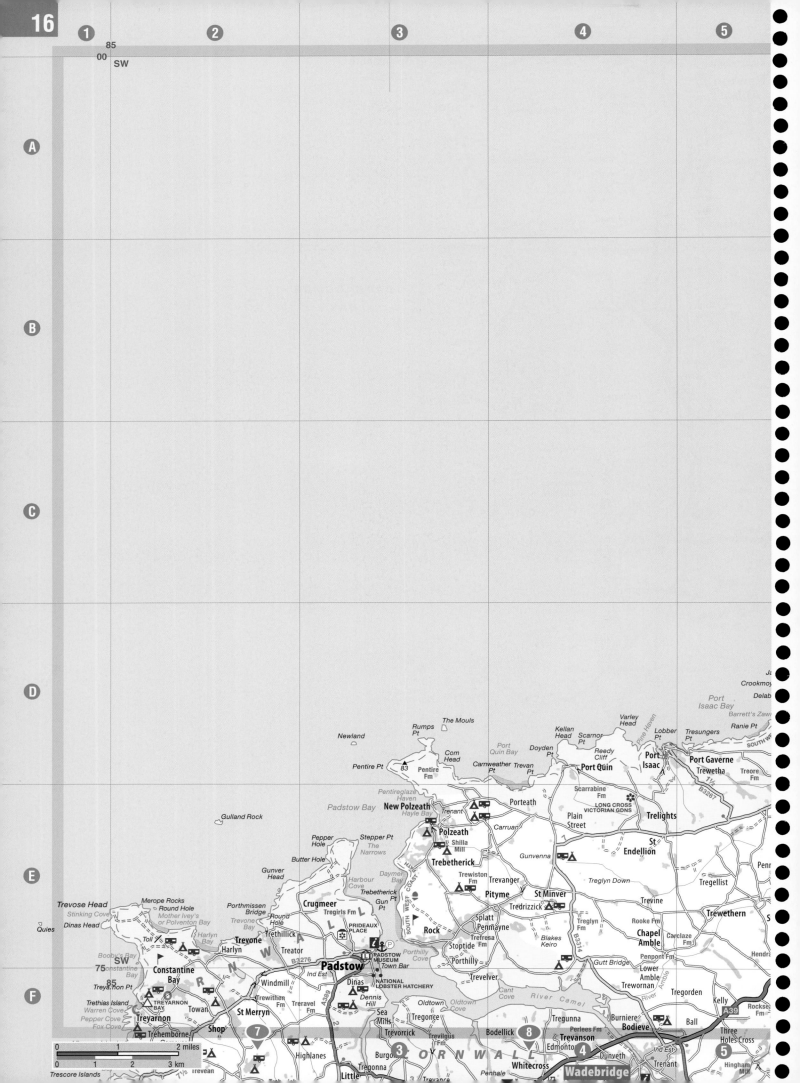

1 **2** **3** **4** **5**

85
00
SW

A

B

C

D

Ja
Crookmoy
Port
Isaac Bay
Delab
Barrett's Zawn
Ranie Pt
Varley
Head
Tresungers
Pt
The Mouls
Rumps
Pt
Kellan
Head
Scarnor
Pt
Lobber
Pt
Newland
Com
Head
Doyden
Pt
Reedy
Cliff
Port Gaverne
Port Quin Bay
Carnweather
Pt
Trevan
Pt
Port Quin
Port Isaac
Trewetha
Treore
Fm
Pentire Pt
83
Pentire
Fm
Port Isaac
SOUTH WE
B3267
Pentireglaze
Haven
Scarrabine
Fm
Plain
Street
Trelights
Padstow Bay
New Polzeath
Trenant
Porteath
LONG CROSS
VICTORIAN GDNS
Gulland Rock
Hayle Bay
Polzeath
Carruan
St
Endellion
Penn
Pepper
Hole
Stepper Pt
The
Narrows
Shilla
Mill
Gunvenna
Tregellist
Butter Hole
Trebetherick
Treviston
Fm
Trevanger
Treglyn Down
Gunver
Head
Daymer
Bay
Pityme
St Minver
Trevine
Trewethern
Harbour
Cove
Trebetherick
Gun Pt
Crugmeer
Tredrizzick
Trevose Head
Merope Rocks
Round Hole
Porthmissen
Bridge
Tregirls
SOUTH WEST COAST
Rock
Splatt
Penmayne
Rooke Fm
Chapel
Amble
Carclaze
Stinking Cove
Mother Ivey's
or Polventon Bay
Trevone
Bay
Round
Hole
PRIDEAUX
PLACE
Treglyn
Penpont Fm
Hendra
Dinas Head
Harlyn
Bay
Frethillick
Trefresa
Fm
Quies
Toll
Trevone
Treator
Porthilly
Cove
Stoptide
Gutt Bridge
S
Booby's Bay
Harlyn
B3276
Padstow
Town Bar
Porthilly
Trelver
Warren Cove
SW
75
Constantine
Bay
Windmill
PADSTOW
MUSEUM
Ind Est
Cant
Cove
River Camel
Lower
Amble
Trewornan
85
Dinas
Treyarnon Pt
Trewithen
Fm
NATIONAL
LOBSTER HATCHERY
Oldtown
Oldtown
Cove
Tregorden
Kelly
A39
Rockse
Fm
Trethias Island
TREYARNON
BAY
Towan
Teraval
A389
Dennis Hill
Tregonce
Tregunna
Burniere
Fm
Bodieve
Ball
Warren Cove
Treyarnon
St Merryn
Sea
Mills
Tregunna
Perlees Fm
Trevanson
Pepper Cove
Fox Cove
Trehemborne
Shop
Trevorrick
Trevilgus
Fm
Bodellick
Whitecross
Edmonto
Burgo
Three
Holes Cross
Tregonna
Trenant
Hingham
Mill
Highlanes
Trevance
Dunveth
Ind Est
Little
Penhale
Wadebridge
Trevean
CORNWALL
Trescore Islands

0   1   2 miles
0   1   2   3 km

7 **8**
3 **4** **5**
7

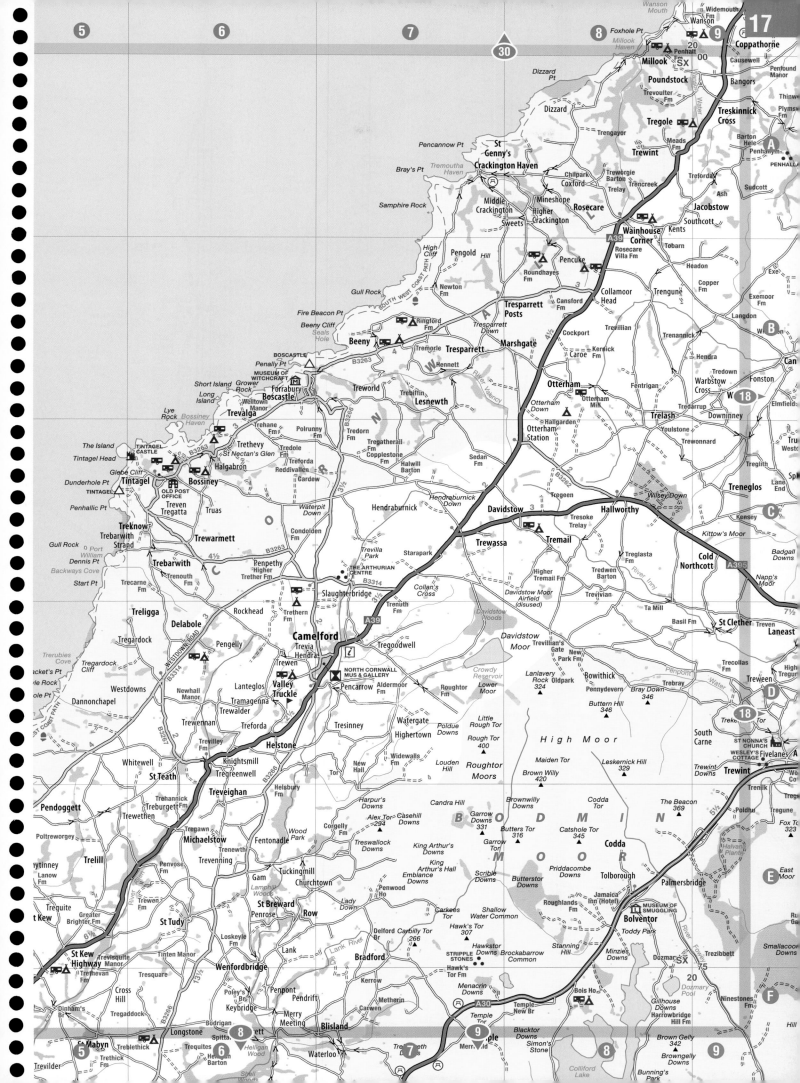

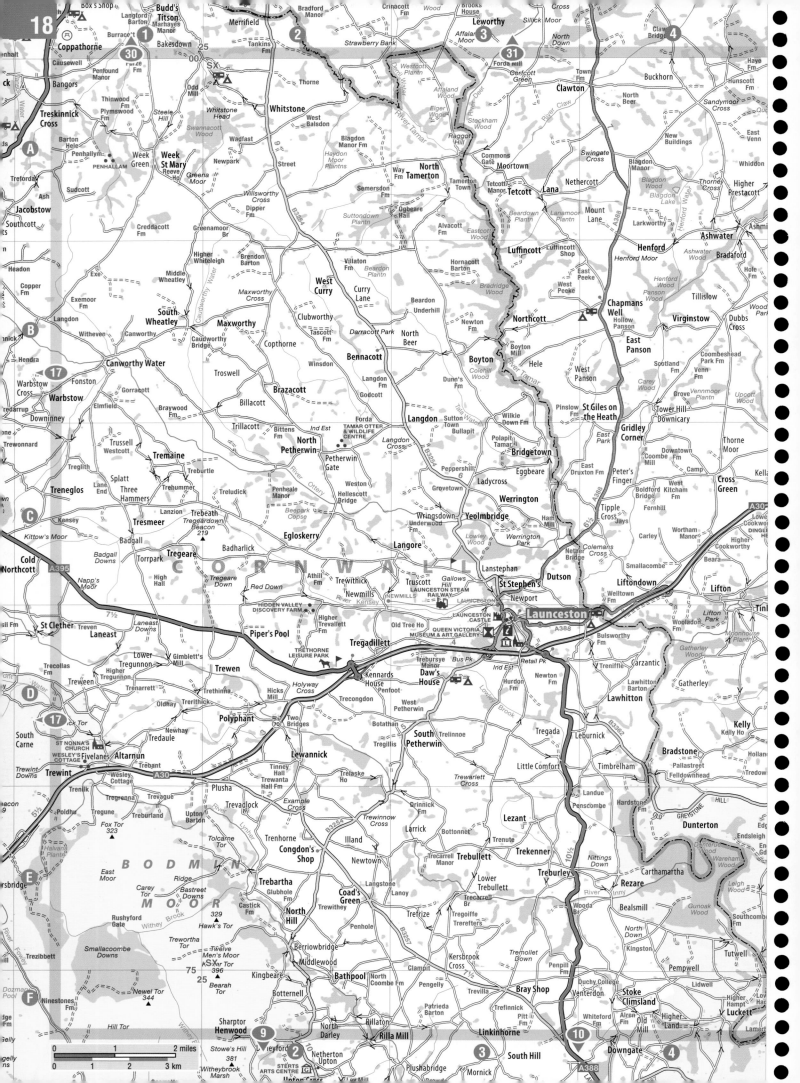

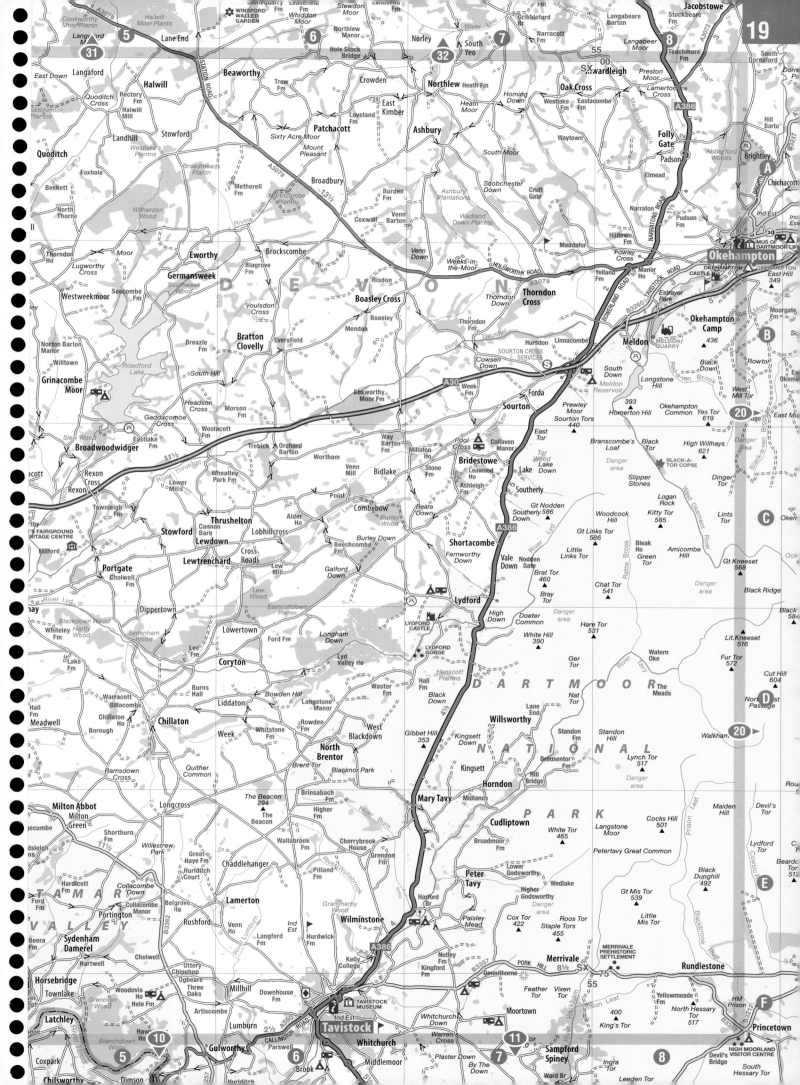

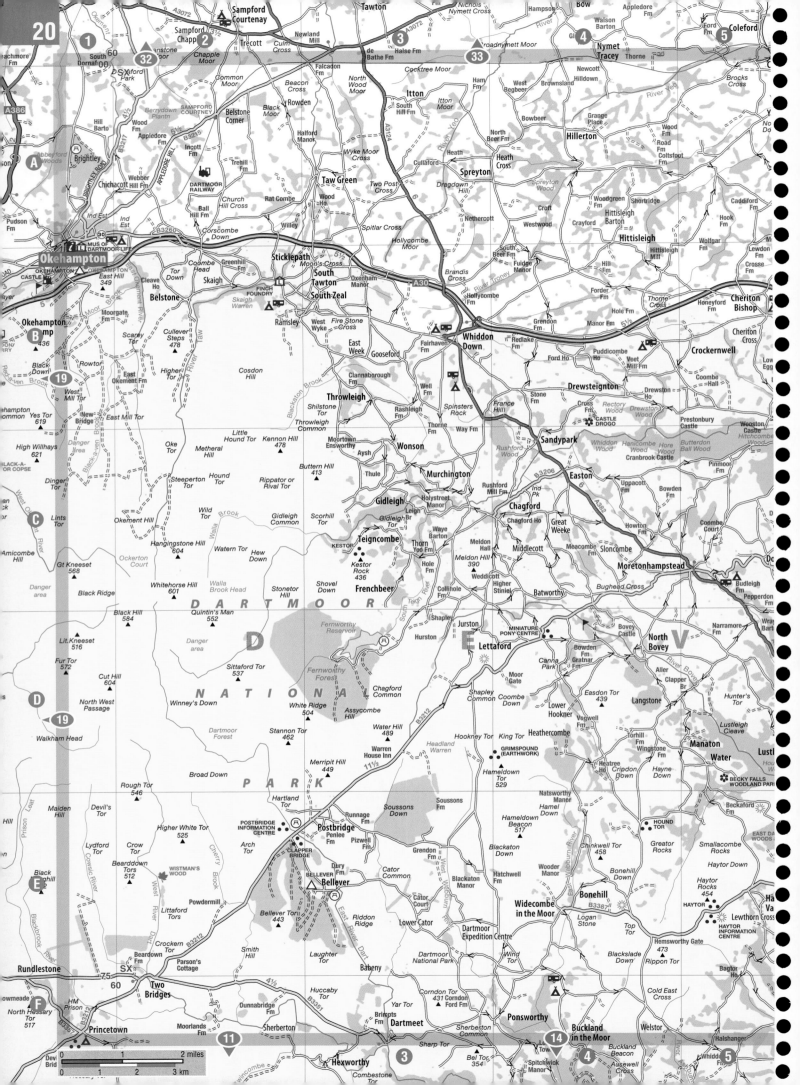

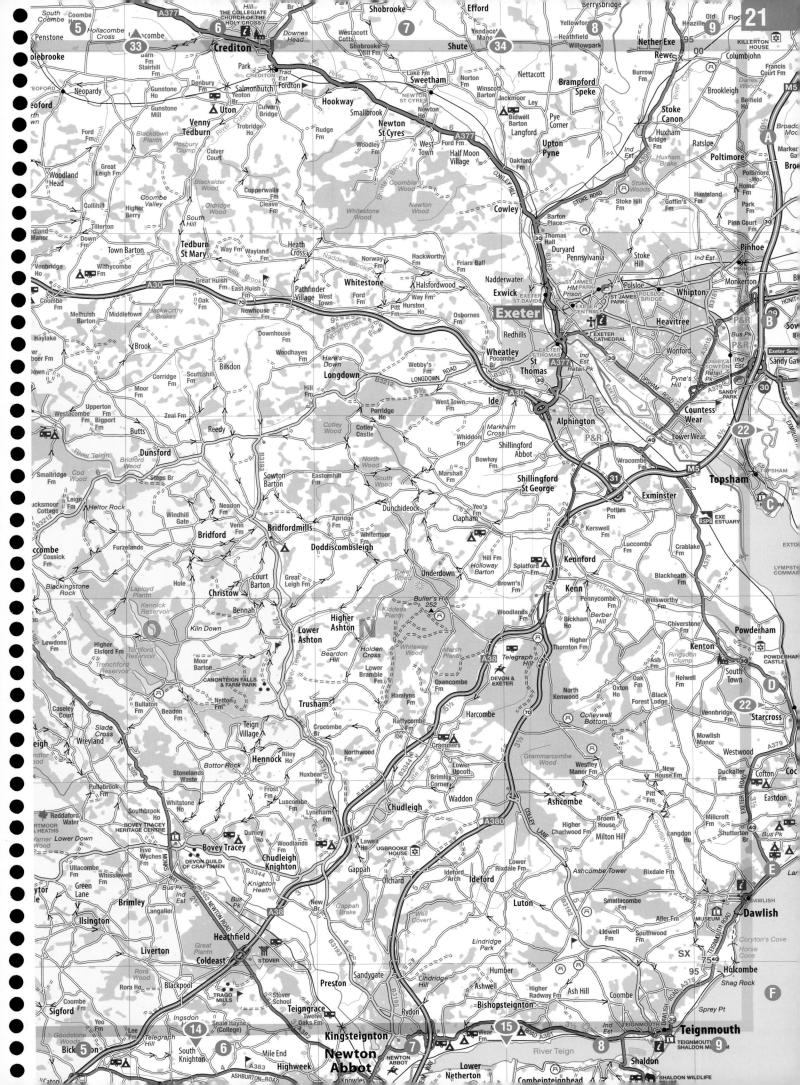

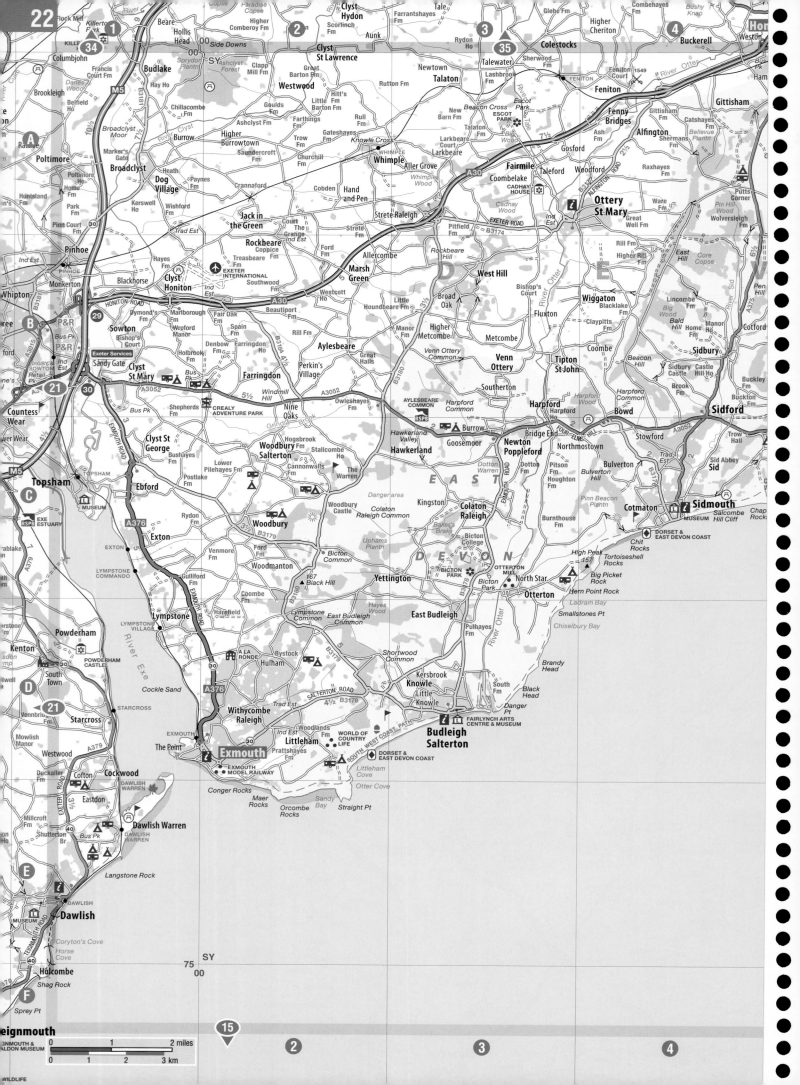

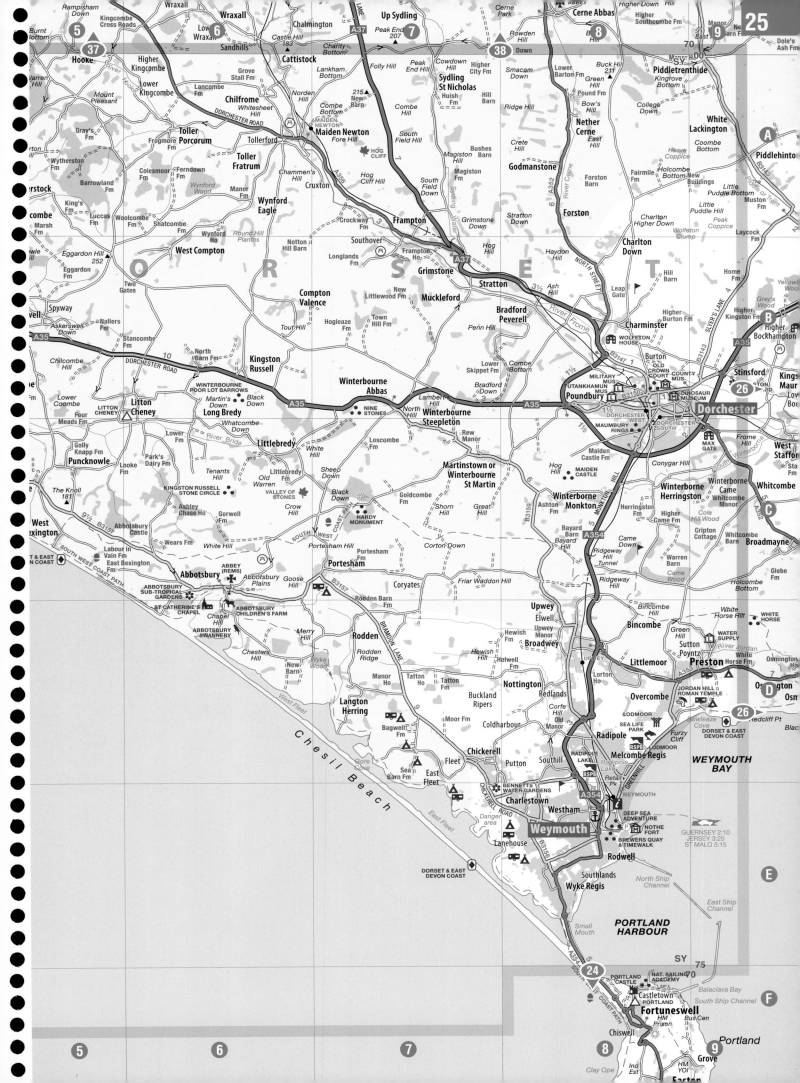

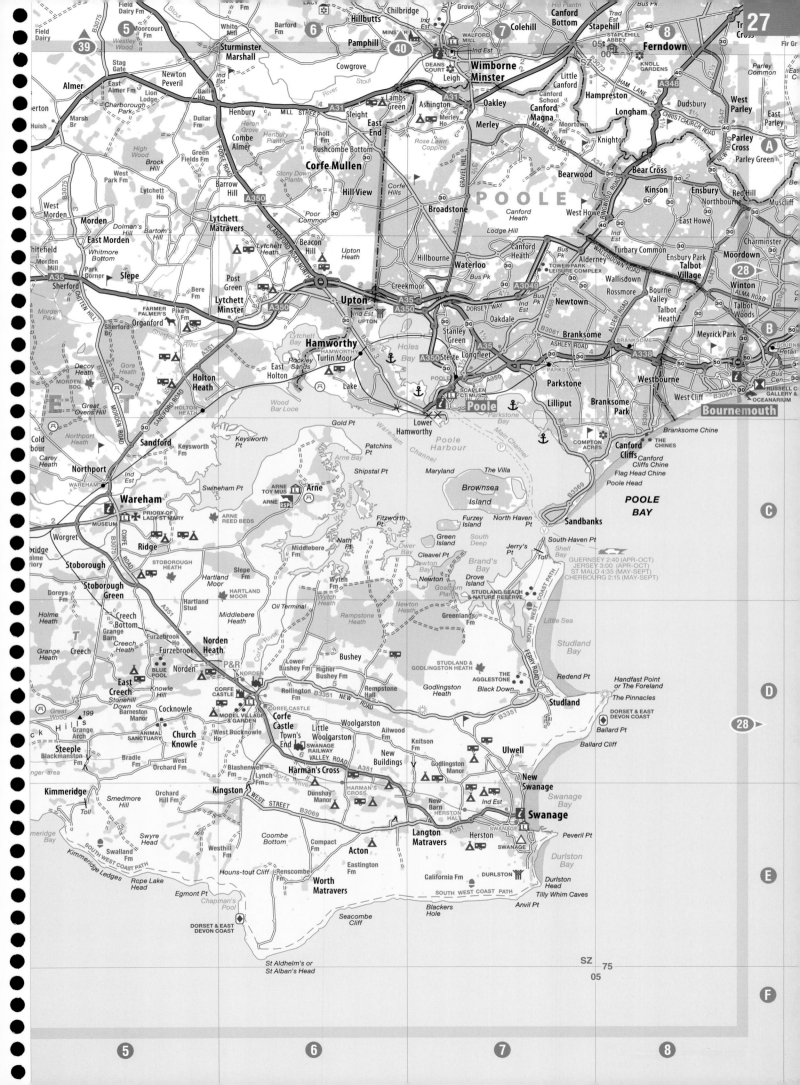

POOLE BAY

CHRISTCHURCH
BAY

DORSET

HAMP

Bournemouth

Place names and features:

MATCHAMS
Ho
Bisterne
Upper Bisterne Fm
Common
Greenberry Br
Holmsley Lodge
Long Slade Bottom
Foxbury Hill
Matcham's Pk
Bisterne Manor
Ripley Wood
Dur Hill Down
Whitten Bottom
Holmsley Ridge
Wilverley Inclosure
Hincheslea Wood

Grove Fm
Week Fm
Lower Bisterne Fm
Whitefield Hill
Shirley Common
Setthorns Cottage

SZ
East Parley Common
Week Common
North Ripley
Martin's Copse
Thorney Hill
Hill Fm
Wootton Coppice Inclosure
Set Thorns Inclosure

Parley Common
Hurn Forest
Avon
Ripley
Shirley
Brownhill Inclosure
Avon Water

West Parley
East Parley
BOURNEMOUTH AIRPORT
Sopley Common
Pithouse Fm
Sopley
North Bockhampton
Bransgore
Beech Ho
Ossemsley
HOLMSLEY ROAD
Wootton
Mead End
SWAY
ARTSWAY

Oudsbury
Parley Cross
Merritown
B3073
Dudmoor Fm
Waterditch
Neacroft
Harrow Lodge
Hinton Park
Beckley Fm
Forest Lodge
Bashley
Tiptoe
Broadley
Arne Mano

Parley Green
ADVENTURE WONDERLAND
Hurn
A338
Town Common
Winkton
Middle Bockhampton
Godwinscroft
Bashley Park
Beckley
New Milton
Ashley
Golden Hill
Hordle

Ensbury
Northbourne
Berry Hill
West Hurn
Blackwater
Winkton Common
South Bockhampton
Burton Common
Hinton
Hinton Ho
SAMMY MILLER MOTORCYCLE MUSEUM
NEW MILTON
B3058
Hordle Grange

East Howe
Red Hill
Muscliff
Mill Throop
Holdenhurst
St Catherine's Hill
Burton
HINTON ADMIRAL
Walkford
Ind Est
Ashley Manor Fm
Hooper's Hill
APP COU Lea

Charminster
Moordown
Stroudon
Jumpers Green
Jumpers Common
Fairmile
LYNDHURST ROAD
Highcliffe
Old Milton
MILFORD ROAD
Downton

Talbot Village
Winton
Queen's Park
Iford
CHRISTCHURCH
ELECTRICITY
Hinton
Taddiford Fm
Cliff

Talbot Woods
WESSEX WAY
Littledown
STONY LANE
A35
HIGHCLIFFE CASTLE
Barton on Sea
Hordle Cliff

Meyrick Park
Springbourne
SEWARD STADIUM
POKESDOWN
West Southbourne
Tuckton
Purewell
Somerford
Stanpit
Friars Cliff

Winton
BOURNEMOUTH Retail Pk
Pokesdown
CHRISTCHURCH
RED HOUSE
CASTLE & NORMAN HOUSE
Christchurch
Stanpit
Mudeford

Bus Cen
Boscombe
BOURNEMOUTH
Wick
Christchurch Harbour
Sandhills

RUSSELL COTES ART GALLERY & MUSEUM
OCEANARIUM
Southbourne
Stanpit Marsh
Hengistbury Head

West Cliff
B3064
Bournemouth

ksome Chine

A347
A338

SZ
75
10

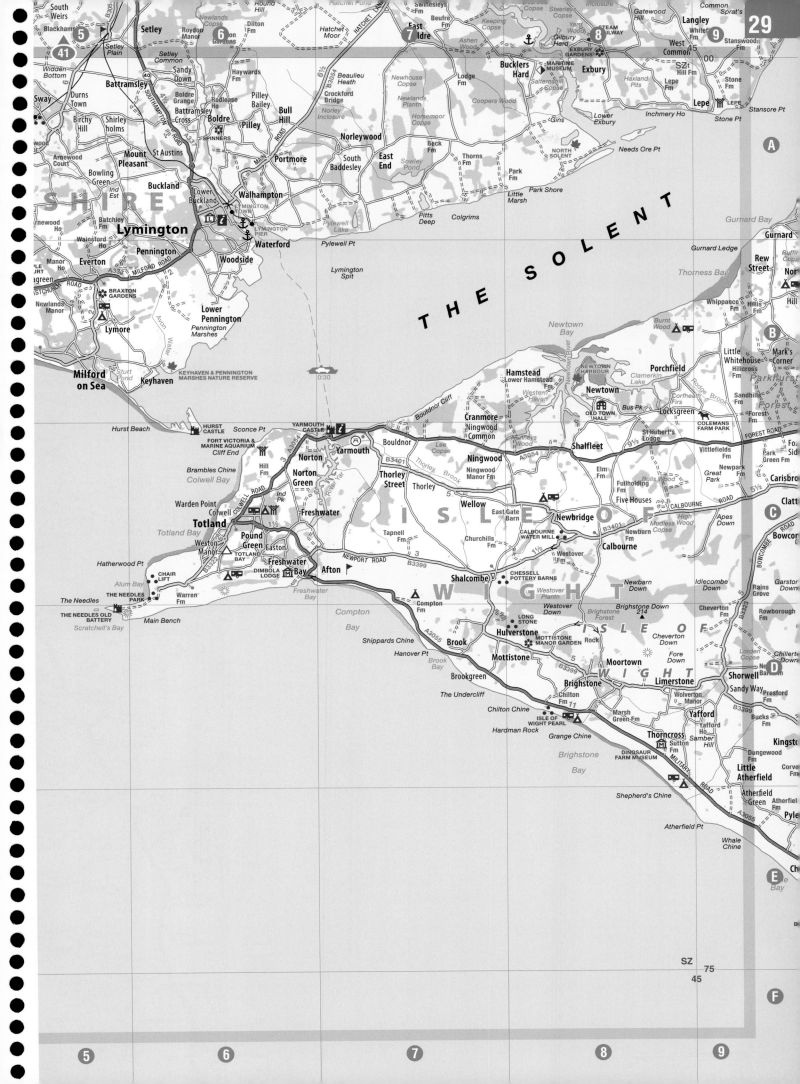

THE SOLENT

ISLE OF WIGHT

A B C D E F

1 2 3 4

10
25
SS

Hartland Pt   Barley Bay   Shipload Bay
Blagdon Fm   Titch
Damehole Pt   Upright Cliff
Blegbury
Hartland Abbey   HART ABBE
HARTLAND QUAY MUS   Stoke
Speke's Mill Mouth   Kernstone Fm   N
Galsha Fm
DOCTON MILL & GARDENS
Milford   D
Mansley Cliff   ELMSCOTT   Elmscott
Docton
Nabor Pt   Sandhole Cliff
Gull Rock   Hardisworthy   Firebeacon Golden Park
South Hole
Embury Beacon 157   Putshole Fm
Ramtor Rock
Tredown   Henaf
Welcombe Mouth   Welcombe
Marsland Mouth   Mead   Darracott   Upc
Marsland Water
Gull Rock   Marsland Cliff   Marsland   Gooseham Mill
Yeol Mouth   Marsland Manor   Hackmar
Cornakey Cliff   Gooseham
Henna Cliff 143
Lucky Hole   Vicarage Cliff   Morwenstow   Rule Cross
Crosstown   Woodford Cross   Shop
Higher Sharpnose Pt   ST JOHN THE BAPTIST CHURCH
Darzle Fm   Middlefields
Hippa Rock   Eastaway Manor   Ham Fm   Stursdon
Stanbury Mouth   Woodford
Lower Sharpnose Pt
Woodlands Fm
Elms
Steeple Pt   Burridge Fm   Penstowe Park
Duckpool   Coombe   Lee Wood   Stowe Wood   ST JAMES'S CHURCH
Houndapit Fm
Stowe Cliffs   Stibb
Long Rock
Killock Fm   C O R N W
Sandy Mouth   C·O·R·N·W
Dunsmouth Fm   Halls
Menachurch Pt
Northcott Mouth   A39   Ivyleaf Fm
Crockwood Fm
Northcott
Poughill   Bush
Maer   Stamford Hill   Colebrook Fm
Wrangle Pt   Flexbury
Bude Haven
Compass Pt   Bude   Stratton
BUDE-STRATTON MUSEUM   A3072
Ebbingford Manor   Ind Est
Grove Park   Launcel Sc
Lynstone   A3073   Marsh   2½
West Grove
Phillips's Pt   Upton   Rodd's Bridge   Brayshill
Thorne
Phillips Fm   Hobbacott
Marhamchurch
Helebridge   Hilton   Rattenbury
A39   Woodknowle   Hackthorne
Widemouth Sand   Helscott   Trelay
Widemouth Bay   Titson
Black Rock   Budd's Titson
Wanson Mouth   Widemouth Fm   Box's Shop   Langford   Marhayes Manor
Wanson   Barton   Burracott
Foxhole Pt   Bakesdown
Millook Haven   Penhalt Fm   Causewell
Millook   Coppathorne   Odd Mill
Dizzard Pt   Penfound   Thinwood
Poundstock   Bangors   Ma
Trevoulter Fm

SS
00
10

17   18

2   3   4

0   1   2 miles
0   1   2   3 km

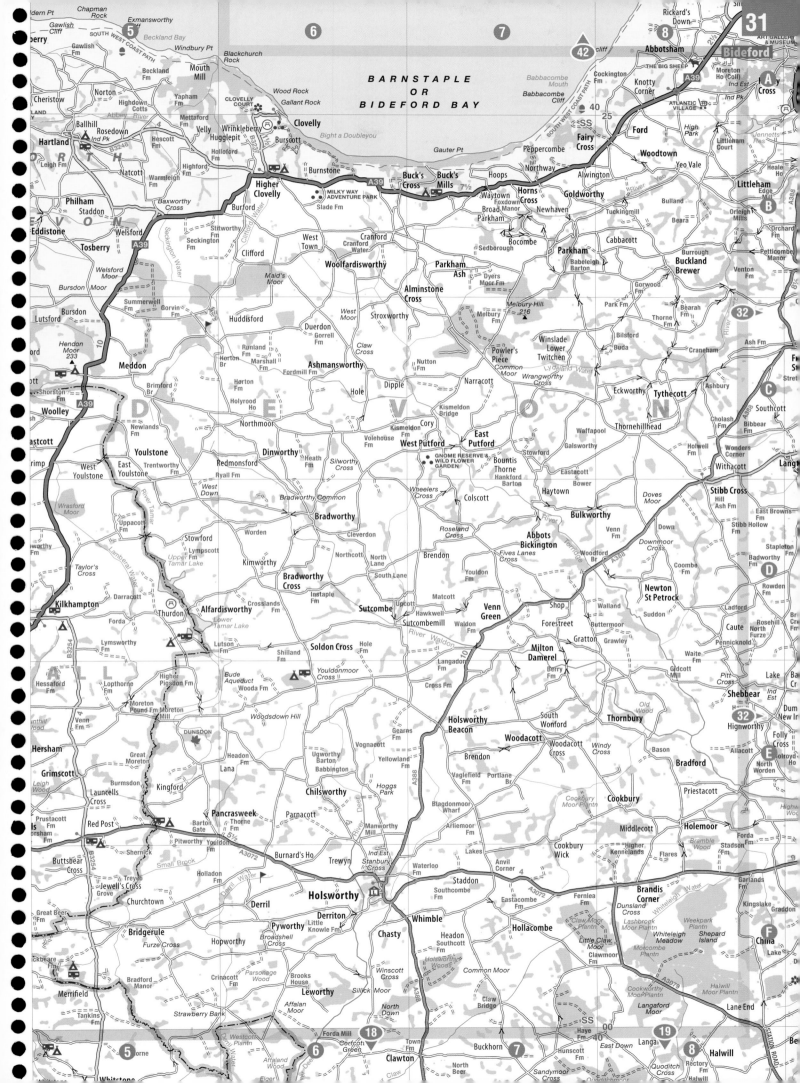

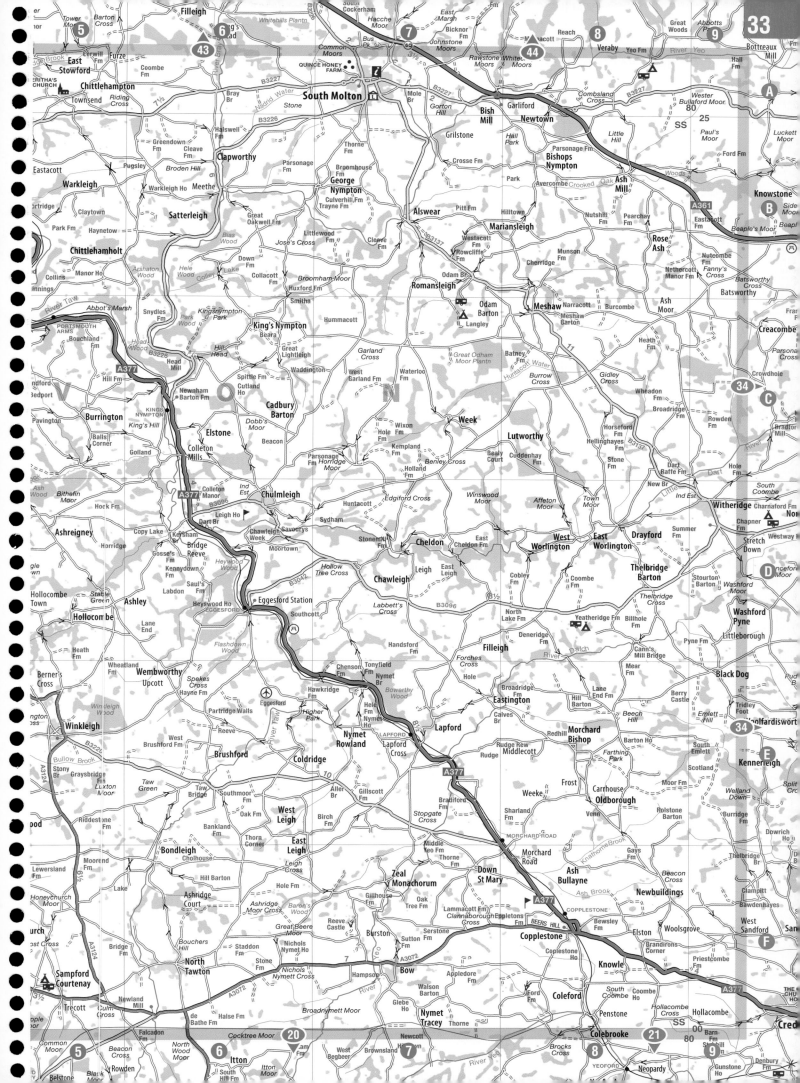

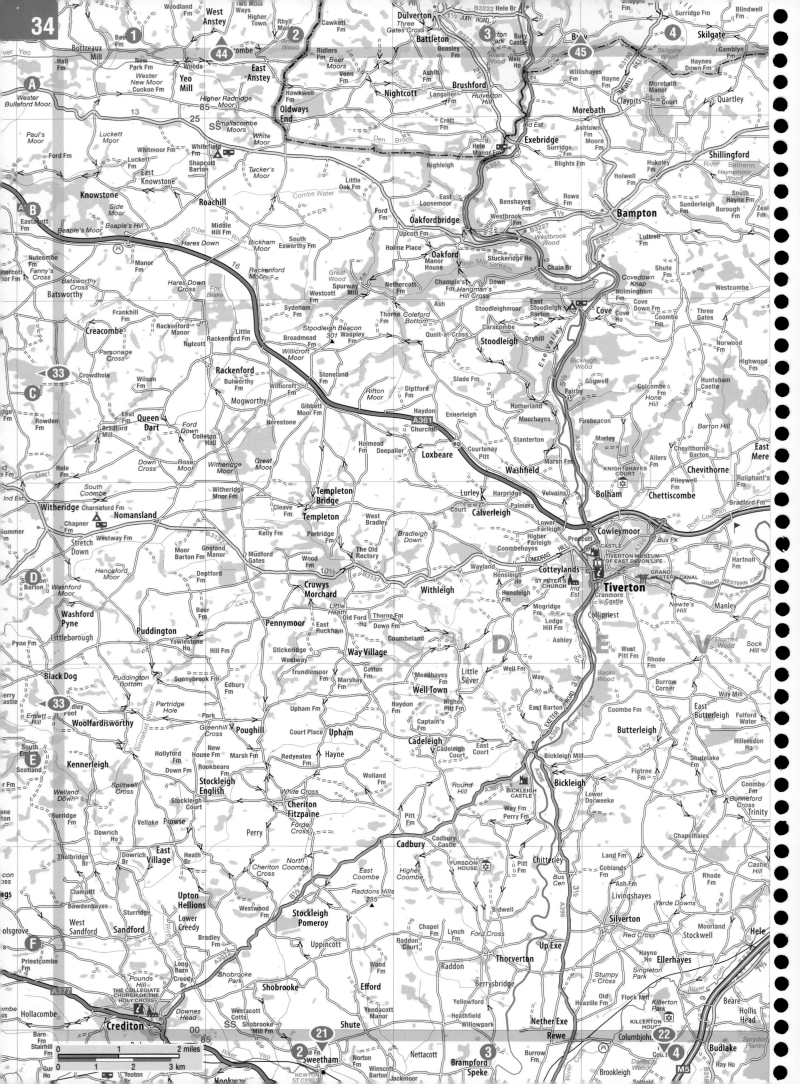

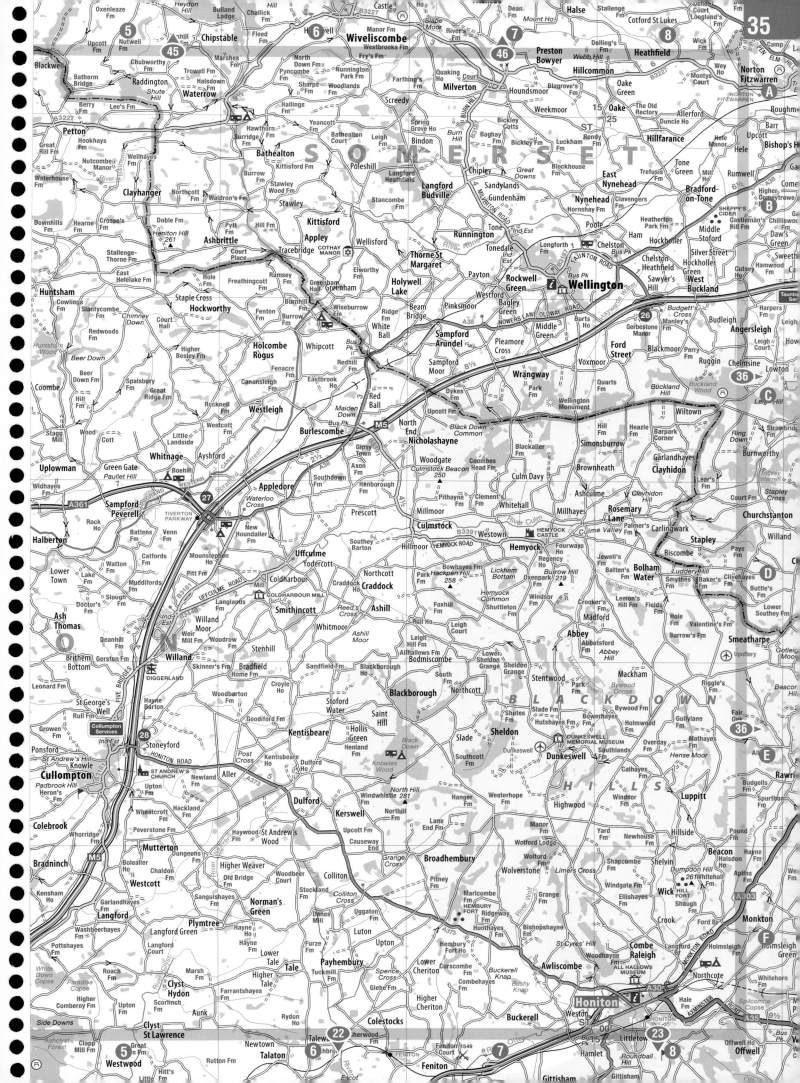

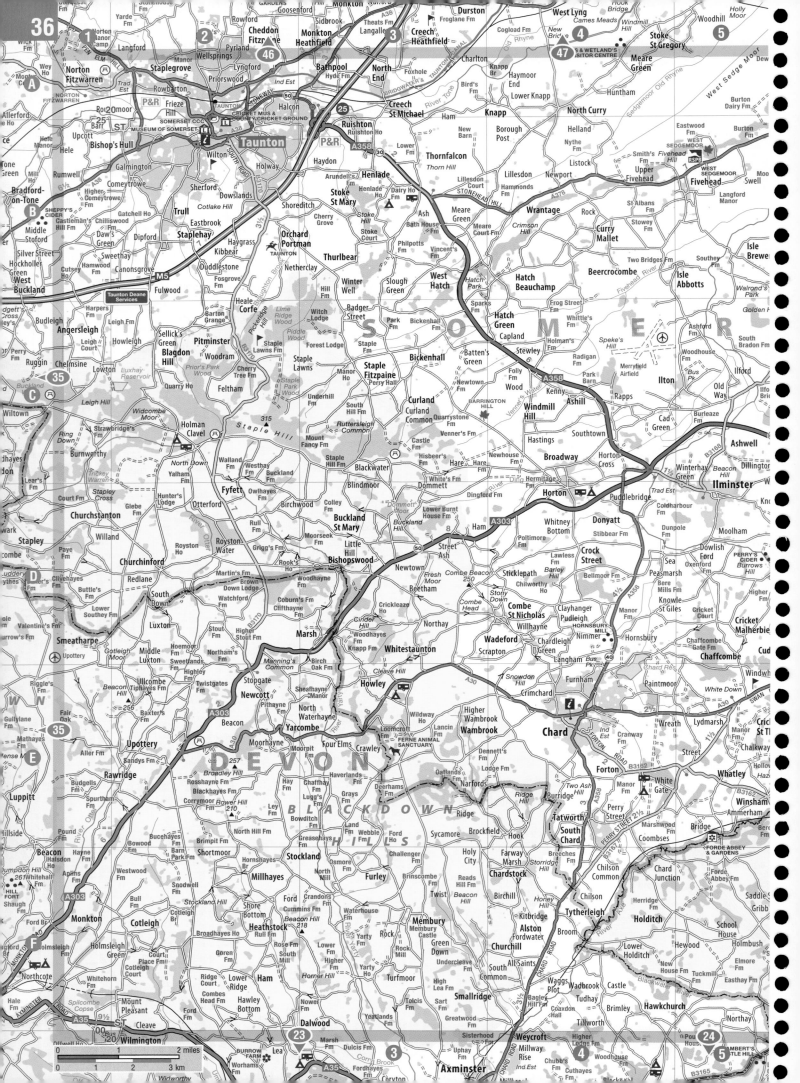

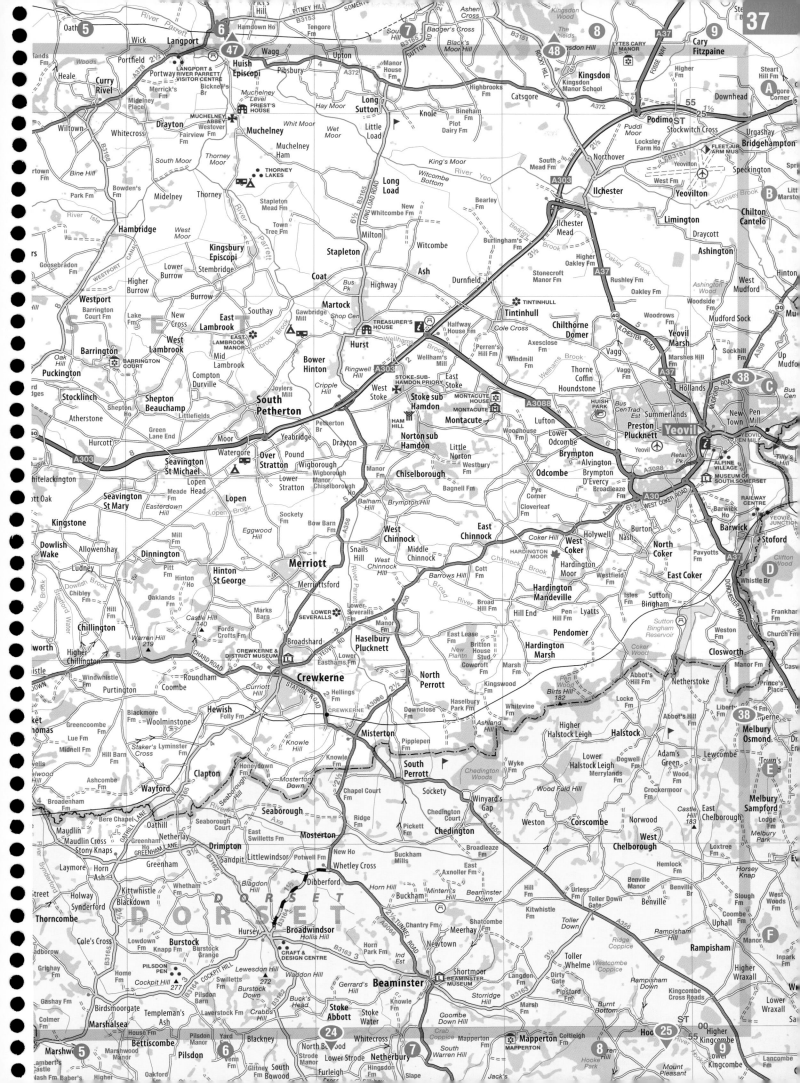

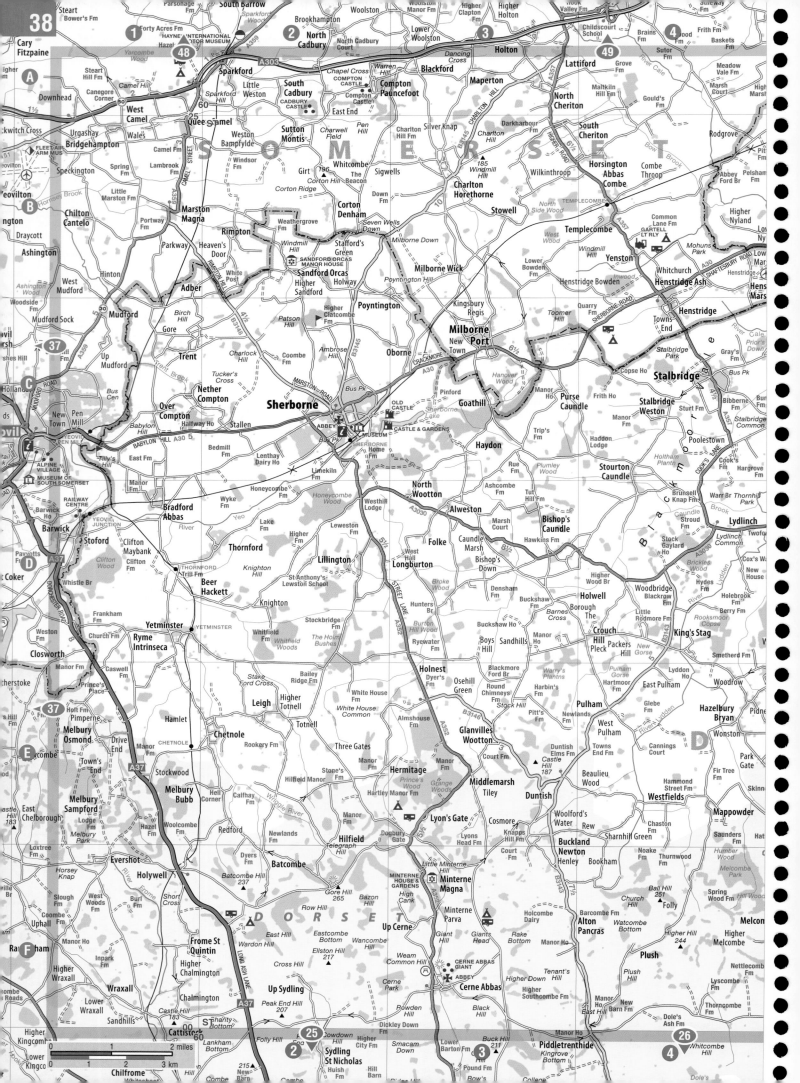

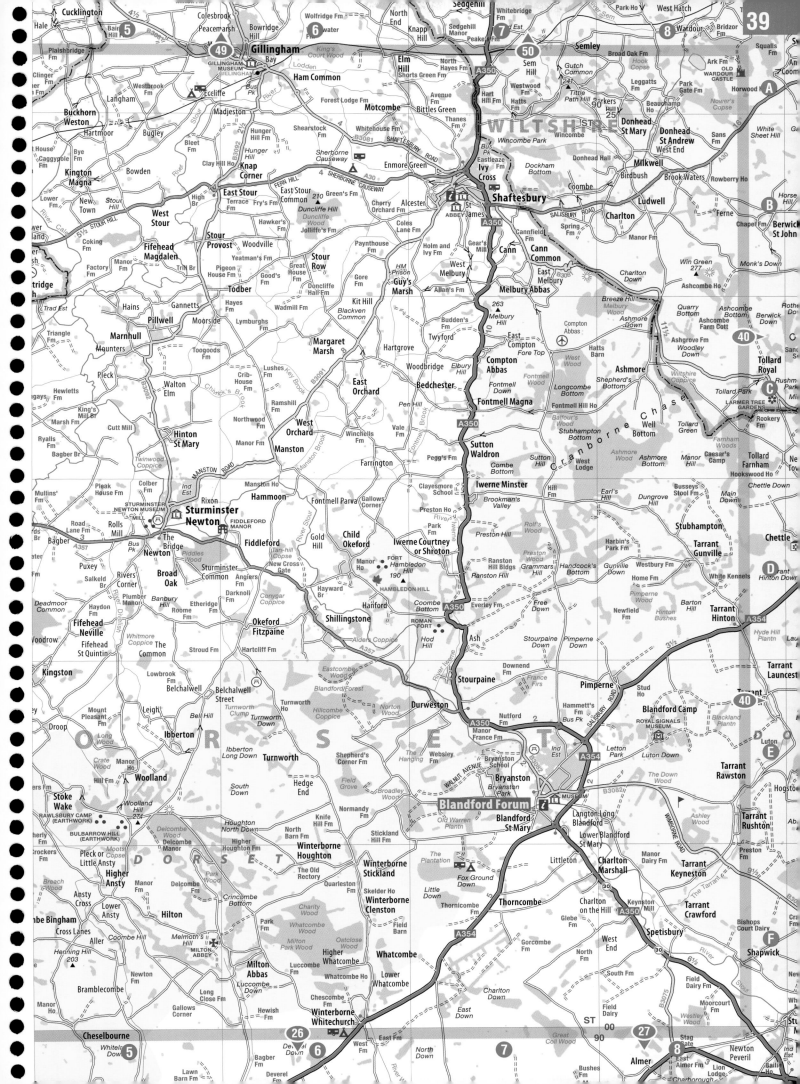

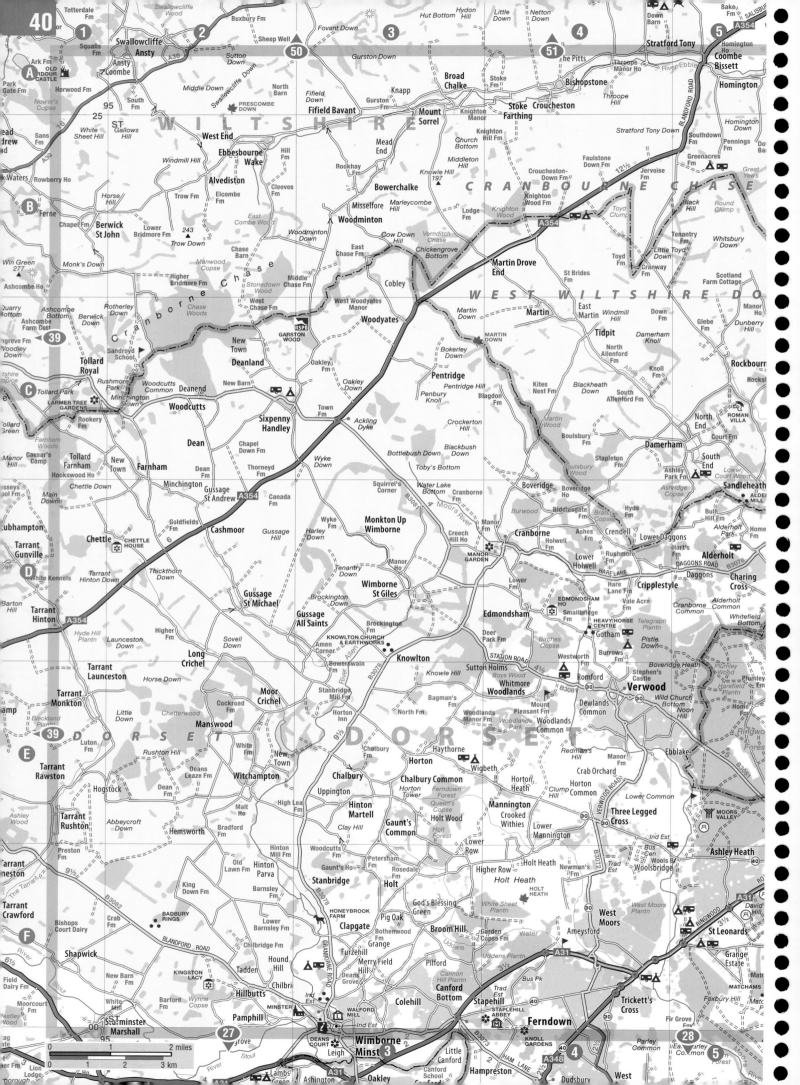

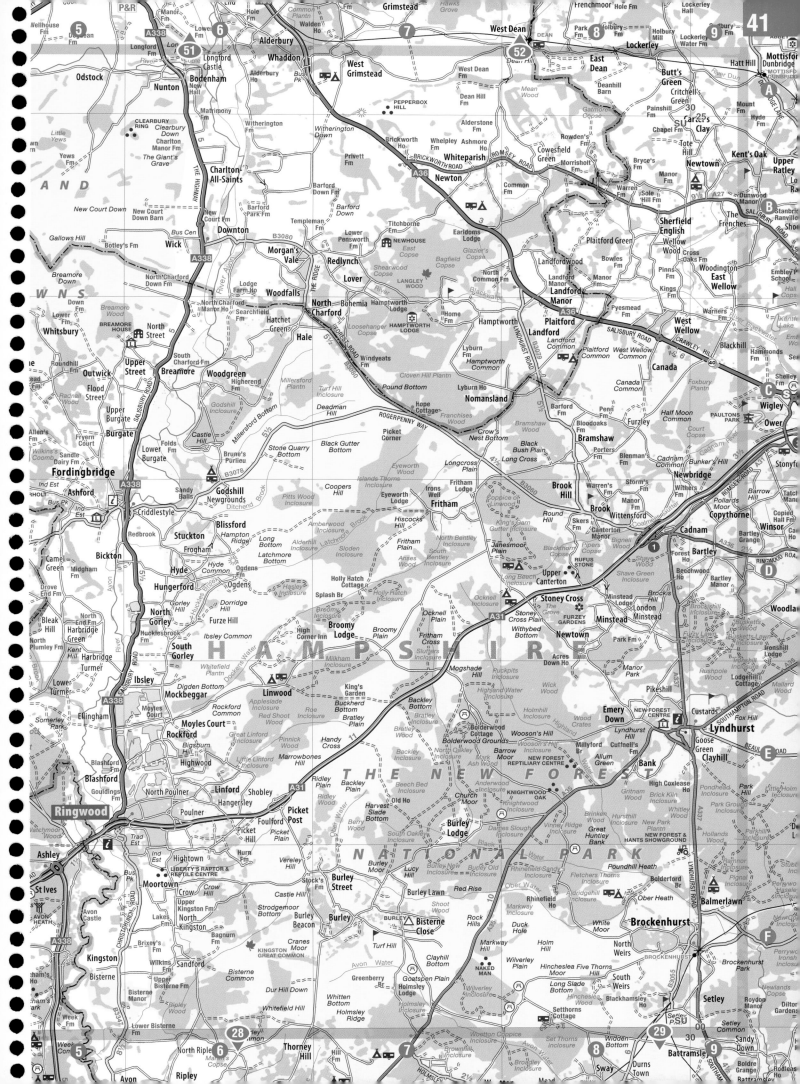

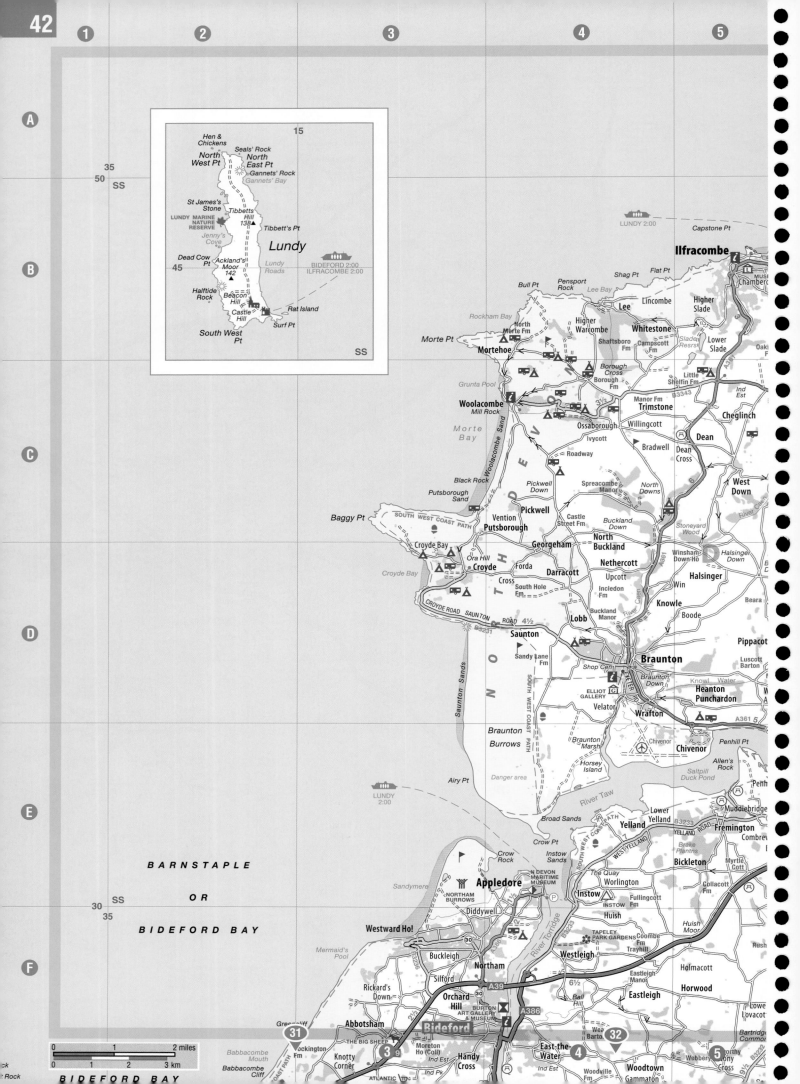

Lundy (inset map)

Hen & Chickens
North West Pt
Seals' Rock
North East Pt
Gannets' Rock
Gannets' Bay
15
St James's Stone
LUNDY MARINE NATURE RESERVE
Tibbetts Hill 138▲
Tibbett's Pt
Jenny's Cove
Dead Cow Pt
Ackland's Moor 142▲
Lundy Roads
BIDEFORD 2:00
ILFRACOMBE 2:00
45
Halftide Rock
Beacon Hill
Castle Hill
Rat Island
South West Pt
Surf Pt
SS

35
50 SS

LUNDY 2:00
Capstone Pt
Ilfracombe
MUSE
Chambers

Bull Pt
Pensport Rock
Shag Pt
Flat Pt
Lee Bay
Lee
Lincombe
Higher Slade
North Morte Fm
Higher Warcombe
Shaftsboro Fm
Campscott Fm
Sladen Resrvr
Whitestone
Lower Slade
Oak
Morte Pt
Rockham Bay
Mortehoe
Borough Cross
Borough Fm
Little Shelfin Fm
Ind Est
Grunta Pool
3½
Manor Fm
B3343
Cheglinch
Woolacombe
Mill Rock
Ossaborough
Willingcott
Trimstone
Dean
Morte Bay
Ivycott
Bradwell
Dean Cross
Roadway
Spreacombe Manor
North Downs
West Down
Black Rock
Pickwell Down
Putsborough Sand
River Cae
Baggy Pt
SOUTH WEST COAST PATH
Vention
Putsborough
Pickwell
Castle Street Fm
Buckland Down
Stoneyard Wood
Croyde Bay
Ora Hill
Georgeham
North Buckland
Winsham Down Ho
Halsinger Down
Croyde Bay
Croyde
Forda
Darracott
Nethercott
Upcott
Halsinger
Cross
South Hole Fm
Incledon Fm
Win
Knowle
Beara
CROYDE ROAD
SAUNTON ROAD 4½
B3231
Lobb
Buckland Manor
Boode
Saunton
Sandy Lane Fm
A361
Pippacot
Shop Cen
Braunton Down
Luscott Barton
Saunton Sands
ELLIOT GALLERY
Braunton
Knowl Water
Velator
Heanton Punchardon
Wrafton
A361 5
Braunton Burrows
Braunton Marsh
Chivenor
Penhill Pt
Horsey Island
Chivenor
Allen's Rock
Airy Pt
Danger area
Saltpill Duck Pond
Penh
LUNDY 2:00
River Taw
Muddlebridge
Broad Sands
Lower Yelland
B3233
Fremington
Crow Pt
Yelland
YELLAND ROAD
Combrew
BARNSTAPLE
Crow Rock
Instow Sands
Bickleton
Myrtle Cott
OR
Sandymere
Appledore
The Quay
Worlington
Collacott Fm
N DEVON MARITIME MUSEUM
Instow
Fullingcott
BIDEFORD BAY
NORTHAM BURROWS
INSTOW Fm
Huish
Huish Moor
Rush
Westward Ho!
Diddywell
Mermaid's Pool
TAPELEY PARK GARDENS
Coombe Trayhill
Westleigh
Holmacott
30 SS
35
Buckleigh
Silford
Northam
6½
Eastleigh Manor
Horwood
Eastleigh
Rickard's Down
Orchard Hill
A39
River Torridge
Lowe Lovacot
BURTON ART GALLERY & MUSEUM
A386
Greencliff
Abbotsham
31
Bideford
East-the-Water
32
Webbery
Woodtown
Cross
Babbacombe Mouth
THE BIG SHEEP
3
Moreton Ho (Coll)
Handy Cross
Ind Est
Bartridge Common
Rock
Babbacombe Cliff
Knotty Corner
Ind Pk
ATLANTIC
Woodville
Gammaton

BIDEFORD BAY

Scale:
0 — 1 — 2 miles
0 — 1 — 2 — 3 km

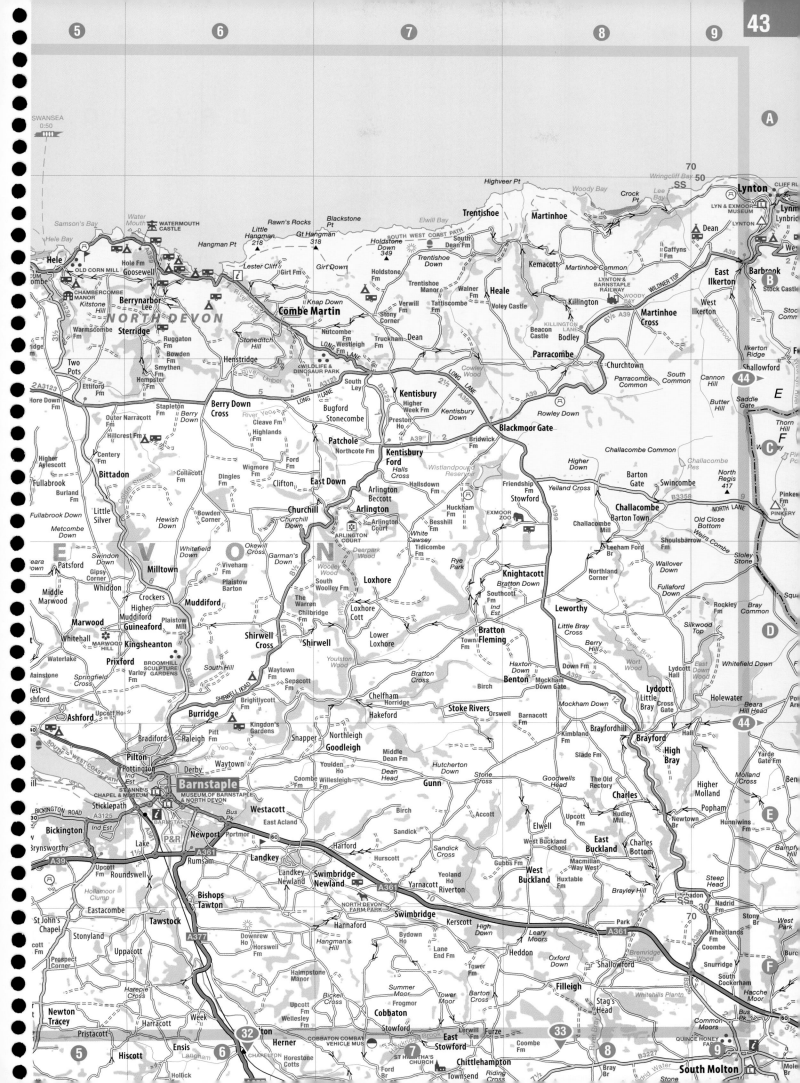

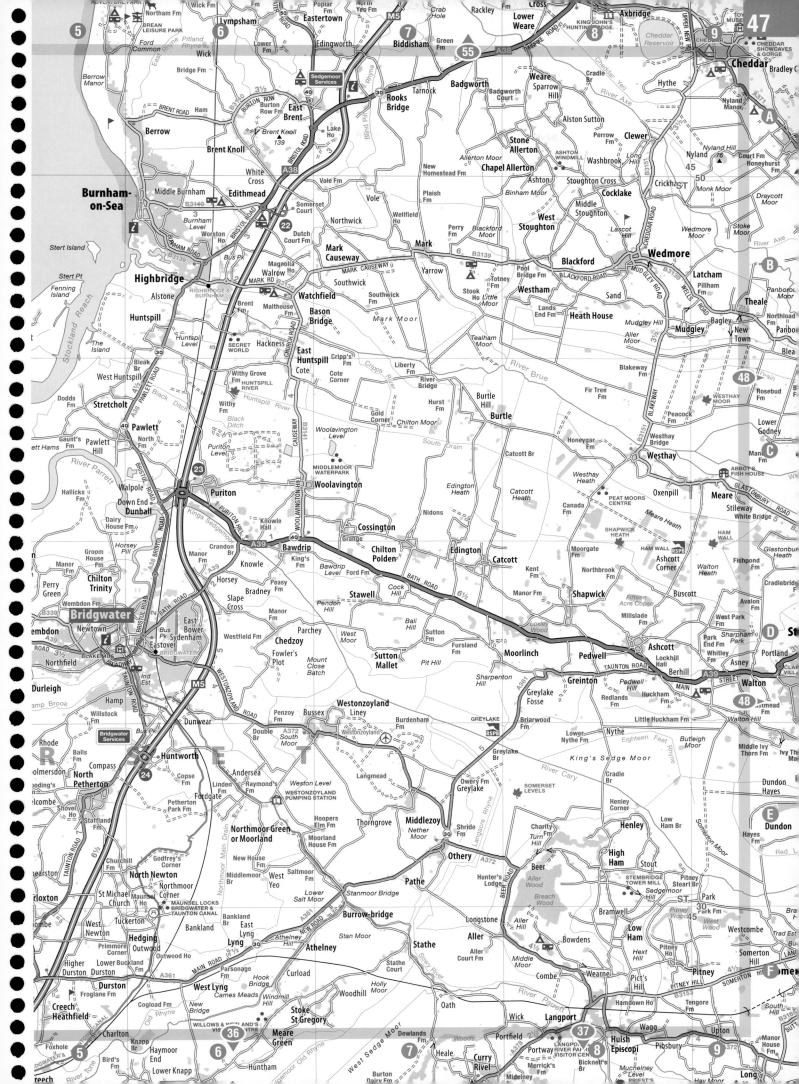

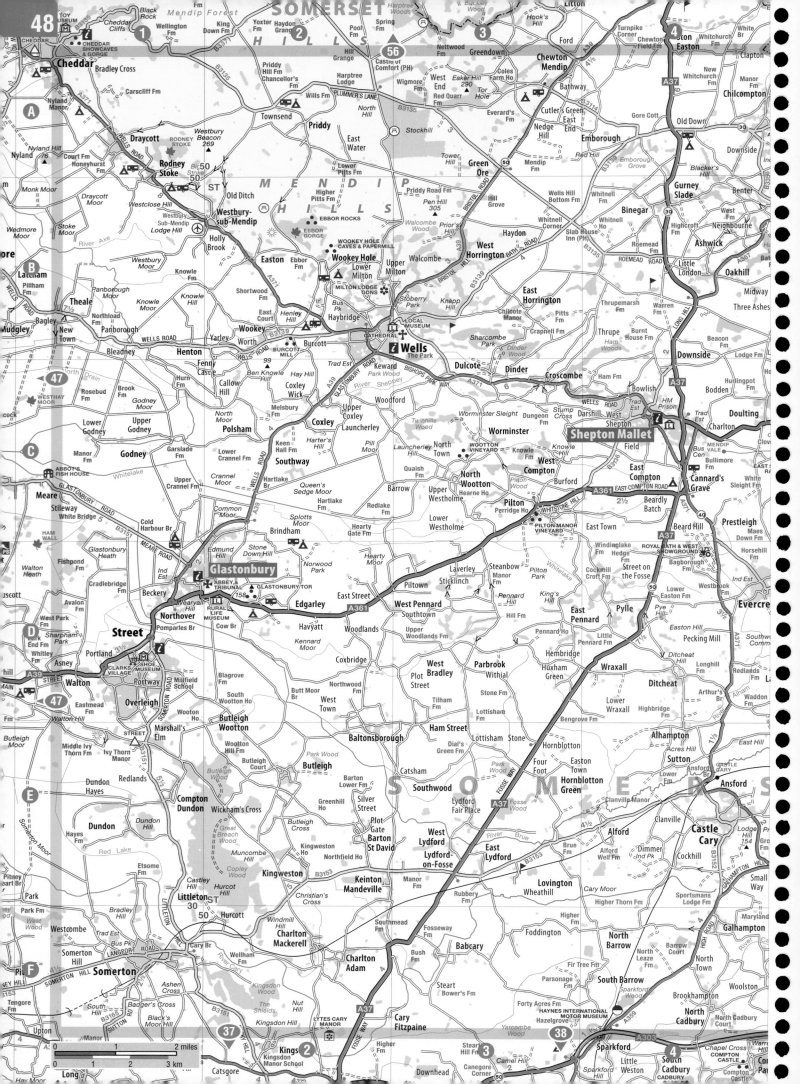

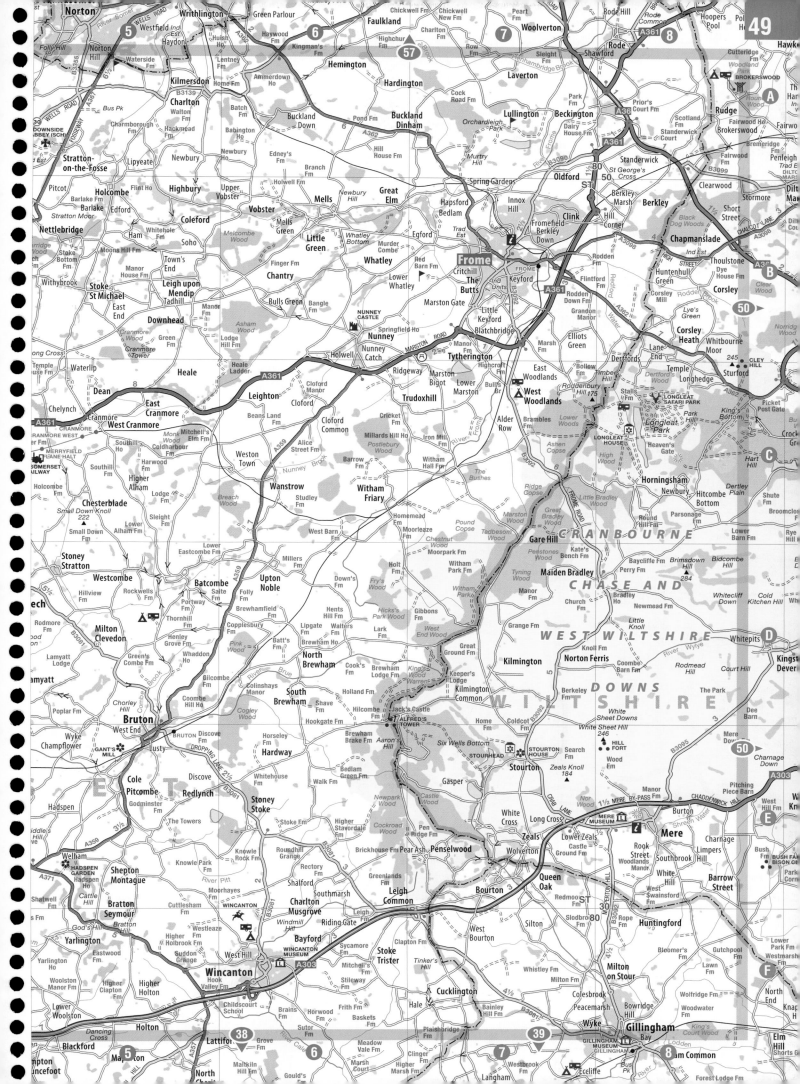

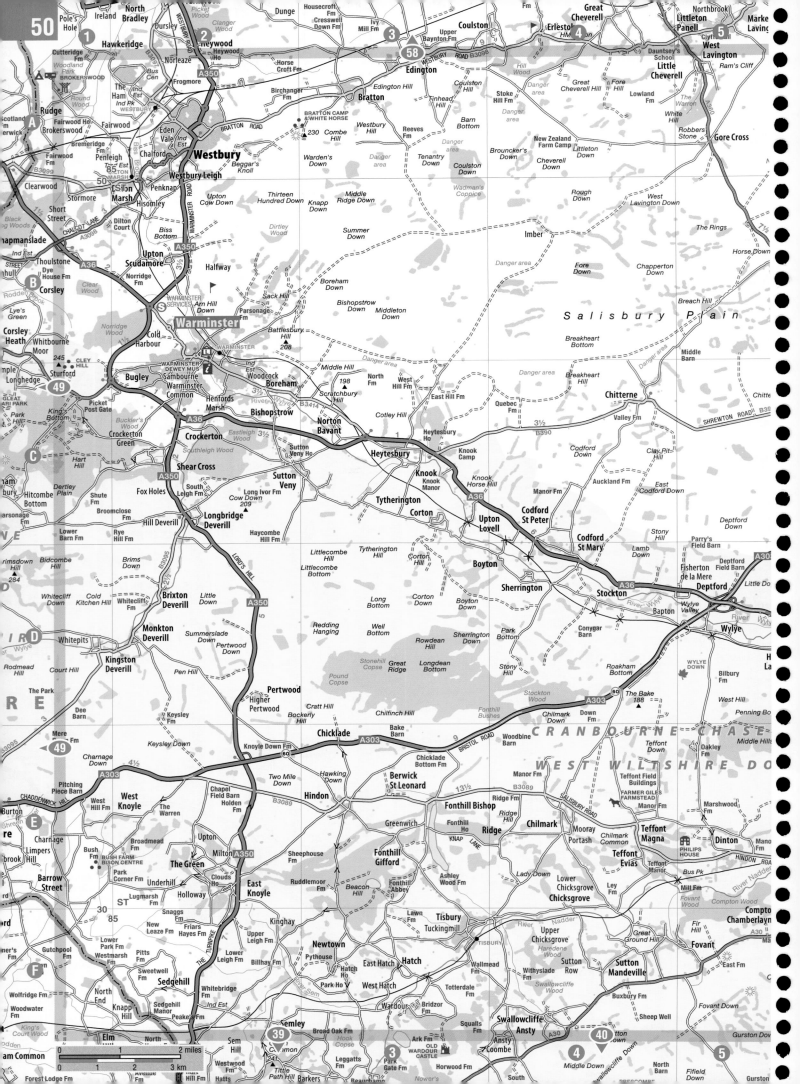

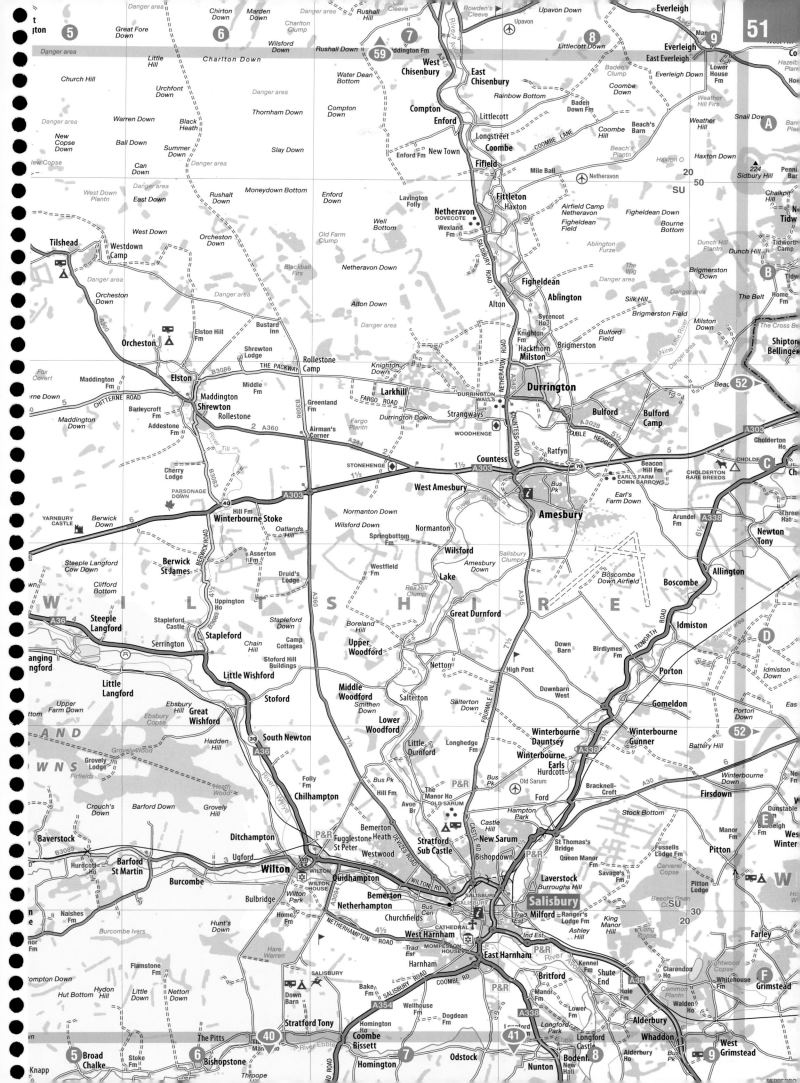

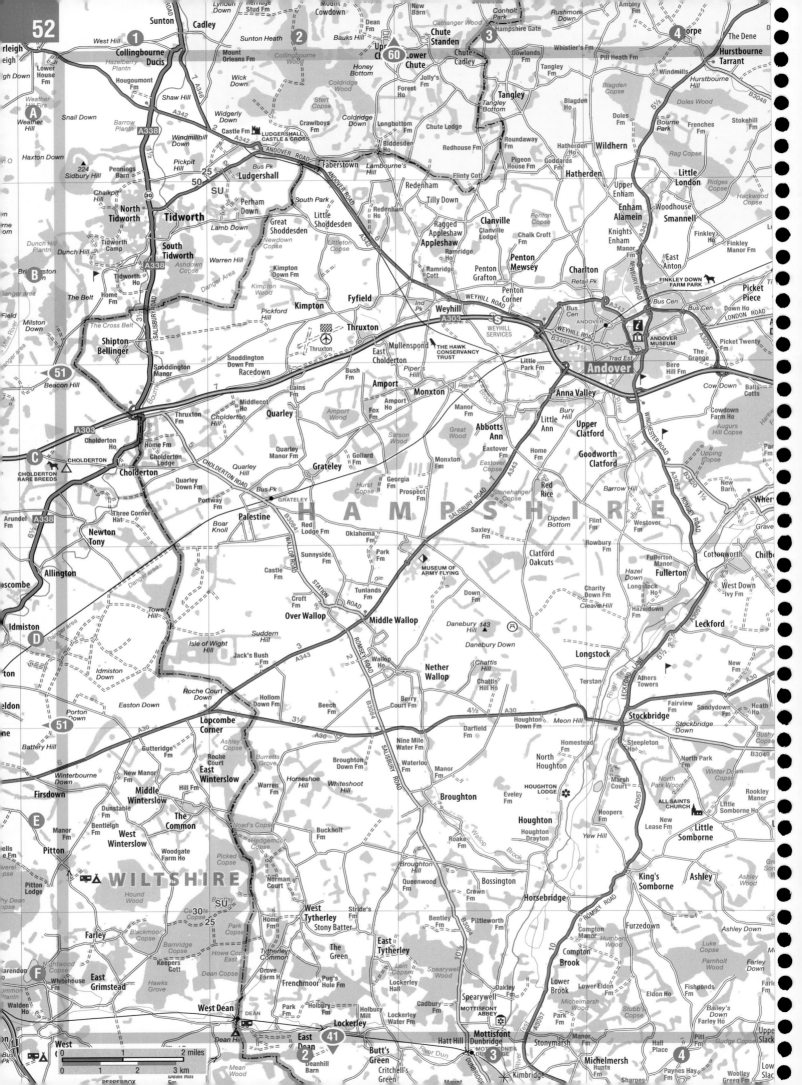

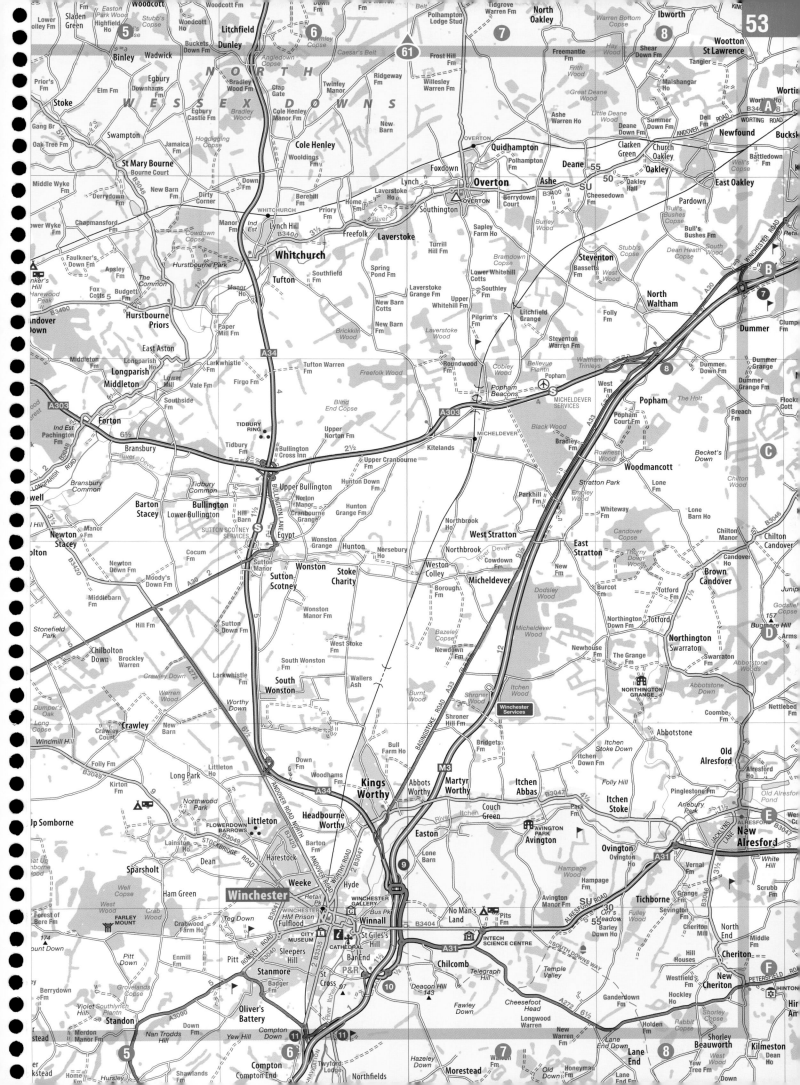

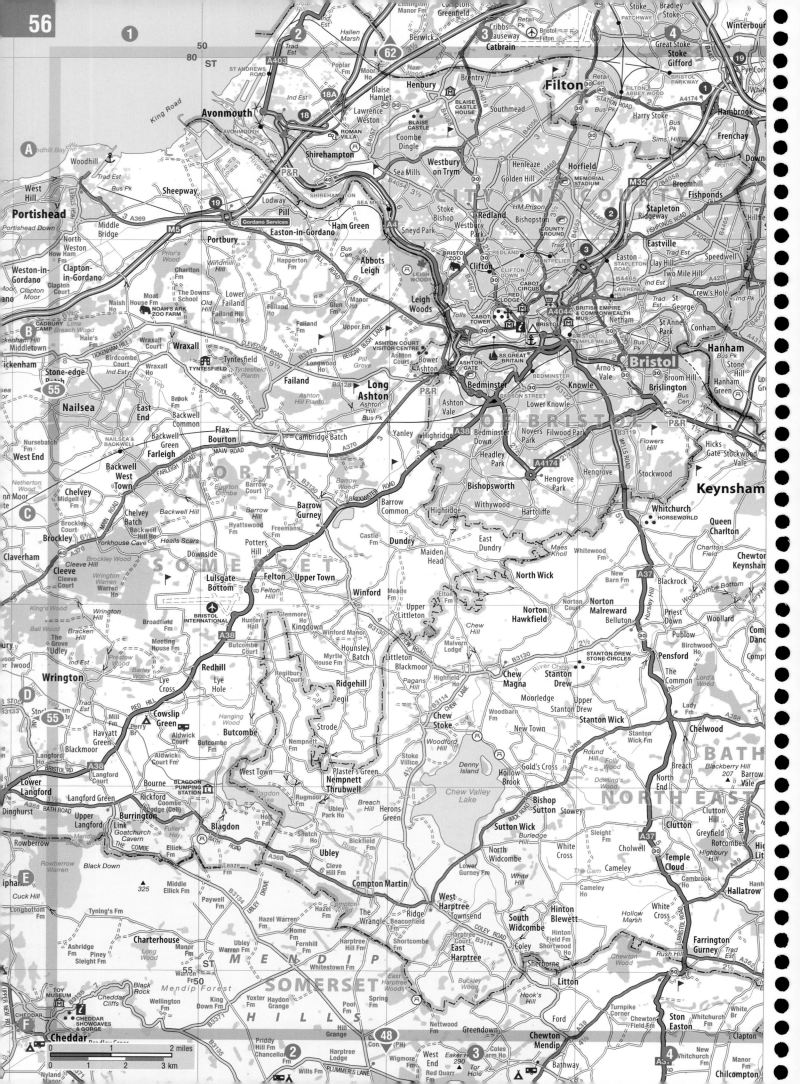

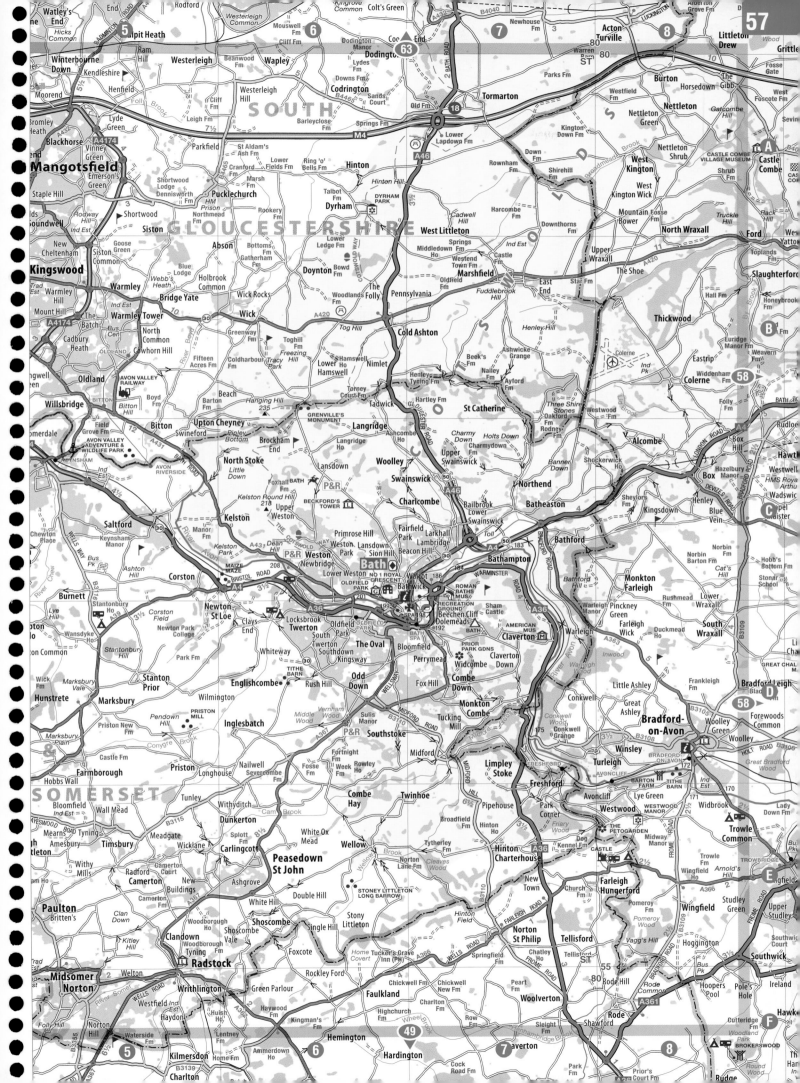

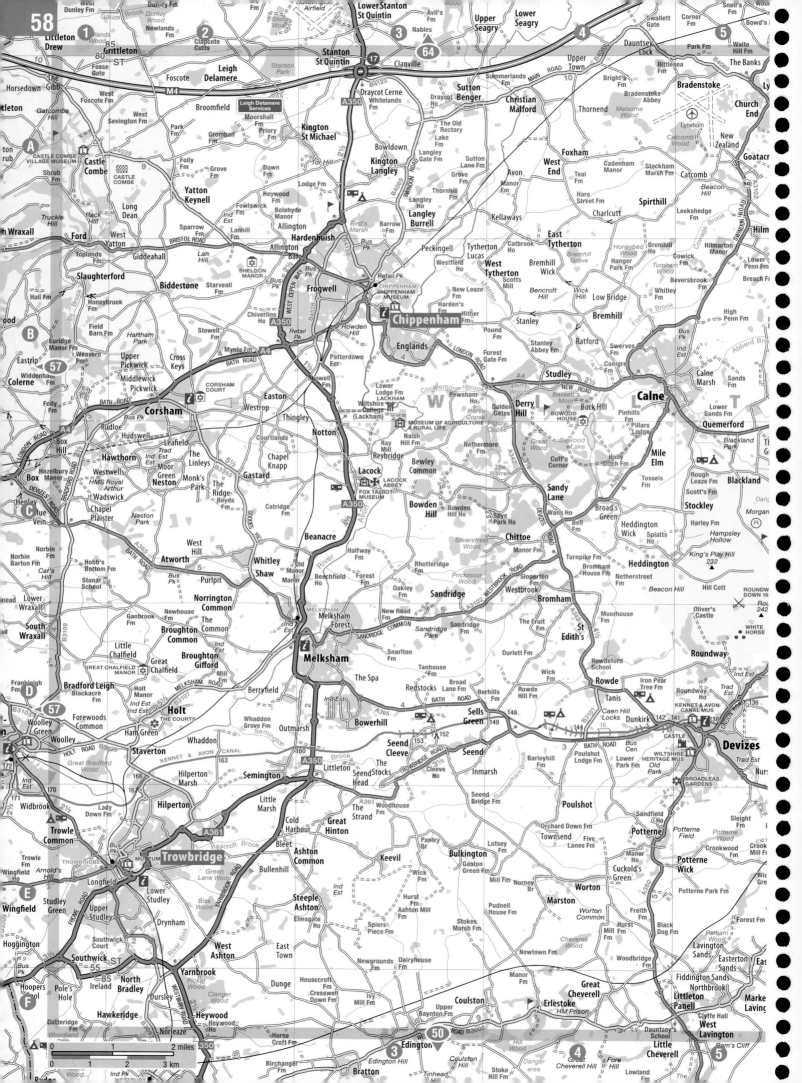

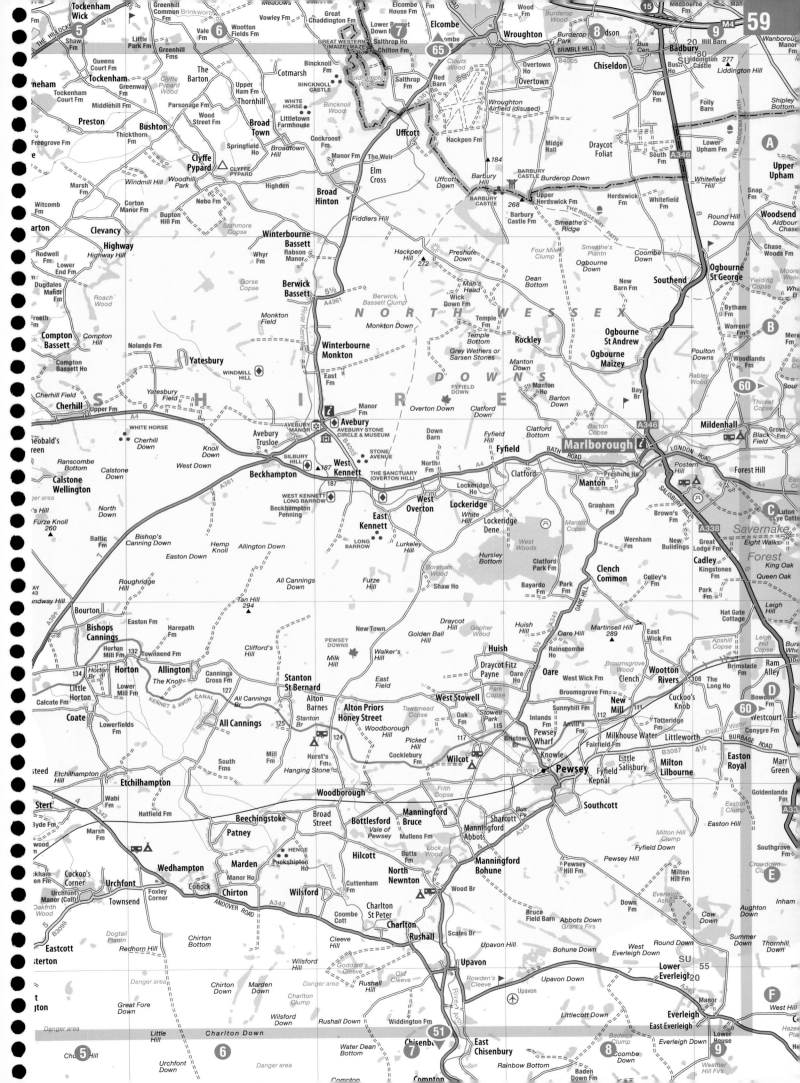

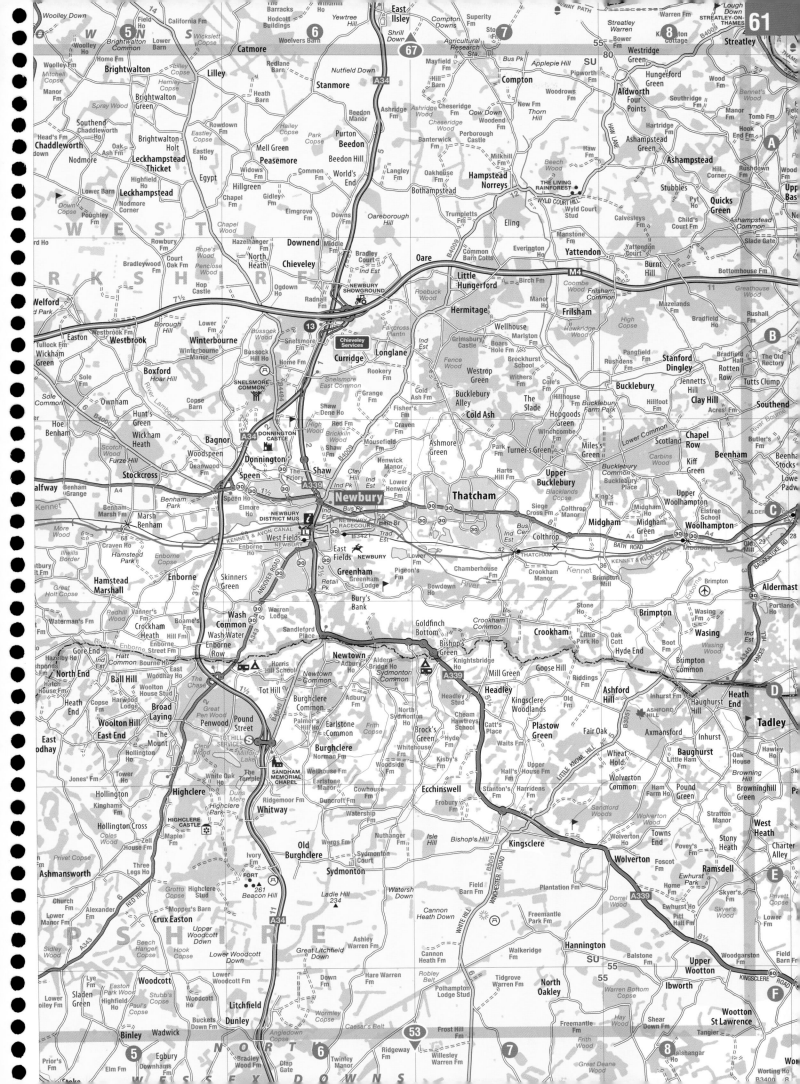

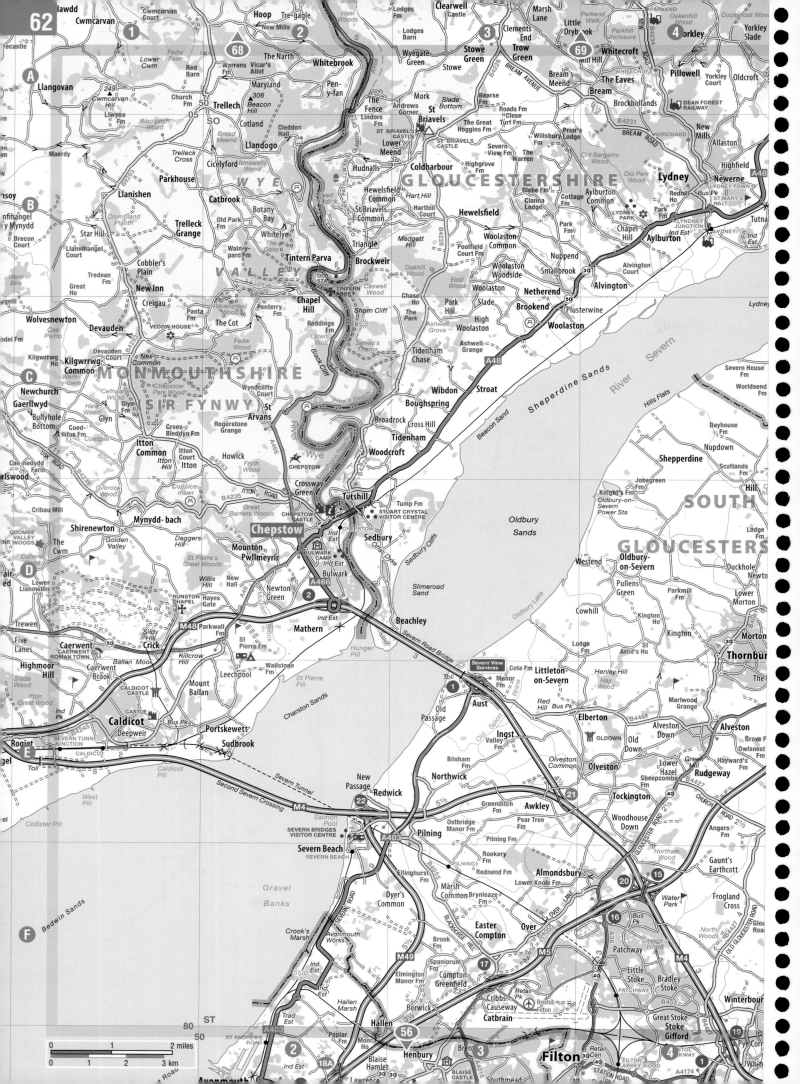

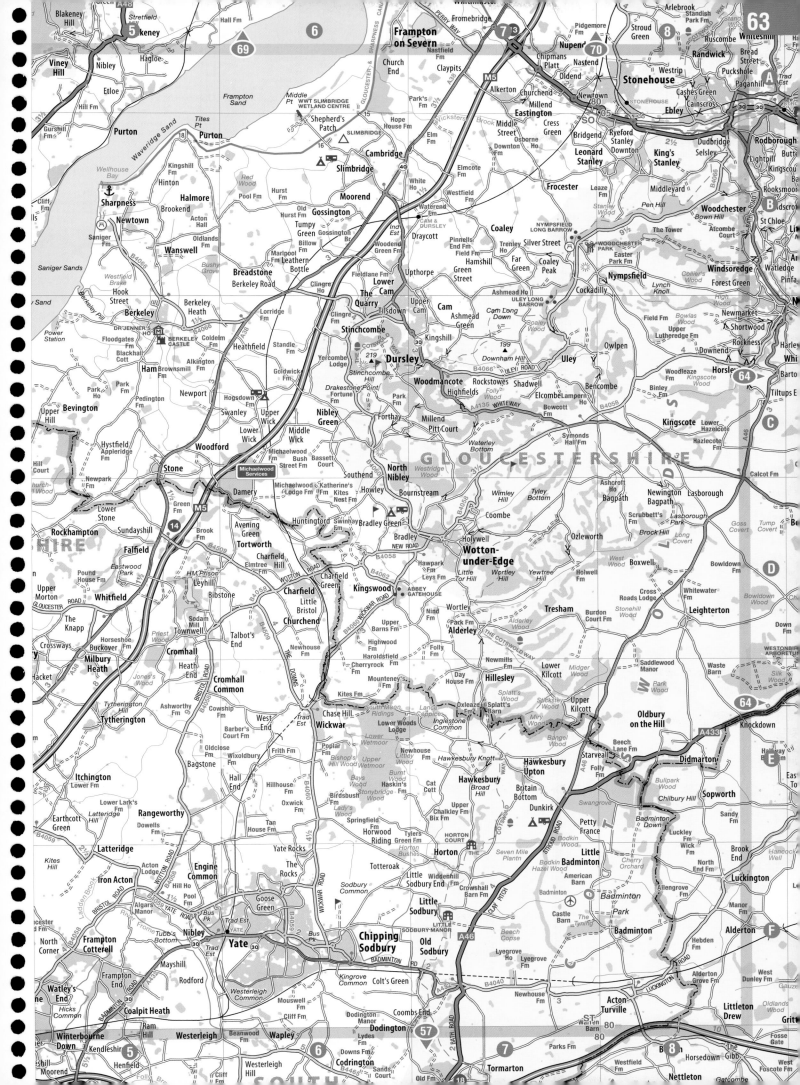

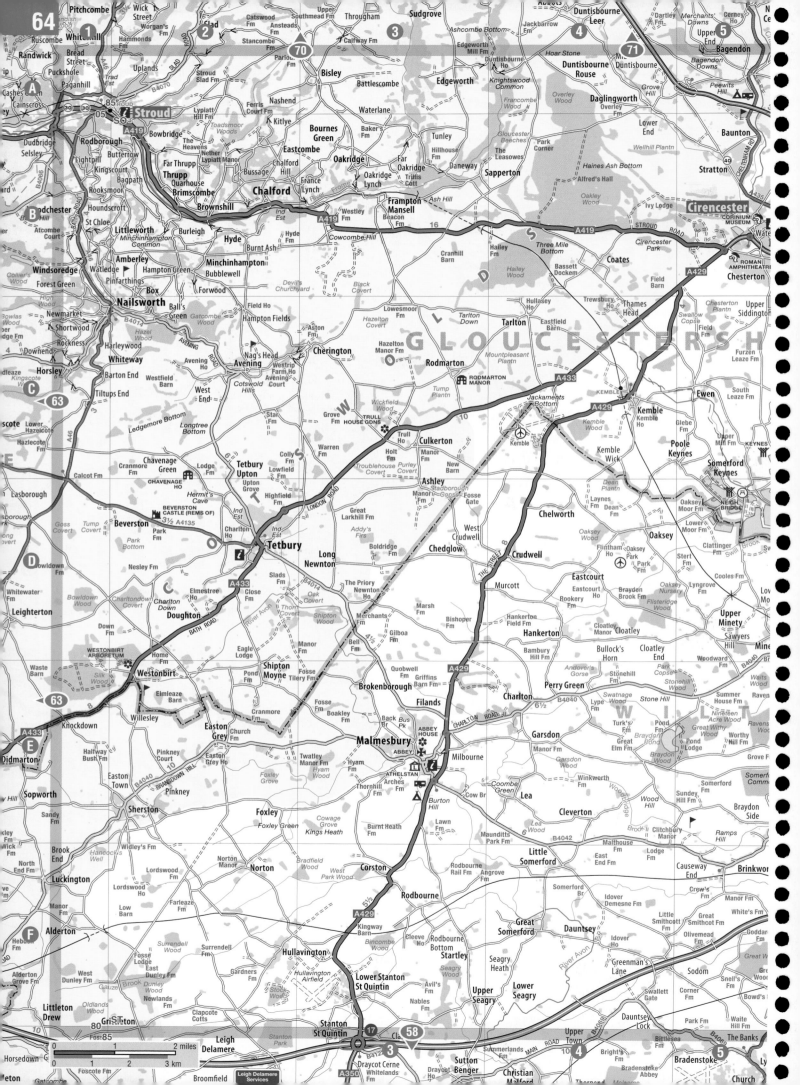

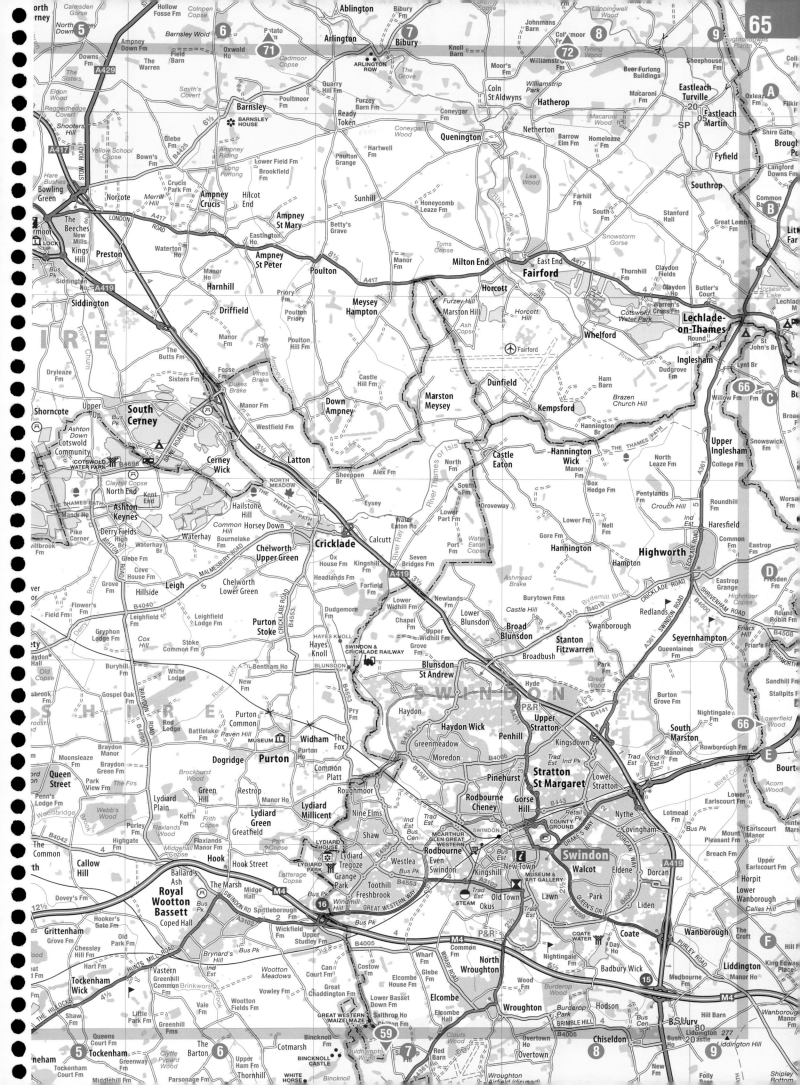

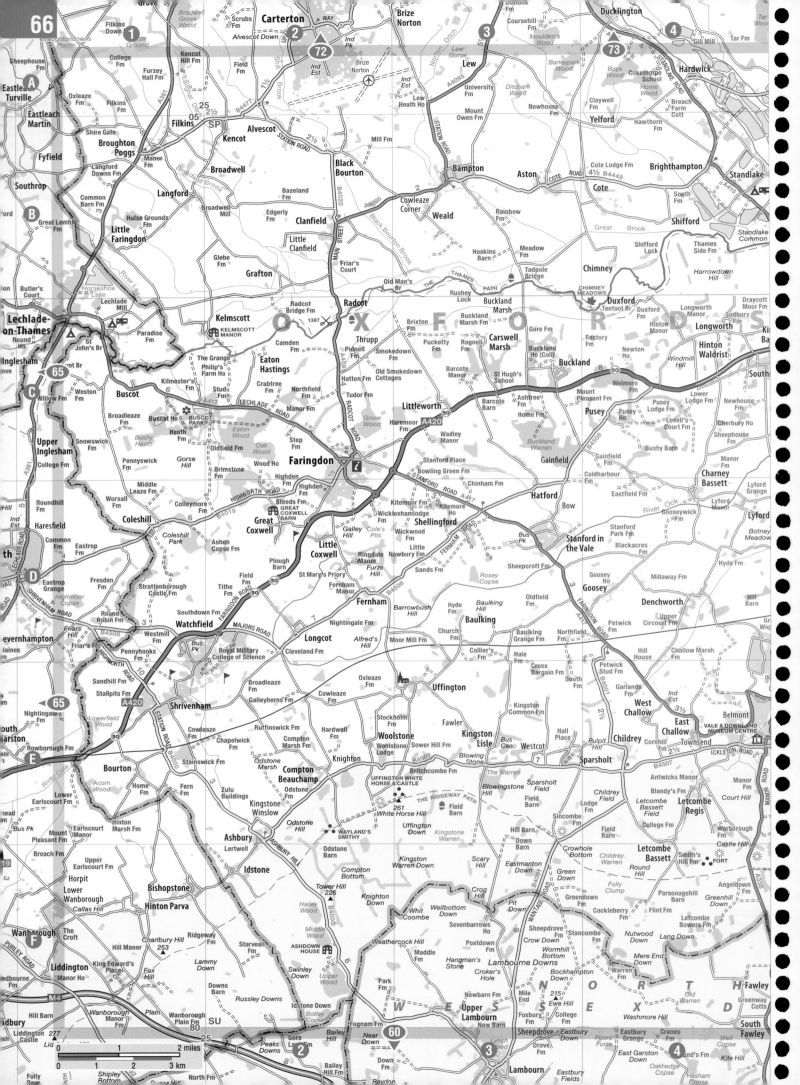

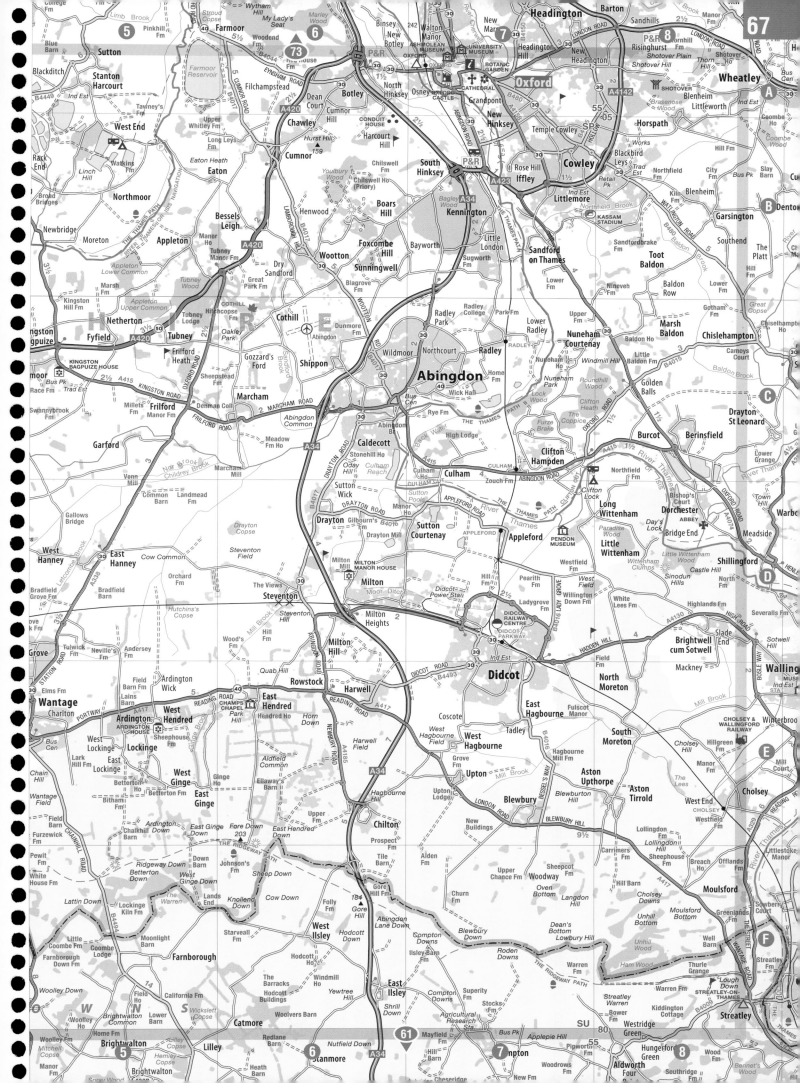

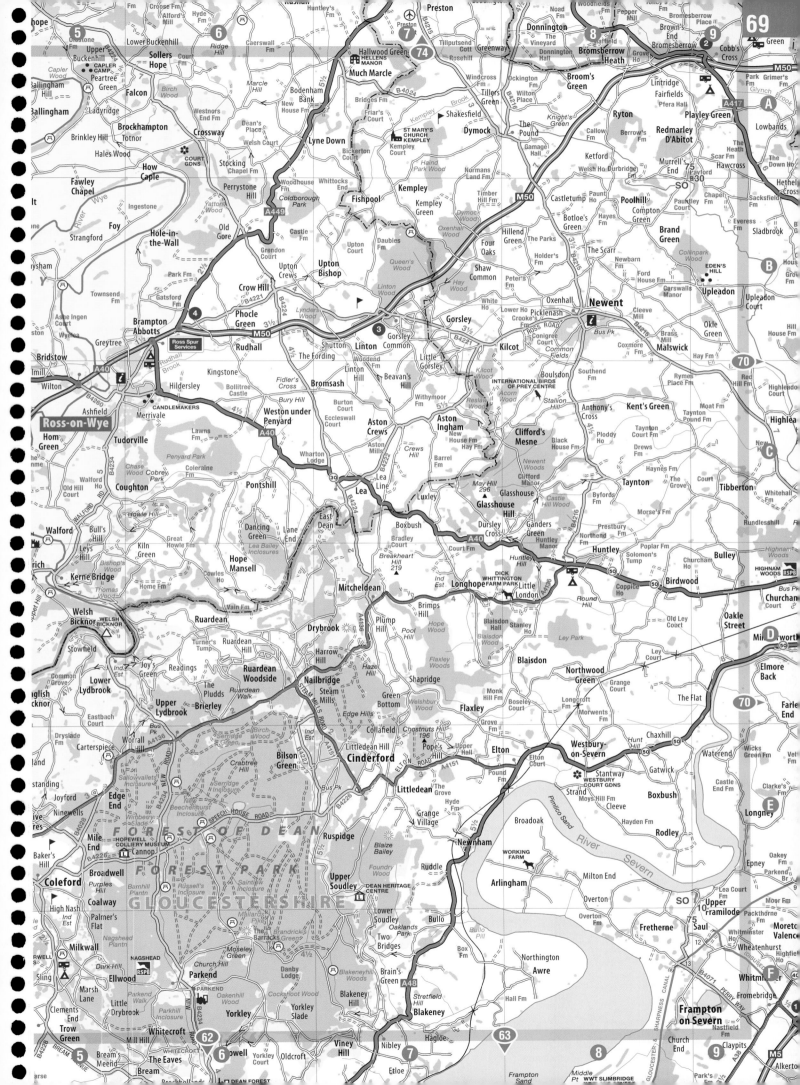

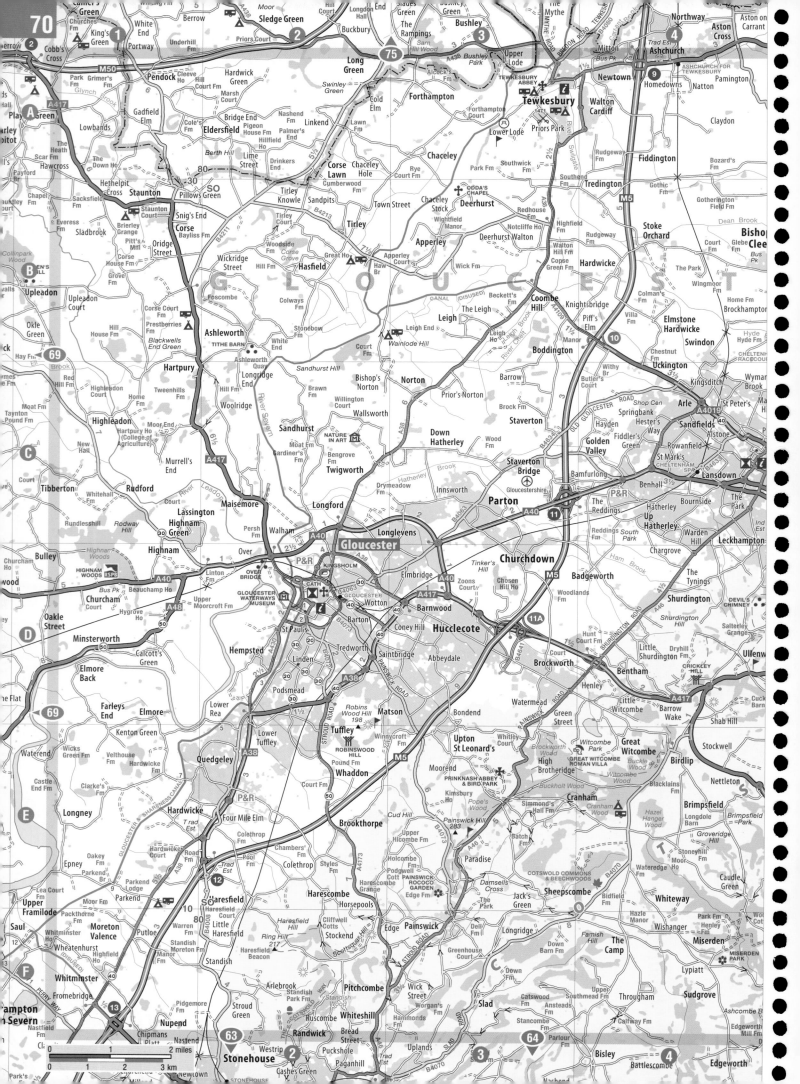

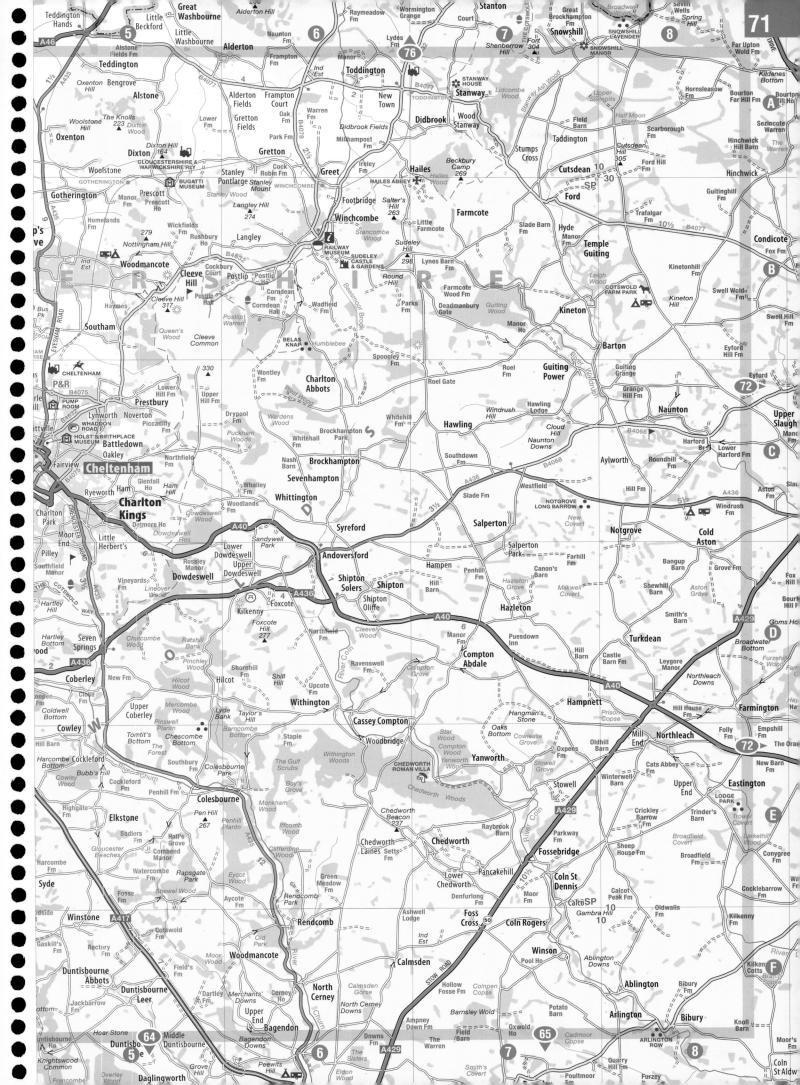

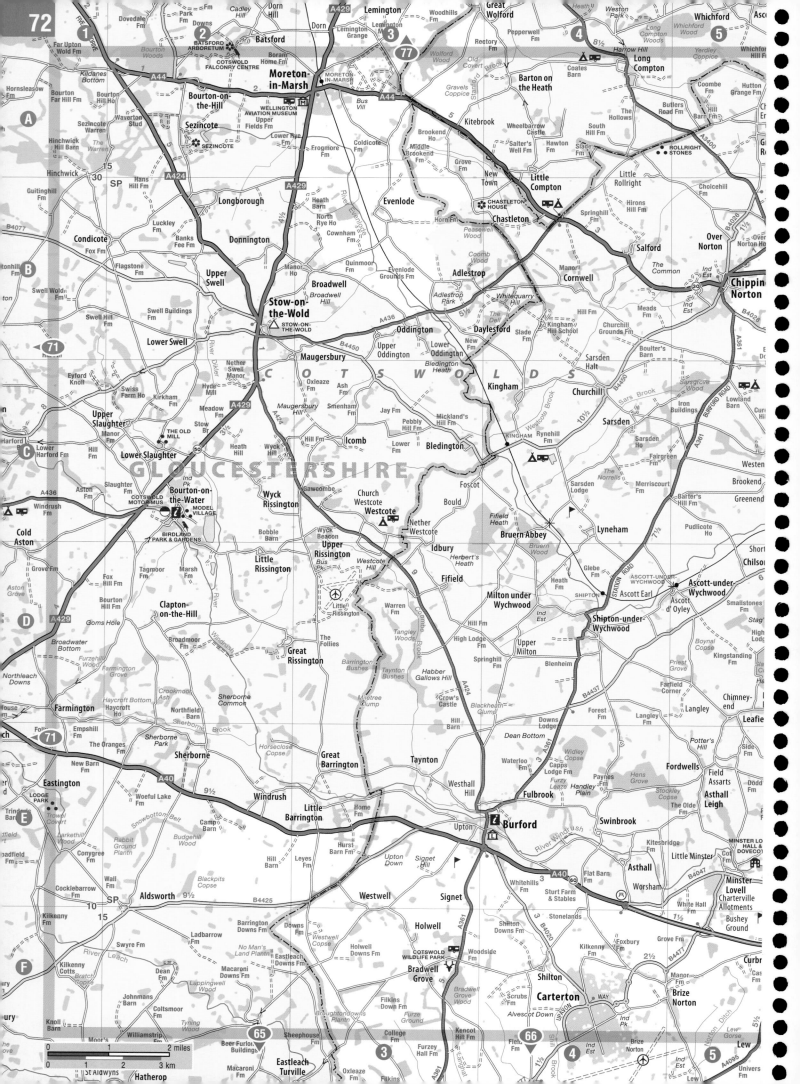

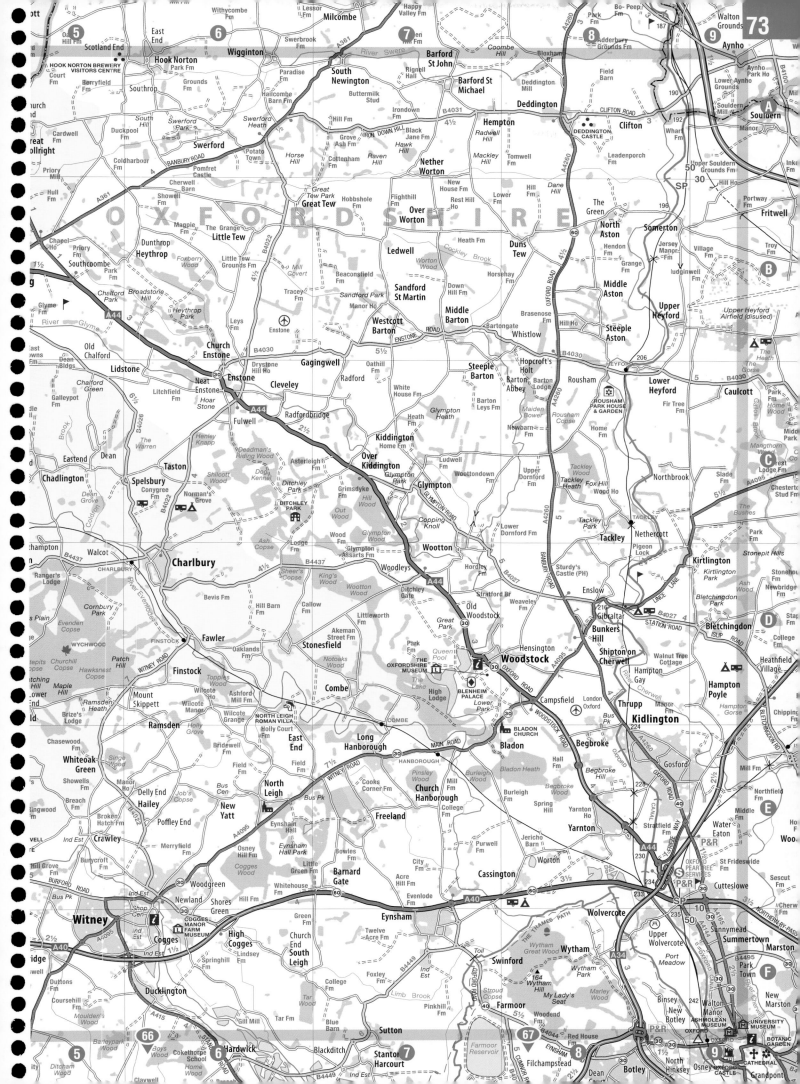

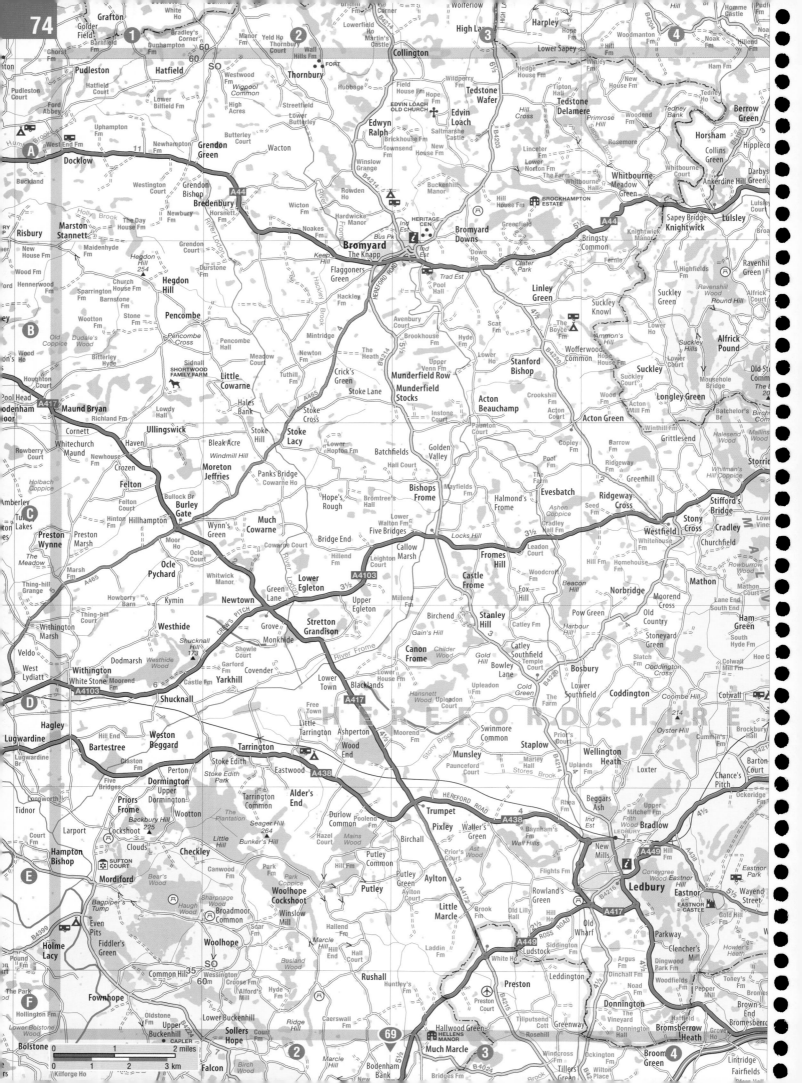

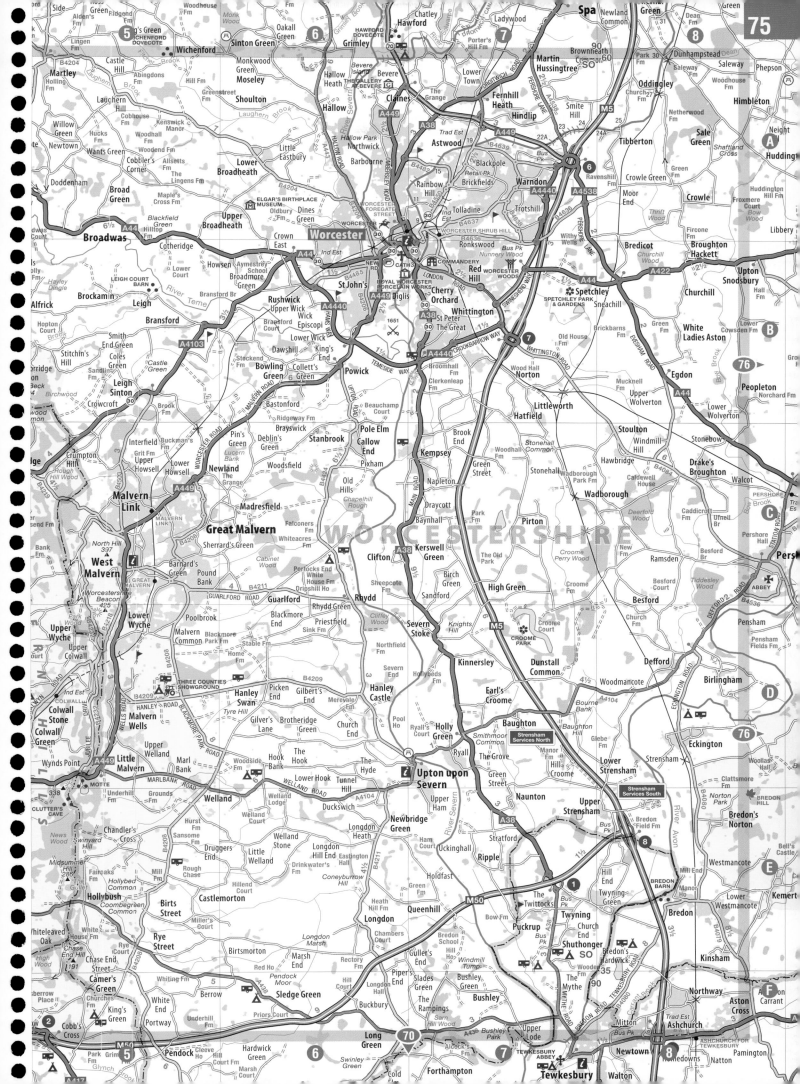

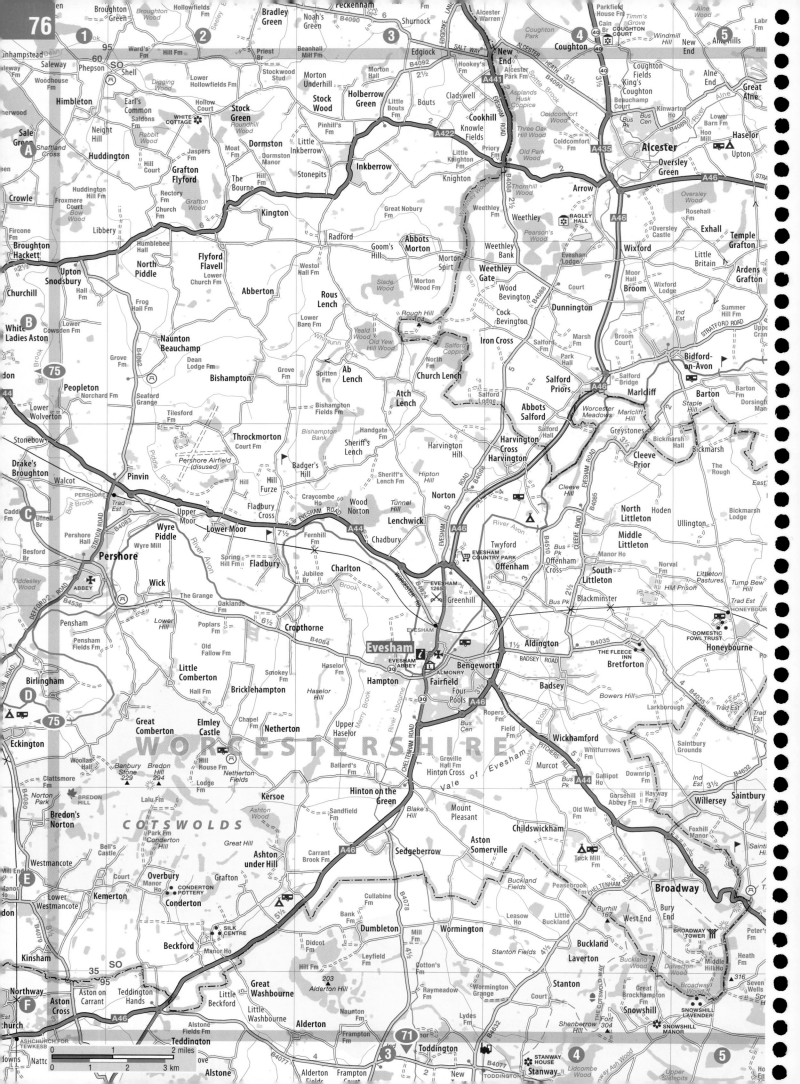

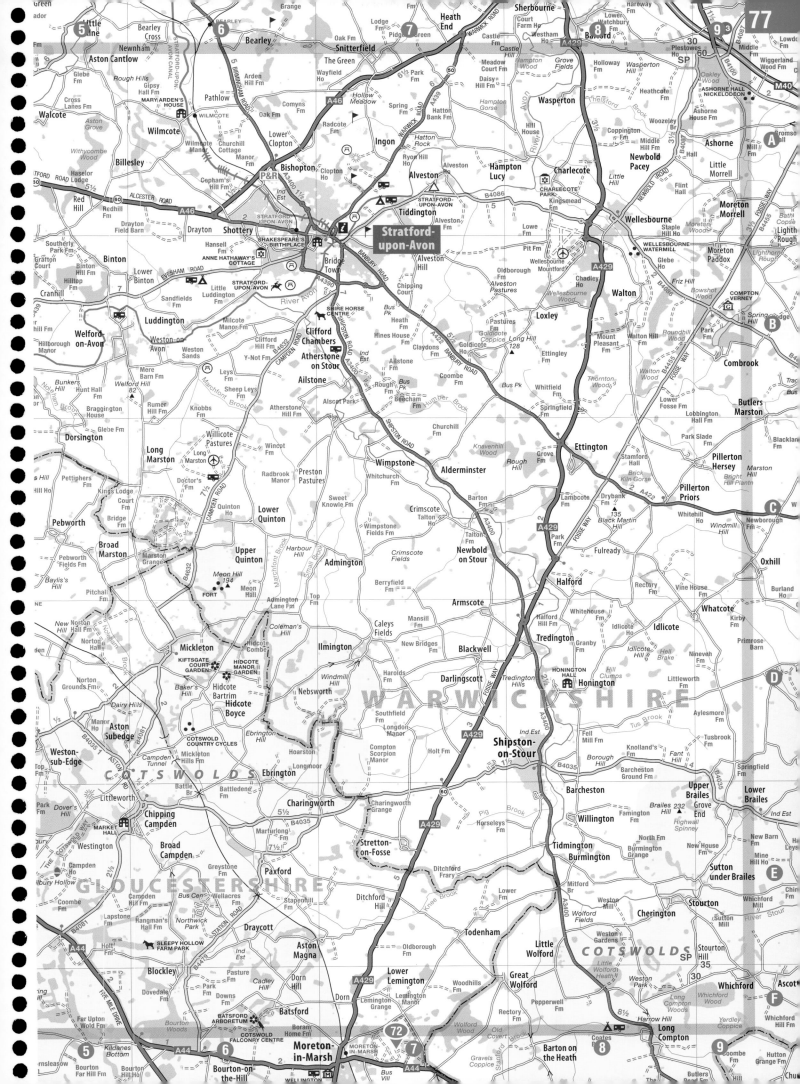

Town plans

Town plan symbols

═══════	**Motorway**
═══════	**Primary route** – dual/single carriageway
───────	**A road** –dual/single carriageway
───────	**B road** – dual/single carriageway
──→──	**Minor through road, one-way street**
▪▪▪▪▪	**Pedestrian roads**
▬▬▬▬	**Shopping streets**
┼┼┼┼┼	**Railway**
╺●╸ *City Hall*	**Tramway with tram stop**
▬	**Railway or bus station**
▬	**Shopping precinct or retail park**
▬	**Park**

Ⓗ	**Hospital**
Ⓟ	**Parking**
▣	**Police station**
PO	**Post office**
♿	**Shopmobility**
⊖ Bank • *West St*	**Underground or metro station**
▲	**Youth hostel**

Tourist information

✝	**Abbey or cathedral**
⌂	**Ancient monument**
⬱	**Aquarium**
⌂	**Art gallery**
↘	**Bird garden**
⌂	**Building of public interest**
⛫	**Castle**
⛪	**Church of interest**
⬚	**Cinema**
✿	**Garden**
⛵	**Historic ship**
⌂	**House**
⌂	**House and garden**
⌂	**Museum**
✦	**Other place of interest**
🚂	**Preserved railway**
⊏⊐	**Railway station**
⌂	**Roman antiquity**
⬚	**Theatre**
	Tourist information centre
🄸	open all year
🄸	summer only
🐘	**Zoo**

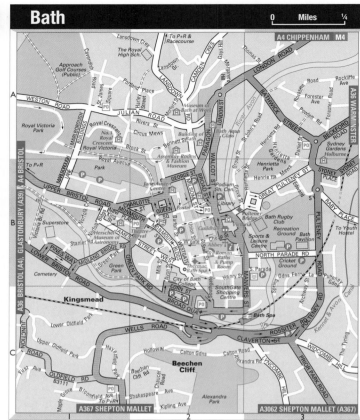

Bath town plan — scale 0 to ¼ Miles. A4 CHIPPENHAM / M4 (top right); A4 BRISTOL, GLASTONBURY (A39), A36 BRISTOL (left); A36 WARMINSTER (right); A367 SHEPTON MALLET, A3062 SHEPTON MALLET (A367) (bottom).

Bath

Alexandra Park	C2	Edward St	B3	Manvers St	B3	Rossiter Rd	C3
Alexandra Rd	C2	Ferry La	B3	Maple Gr	C1	Royal Ave	A1
Approach Golf		First Ave	C1	Margaret's Hill	A2	Royal Cr	A1
Courses (Public)	A1	Forester Ave	A3	Marlborough		Royal High School,	
Bath Aqua Glass ⌂	A2	Forester Rd	A3	Buildings	A1	The	A1
Archway St	C3	Gays Hill	A2	Marlborough La	B1	Royal Victoria Park	A1
Assembly Rooms		George St	B2	Midland Bridge Rd	B1	St James Sq	A1
and Fashion		Great Pulteney St	B3	Milk St	B2	St John's Rd	A3
Museum ⌂	A2	Green Park	B1	Milsom St	B2	Shakespeare Ave	C2
Avon St	B2	Green Park Rd	B1	Monmouth St	B2	Southgate	C2
Barton St	B2	Grove St	B2	Morford St	A2	South Pde	B3
Bath Abbey ✝	B2	Guildhall ⌂	B2	Museum of Bath		Sports & Leisure	
Bath City College	B2	Harley St	A2	at Work ⌂	A2	Centre	B3
Bath Pavilion	B3	Hayesfield Park	C1	New King St	B1	Spring Gdns	C3
Bath Rugby Club	B3	Henrietta Gdns	B3	No 1 Royal		Stall St	B2
Bath Spa Station ⊏⊐	C3	Henrietta Mews	B3	Crescent ⌂	A1	Stanier Rd	B1
Bathwick St	A3	Henrietta Park	B3	Norfolk Bldgs	B1	Superstore	B1
Beckford Road	A3	Henrietta Rd	B3	Norfolk Cr	B1	Sydney Gdns	A3
Beechen Cliff Rd	C2	Henrietta St	B3	North Parade Rd	B3	Sydney Pl	A3
Bennett St	A2	Henry St	B2	Oldfield Rd	C1	Sydney Rd	B3
Bloomfield Ave	C1	Herschel Museum of		Paragon	A2	Theatre Royal ⬚	B2
Broad Quay	C2	Astronomy ⌂	A1	Pines Way	B1	Thermae Bath	
Broad St	B2	Holburne		Podium Shopping		Spa ✦	B2
Brock St	A1	Museum ⌂	B3	Centre	B2	The Tyning	C3
Building of Bath		Holloway	C2	Police Station ▣	B2	Thomas St	A3
Museum ⌂	A2	Information Ctr 🄸	B2	Portland Pl	A2	Union St	B2
Bus Station	C2	James St West	B1/B2	Post Office		Upper Bristol Rd	B1
Calton Gdns	C2	Jane Austen		PO	A1/A3/B2/C1/C2	Upper Oldfield	
Calton Rd	C2	Centre ⌂	B2	Postal Museum ⌂	B2	Park	C1
Camden Cr	A1	Julian Rd	A1	Powlett Rd	A3	Victoria Art	
Cavendish Rd	A1	Junction Rd	C1	Prior Park Rd	C3	Gallery ⌂	B2
Cemetery	B1	Kipling Ave	C2	Pulteney Bridge ✦	B2	Victoria Bridge Rd	B1
Charlotte St	B2	Lansdown Cr	A1	Pulteney Gdns	B3	Walcot St	B2
Chaucer Rd	C2	Lansdown Gr	A2	Pulteney Rd	B3/C3	Wells Rd	C1
Cheap St	B2	Lansdown Rd	A2	Queen Sq	B2	Westgate Buildings	B2
Circus Mews	A2	Library	B2	Raby Pl	B3	Westgate St	B2
Claverton St	C2	London Rd	A3	Recreation Ground	B3	Weston Rd	A1
Corn St	C2	London St	A2	Rivers St	A2	Widcombe Hill	C3
Cricket Ground	B3	Lower Bristol Rd	B1	Rockliffe Ave	A3		
Daniel St	A3	Lower Oldfield		Rockliffe Rd	A3		
		Park	C1	Roman Baths &			
		Lyncombe Hill	C3	Pump Room ⌂	B2		

Bristol

Acramans Rd	C4	Ambrose Rd	B2	Ashton Gate Rd	C2	Barossa Pl	C4
Albert Rd	C6	Amphitheatre	C3	Ashton Rd	C1	Barton Manor	B6
Alfred Hill	A4	Anchor Rd	B3	at-Bristol ✦	B3	Barton Rd	B6
All Saints' St	A4	Anvil St	B6	Avon Bridge	C1	Barton Vale	B6
All Saints' ⛪	B4	Argyle Pl	B2	Avon Cr	C1	Bath Rd	C6
Allington Rd	C3	Arlington Villas	A2	Avon St	B6	Bathurst Basin	C4
Alpha Rd	C4	Arnolfini Arts Centre,		Baldwin St	B4	Bathurst Parade	C4
Ambra Vale	B1	The ✦	B4	Baltic Wharf	B3	Beauley Rd	C3
Ambra Vale East	B2	Art Gallery ⌂	A3	Baltic Wharf Leisure		Bedminster Bridge	C5
				Centre & Caravan		Bedminster Parade	C4
				Park ✦	C2	Bellevue	B2

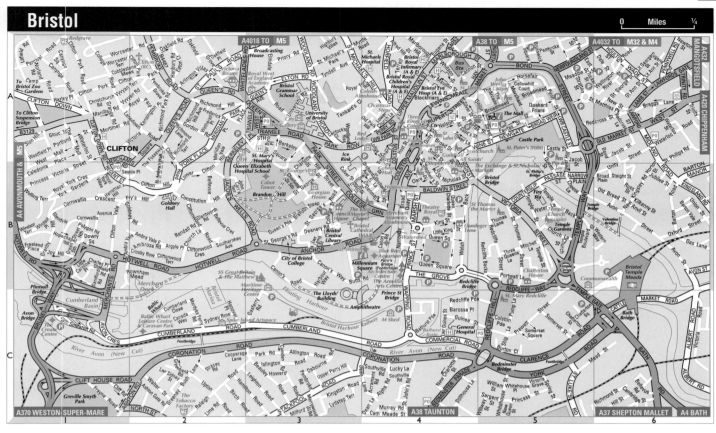

Bristol

0   Miles   ¼

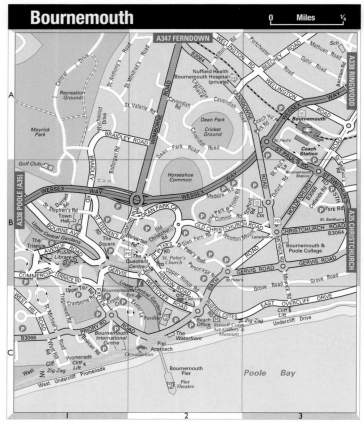

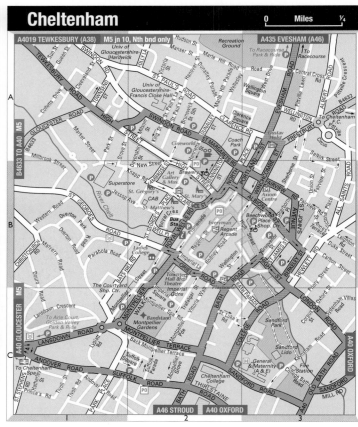

Bournemouth

Ascham Rd A3
Avenue Rd B1
Bath Rd C2
Beacon Rd C1
Beach Office C2
Beechey Rd A3
Bodorgan Rd B1
Bourne Ave B1
Bournemouth ≥ . . A3
Bournemouth &
  Poole College . . B3
Bournemouth
  Eye ✦ C2
Bournemouth
  International Ctr . C1
Bournemouth Pier . C2
Bournemouth
  Station ⟳ B3
Braidley Rd A1
Cavendish Place . . . A2
Cavendish Rd A2
Central Drive A1
Christchurch Rd . . . B3
Cliff Lift C1/C3
Coach House Pl. . . . A3
Coach Station A3
Commercial Rd. . . . B1
Cotlands Rd. A3
Courts B3
Cranborne Rd C1

Cricket Ground . . . A2
Cumnor Rd B2
Dean Park A2
Dean Park Cr B2
Dean Park Rd B2
Durrant Rd B1
East Overcliff Dr . . C3
Exeter Cr C1
Exeter La C1
Exeter Rd C2
Gervis Place B1
Gervis Rd B2
Glen Fern Rd B2
Golf Club B1
Grove Rd B3
Hinton Rd C2
Holdenhurst Rd . . . B3
Horseshoe
  Common B2
Nuffield Health
  Bournemouth Hosp
  (private) ⊞ A2
Lansdowne ⟳ B3
Lansdowne Rd A2
Lorne Park Rd B2
Lower Central
  Gdns B1/C2
Madeira Rd B2
Methuen Rd. A3
Meyrick Park A1
Meyrick Rd B3

Milton Rd A2
Oceanarium ✇ . . . C2
Odeon Cinema ☺ . . C2
Old Christchurch
  Rd B2
Ophir Rd A3
Oxford Rd B3
Park Rd A3
Parsonage Rd B2
Pavilion ⊞ C2
Pier Approach C2
Pier Theatre ⊞ . . . C2
Police Station
  ⊠ A3/B3
Portchester Rd . . . A3
Post Office ⊡ . . . B1/B3
Priory Rd C1
Quadrant, The. . . . B2
Recreation Ground A1
Richmond Hill Rd . . B1
Russell Cotes Art
  Gallery & Mus ☆ . C2
Russell Cotes Rd . . C2
St Anthony's Rd . . . A1
St Michael's Rd . . . C1
St Paul's ⟳ A3
St Paul's La B3
St Paul's Rd B3
St Peter's ⟳ B2
St Peter's Rd B2
St Stephen's Rd . B1/B2

Milton Rd A2
St Swithin's ⟳ . . . B3
St Swithun's Rd. . . B3
St Swithun's Rd
  South B3
St Valerie Rd A2
St Winifred's Rd . . A2
Stafford Rd B2
Terrace Rd B1
The Square B1
The Triangle B1
Town Hall B1
Tregonwell Rd. . . . C1
Trinity Rd B2
Undercliff Drive . . . C3
Upper Central Gdns B1
Upper Hinton Rd. . . B2
Upper Terr Rd C1
Waterfront, The ✦ . C2
Wellington Rd . . A2/A3
Wessex Way. A3/B1/B2
West Cliff
  Promenade C1
West Hill Rd C1
West Undercliff
  Promenade C1
Westover Rd B2
Wimborne Rd A2
Wootton Mount . . . B2
Wychwood Dr A1
Yelverton Rd B2
York Rd B3
Zig-Zag Walks . .C1/C3

Cheltenham

Albert Rd A3
Albion St B3
All Saints Rd B3
Ambrose St B2
Andover Rd C1
Art Gallery &
  Museum ⋔ B2
Axiom Centre ⋔ . . B3
Back Montpellier
  Terr. C2
Bandstand ✦ C2
Bath Pde B2
Bath Rd C2
Bays Hill Rd C1
Beechwood Place
  Shopping Centre . B3
Bennington St B2
Berkeley St B3
Brewery A2
Brunswick St
  South A2
Bus Station B2
CAB. B2
Carlton St. B3
Central Cross Road A3
Cheltenham
  College. C2
Cheltenham FC. . . . A3
Cheltenham
  General (A&E) ⊞ . C3
Christchurch Rd . . . B1
Cineworld ☺ A2
Clarence Rd. A2
Clarence Sq. A2
Clarence St B2
Cleeveland St A1
Coach Park A2
College Baths Rd . . C3
College Rd C2
Colletts Dr A1
Corpus St C3
Devonshire St A2

Douro Rd B1
Duke St B3
Dunalley Pde A2
Dunalley St A2
Everyman ⊞ B2
Evesham Rd A3
Fairview Rd B3
Fairview St. B3
Fire Station C3
Folly La C1
Gloucester Rd A1
Grosvenor St B3
Grove St A1
Gustav Holst ⋔ . . A3
Hanover St A2
Hatherley St C1
Henrietta St A2
Hewlett Rd B3
High St B2/B3
Hudson St A2
Imperial Gdns C2
Imperial La C2
Imperial Sq C2
Information Ctr ☑ . B2
Keynsham Rd C3
King St A2
Knapp Rd B2
Ladies College ⋔ . B2
Lansdown Cr C1
Lansdown Rd C1
Leighton Rd B3
London Rd C3
Lypiatt Rd C1
Malvern Rd B1
Manser St. B2
Market St A1
Marle Hill Pde A2
Marle Hill Rd A2
Millbrook St A1
Milsom St A2
Montpellier Gdns . . C2
Montpellier Gr C2
Montpellier Pde . . . C2
Montpellier Spa Rd C2

Montpellier St. . . . C1
Montpellier Terr. . . C2
Montpellier Walk . . C2
New St B2
North Pl B2
Old Bath Rd C3
Oriel Rd B2
Overton Park Rd . . B1
Overton Rd B1
Oxford St C3
Parabola Rd B1
Park Pl C1
Park St A1
Pittville Circus . . . A3
Pittville Cr A3
Pittville Lawn A3
Playhouse ⊞ B2
Police Sta ⊠ . . . B1/C1
Portland St B3
Post Office ⊡ . . B2/C2
Prestbury Rd A3
Prince's Rd C1
Priory St B3
Promenade B2
Queen St A1
Recreation Ground A2
Regent Arcade . . . B2
Regent St B2
Rodney Rd B2
Royal Cr B2
Royal Wells Rd . . . B2
St George's Pl B2
St Georges Rd B1
St Gregory's ⋔ . . . B2
St James St B3
St John's Ave B3
St Luke's Rd C2
St Margarets Rd . . . A2
St Mary's ⋔ B2
St Matthew's ⋔ . . B2
St Paul's La A2
St Paul's Rd A2
St Paul's St. A2
St Stephen's Rd . . . C1

Sandford Lido C3
Sandford Mill Road C3
Sandford Park . . . C3
Sandford Rd C2
Selkirk St A3
Sherborne Pl B3
Sherborne St B3
Suffolk Pde C2
Suffolk Rd C1
Suffolk Sq C1
Sun St A1
Swindon Rd B2
Sydenham Villas
  Rd C3
Tewkesbury Rd . . . A1
The Courtyard B1
Thirlstaine Rd C2
Tivoli Rd C1
Tivoli St C1
Town Hall and
  Theatre ⊞ B2
Townsend St A1
Trafalgar St C2
Union St B3
University of
  Gloucestershire
  (Francis Close
  Hall) A2
University of
  Gloucestershire
  (Hardwick) A1
Victoria Pl B3
Victoria St A2
Vittoria Walk C2
Wel Pl B2
Wellesley Rd A2
Wellington Rd A3
Wellington Sq A3
Wellington St B2
West Drive A3
Western Rd B1
Winchcombe St . . . B3

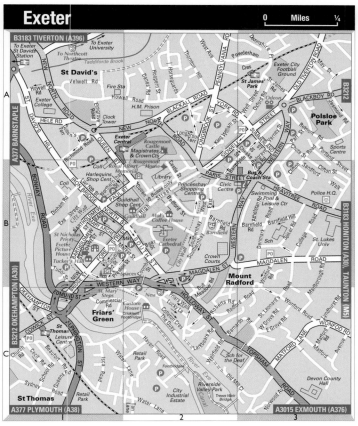

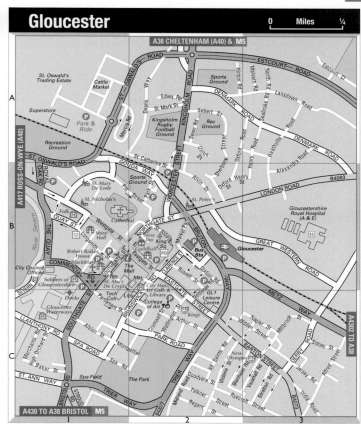

Exeter

Alphington St	C1	Devonshire Pl	A3	Magdalen St	B2	Royal Albert		GL1 Leisure Centre	C2	Metz Way	C3	St Oswald's Rd	A1
Athelstan St	B3	Dinham Rd	B1	Magistrates and		Memorial Mus 🏛	B2	Gloucester		Midland Rd	C2	St Oswald's	
Bampfylde St	B2	East Grove Rd	C3	Crown Courts	A2	St David's Hill	A1	Cathedral ✝	B1	Millbrook St	C3	Trading Estate	A1
Barnardo Rd	C3	Edmund St	B1	Market	B2	St James' Park		Gloucester		Market	B2	St Peter's 🏛	B2
Barnfield Hill	B3	Elmgrove Rd	C1	Market St	B2	Station ≥	A3	Station ≥	B2	Montpellier	C1	Seabroke Rd	A3
Barnfield Rd	B2/B3	Exe St	B1	Marlborough Rd	C3	St James' Rd	A3	Gloucestershire		Napier St	C3	Sebert St	A2
Barnfield		Exeter Cathedral ✝	B2	Mary Arches St	B1	St Leonard's Rd	C3	Royal Hospital		Nettleton Rd	C2	Severn Rd	C1
Theatre 🎭	B2	Exeter Central		Matford Ave	C3	St Lukes University	B3	(A & E) 🏥	B3	New Inn 🏛	B2	Sherborne St	B2
Bartholomew St		Station ≥	A1	Matford La	C3	St Mary Steps 🏛	C1	Gloucester		New Olympus 🎭	C3	Shire Hall 🏛	B1
East	B1	Exeter City Football		Matford Rd	C3	St Nicholas		Waterways Mus 🏛	C1	North Rd	A3	Sidney St	C3
Bartholomew St		Ground	A3	May St	A3	Priory 🏛	B1	Goodyere St	C2	Northgate St	B2	Soldiers of	
West	B1	Exeter College	A1	Mol's Coffee		St Thomas		Gouda Way	A1	Oxford Rd	A2	Gloucestershire	
Bear St	B2	Exeter Picture		House 🏛	B2	Station ≥	C1	Great Western Rd	B2	Oxford St	B2	Museum 🏛	B1
Beaufort Rd	C1	House 🎭	B1	New Theatre 🎭	C2	Sandford Walk	B3	Brunswick Rd	C2	Park & Ride		Southgate St	B1/C1
Bedford St	B2	Fire Station	A1	New Bridge St	B1	School for the Deaf	C2	Bruton Way	B2	Gloucester	A1	Spa Field	C1
Belgrave Rd	A3	Fore St	B1	New North Rd	A1/A2	School Rd	C2	Bus Station	B2	Park Rd	C2	Spa Rd	C1
Belmont Rd	A3	Friars Walk	C2	North St	B1	Sidwell St	A2	Cattle Market	A1	Park St	B2	Sports Ground	A2/B2
Blackall Rd	A2	Guildhall 🏛	B2	Northernhay St	B1	Smythen St	B1	City Council		Parliament St	C1	Station Rd	B2
Blackboy Rd	A3	Guildhall		Norwood Ave	C3	South St	B2	Offices	B2	Pitt St	B1	Stratton Rd	C3
Bonhay Rd	B1	Shopping Centre	B2	Odeon 🎦	A3	Southernhay East	B2	City Museum,		Police Station 🏛	B1	Stroud Rd	C1
Bull Meadow Rd	C2	Harlequins		Okehampton St	C1	Southernhay West	B2	Art Gallery and		Post Office 🏤	B2	Superstore	A1
Bus & Coach Sta	B3	Shopping Centre	B1	Old Mill Cl	B2	Spacex Gallery 🏛	B1	Library 🏛	B2	Quay St	B1	Swan Rd	A2
Castle St	B2	Haven Rd	C2	Old Tiverton Rd	A3	Spicer Rd	B3	King's 🏫	C2	Recreation Gd	A1/A2	Technical College	C1
Cecil Rd	C1	Heavitree Rd	B2	Oxford Rd	A3	Sports Centre	B2	King's Sq	C2	Regent St	C2	The Mall	C2
Cheeke St	A3	Hele Rd	A1	Paris St	B2	Summerland St	A3	College of Art	C2	Robert Raikes		The Park	C2
Church Rd	C1	High St	B2	Parr St	A3	Swimming Pool &		Commercial Rd	B1	House 🏛	B1	The Quay	C1
Chute St	A3	HM Prison	A2	Paul St	B1	Leisure Centre	C2	Cromwell St	C2	Royal Oak Rd	B1	Trier Way	C1/C2
City Industrial		Holloway St	C2	Pennsylvania Rd	A2	Sydney Rd	C1	Deans Way	A2	Russell St	C2	Union St	A2
Estate	C2	Hoopern St	A2	Police HQ 🏛	B3	Tan La	C1	Denmark Rd	A3	Ryecroft St	C2	Vauxhall Rd	C3
City Wall	B1/B2	Horseguards	A2	Portland Street	A3	The Quay	C2	Derby Rd	C3	St Aldate St	B2	Victoria St	C2
Civic Centre	B2	Howell Rd	A1	Post Office		Thornton Hill	A2	Docks ⚓	C1	St Ann Way	C1	Wellington St	C2
Clifton Rd	B3	Information Ctr 🛈	B2	🏤	A3/B1/B3/C1	Topsham Rd	C3	Eastgate St	B2	St Catherine St	A2	Westgate St	B1
Clifton St	B3	Iron Bridge	B1	Powderham Cr	A3	Tucker's Hall 🏛	B1	Edwy Pde	A2	St Mark St	A2	Widden St	C2
Clock Tower	A1	Isca Rd	C1	Preston St	B1	Tudor St	B1	Estcourt Cl	A3	St Mary De Crypt 🏛	B1	Worcester St	B2
College Rd	B3	Jesmond Rd	A3	Princesshay		Velwell Rd	A1	Estcourt Rd	A3	St Mary De Lode 🏛	B1	
Colleton Cr	C2	King William St	A2	Shopping Centre	B2	Verney St	A3	Falkner St	C2	St Nicholas's 🏛	B1	
Commercial Rd	C1	King St	B1	Queen St	A1	Water La	C1/C2	Folk Museum 🏛	B1		
Coombe St	B2	Larkbeare Rd	C2	Queens Rd	C1	Weirfield Rd	C2			
Cowick St	C1	Leisure Centre	C1	Queen's Terr	A1	Well St	A3			
Crown Courts	B2	Library	B2	Radford Rd	C2	West Ave	A2			
Custom House 🏛	C2	Longbrook St	A2	Richmond Rd	A1	West Grove Rd	C1			
Danes' Rd	A2	Longbrook Terr	A2	Roberts Rd	C2	Western				
Denmark Rd	B3	Lower North St	B1	Rougemont		Way	A3/B1/B2			
Devon County Hall	C3	Lucky La	C2	Castle 🏛	A2	Wonford Rd	B3/C3			
		Lyndhurst Rd	C3	Rougemont		York Rd	A2			
		Magdalen Rd	B3	House ✦	B2					

Gloucester

Albion St	C1				
Alexandra Rd	B3				
Alfred St	C3				
All Saints Rd	C2				
Alvin St	B2				
Arthur St	C2				
Baker St	C2				
Barton St	C2				
Blackfriars ✝	B1				
Blenheim Rd	C2				
Bristol Rd	C1				
Brunswick Rd	C2				
Bruton Way	B2				
Bus Station	B2				
Cattle Market	A1				
City Council					
Offices	B2				
City Museum,					
Art Gallery and					
Library 🏛	B2				
Clarence St	B2				
College of Art	C2				
Commercial Rd	B1				
Cromwell St	C2				
Deans Way	A2				
Denmark Rd	A3				
Derby Rd	C3				
Docks ⚓	C1				
Eastgate St	B2				
Edwy Pde	A2				
Estcourt Cl	A3				
Estcourt Rd	A3				
Falkner St	C2				
Folk Museum 🏛	B1				

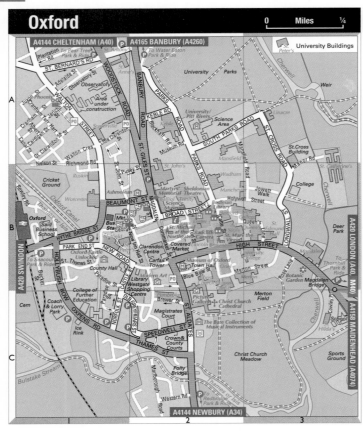

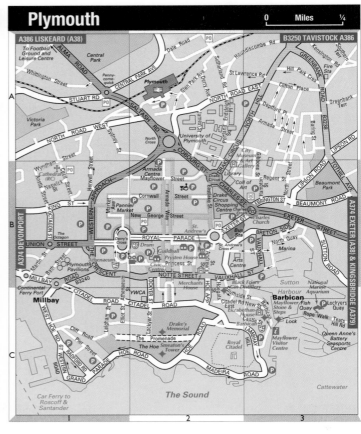

Oxford

Adelaide St A1
Albert St. A1
All Souls (Coll) . . . B2
Ashmolean
  Museum 🏛 B2
Balliol (Coll) B2
Banbury Rd A2
Bate Collection
  of Musical
  Instruments 🏛 . . C2
Beaumont St B1
Becket St B1
Blackhall Rd A2
Blue Boar St. B2
Bodleian Library
  🏛 B2
Botanic Garden ❀ . B3
Brasenose (Coll) . . B2
Brewer St. C2
Broad St. B2
Burton-Taylor
  Theatre B2
Bus Station B1
Canal St A1
Cardigan St A1
Carfax Tower B2
Castle 🏰 B1
Castle St. B1
Catte St B2
Cemetery C1
Christ Church
  (Coll) B2
Christ Church
  Cathedral † C2
Christ Church
  Meadow C2
Clarendon Centre . B2
Coach and Lorry
  Park C1
College B3
College of Further
  Education C1
Cornmarket St . . . B2

Corpus Christi
  (Coll) B2
County Hall B1
Covered Market . . B2
Cowley Pl C3
Cranham St A1
Cranham Terr A1
Cricket Ground . . . B1
Crown & County
  Courts C2
Deer Park B3
Exeter (Coll) B2
Folly Bridge C2
George St B1
Great Clarendon St A1
Hart St A1
Hertford (Coll) . . . B2
High St B2
Hollybush Row . . . B1
Holywell St B2
Hythe Bridge St. . . B1
Ice Rink C1
Information Ctr 🅿 . B2
Jericho St A1
Jesus (Coll) B2
Jowett Walk B3
Juxon St A1
Keble (Coll) A2
Keble Rd. A2
Library B2
Linacre (Coll) A3
Lincoln (Coll) B2
Little Clarendon St. A1
Longwall St B3
Magdalen (Coll) . . B3
Magdalen Bridge . . B2
Magdalen St B2
Magistrate's Court. C2
Manchester (Coll) . B2
Manor Rd B3
Mansfield (Coll) . . A3
Mansfield Rd. A3
Market B1
Marlborough Rd . . C2
Martyrs'
  Memorial ✦ B2

Merton Field B3
Merton (Coll) B3
Merton St. B2
Museum of
  Modern Art B2
Museum of
  Oxford 🏛 B2
Museum Rd A2
New College (Coll). B3
New Inn Hall St . . . B1
New Rd B1
New Theatre 🎭 . . . B2
Norfolk St C1
Nuffield (Coll). . . . B1
Observatory A1
Observatory St . . . A1
Odeon 🎬 B1/B2
Old Fire Station 🎭 . B1
Old Greyfriars St. . C2
Oriel (Coll). B2
Oxford Station 🚉 . . B1
Oxford Story,
  The ✦ B2
Oxford University
  Research Centres A1
Oxpens Rd C1
Paradise Sq C1
Paradise St B1
Park End St B1
Parks Rd A2/B2
Pembroke (Coll). . . C2
Phoenix 🎬 A1
Picture Gallery 🏛 . B2
Plantation Rd A1
Playhouse 🎭 B2
Police Station 👮 . . C2
Post Office 🅿 . . A1/B2
Pusey St B1
Queen's La B2
Queen's (Coll) B3
Radcliffe
  Camera 🏛 B2
Rewley Rd B1
Richmond Rd A1
Rose La B2
Ruskin (Coll) B1

Saïd Business
  School B1
St Aldates C2
St Anne's (Coll) . . . A1
St Antony's (Coll) . A1
St Bernard's Rd. . . A1
St Catherine's
  (Coll) B3
St Cross Building . . A3
St Cross Rd A3
St Edmund Hall
  (Coll) B3
St Giles St B2
St Hilda's (Coll). . . C3
St John St. B1
St John's (Coll) . . . B1
St Mary the
  Virgin 🏛 B2
St Michael at the
  Northgate 🏛 . . . B2
St Peter's (Coll) . . . B1
St Thomas St B1
Science Area A2
Science Mus 🏛 . . . A2
Sheldonian
  Theatre 🏛 B2
Somerville (Coll) . . A1
South Parks Rd . . . A2
Speedwell St C2
Sports Ground . . . C3
Thames St C2
Town Hall B2
Trinity (Coll) B2
Turl St. B2
University College
  (Coll) B3
University Museum &
  Pitt Rivers Mus . . A2
University Parks. . . A2
Wadham (Coll) . . . B2
Walton Cr A1
Walton St A1
Western Rd C2
Westgate Sh Ctr . . B2
Woodstock Rd. . . . A1
Worcester (Coll) . . B1

Plymouth

Alma Rd A1
Anstis St B1
Armada Centre . . . B2
Armada St A3
Armada Way B2
Arts Centre B2
Athenaeum 🎭 B1
Athenaeum St. . . . C1
Barbican C3
Barbican 🎭 C3
Baring St A3
Bath St B1
Beaumont Park. . . . B3
Beaumont Rd B3
Black Friars Gin
  Distillery ✦ C2
Breton Side B3
Bus Station B2
Castle St. C3
Cathedral (RC) † . . B1
Cecil St B1
Central Park A1
Central Park Ave. . . A1
Charles Church 🏛 . B3
Charles Cross 🔄 . . B2
Charles St B2
City Museum and
  Art Gallery 🏛 . . A2
Citadel Rd C2
Citadel Rd East . . . C2
Civic Centre 🏛 . . . B2
Cliff Rd C1
Clifton Pl A3
Cobourg St A2
College of Art B2
Continental Ferry
  Port. C1
Cornwall St B2

Dale Rd A2
Deptford Pl A3
Derry Ave A2
Derry's Cross 🔄 . . B1
Drake Circus B2
Drake Circus
  Shopping Centre . B2
Drake's
  Memorial ✦ C2
Drum 🎭 B2
Eastlake St. B2
Ebrington St B3
Elizabethan
  House 🏛 C3
Elliot St. C1
Endsleigh Pl A2
Exeter St B2
Fire Station B1
Fish Quay C3
Gibbons St. A3
Glen Park Ave A3
Grand Pde C1
Great Western Rd . C1
Greenbank Rd. . . . A3
Greenbank Terr . . . A3
Guildhall 🏛 B2
Hampton St B3
Harwell St B1
Hill Park Cr A3
Hoe Approach. . . . C2
Hoe Rd C2
Hoegate St. C2
Houndiscombe Rd . A2
Information Ctr 🅿 . C3
James St A2
Kensington Rd . . . A3
King St B1
Lambhay Hill C3
Leigham St C1
Library B2

Lipson Rd A3/B3
Lockyer St C2
Lockyers Quay . . . C3
Madeira Rd C2
Marina C3
Market Ave B2
Martin St B1
Mayflower Stone
  & Steps ✦ C3
Mayflower St. B2
Mayflower Visitor
  Centre ✦ C3
Merchants
  House 🏛 B2
Millbay Rd B1
National Marine
  Aquarium ✦ C3
Neswick St B1
New George St . . . B2
New St C3
North Cross 🔄 . . . A2
North Hill A3
North Rd East A1
North Rd West. . . . A1
North St B3
Notte St B2
Octagon St. B1
Pannier Market . . . B2
Pennycomequick
  🔄 A1
Pier St C1
Plymouth Pavilions B1
Plymouth
  Station 🚉 A2
Police Station 👮 . . B3
Portland Sq. A2
Post Office
  🅿 A1/B1/B2
Princess St B2

Prysten House 🏛 . . B2
Queen Anne's Battery
  Seasports Centre . C3
Radford Rd C1
Regent St B2
Rope Walk C3
Royal Citadel 🏰 . . C2
Royal Pde. B2
St Andrew's 🏛 . . . B2
St Andrew's
  Cross 🔄 B2
St Andrew's St. . . . B2
St Lawrence Rd . . . A2
Saltash Rd A2
Smeaton's
  Tower ✦ C2
Southern Terr A3
Southside St C2
Stuart Rd A1
Sutherland Rd A2
Sutton Rd. B3
Sydney St A1
Teats Hill Rd C3
The Crescent B1
The Hoe C2
The Octagon 🔄 . . . B1
The Promenade . . . C2
Tothill Ave B3
Union St. B1
University of
  Plymouth A2
Vauxhall St. B2/3
Victoria Park. A1
West Hoe Rd C1
Western Approach. B1
Whittington St . . . A1
Wyndham St B1
YMCA B2
YWCA C2

Salisbury

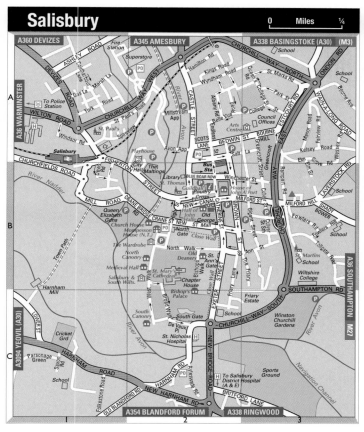

Stratford-upon-Avon

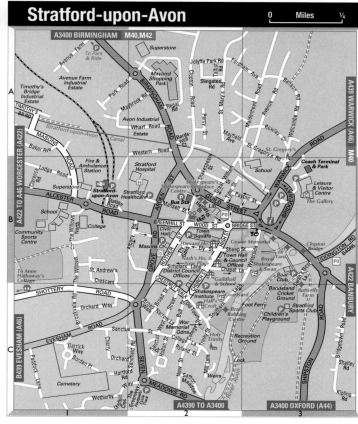

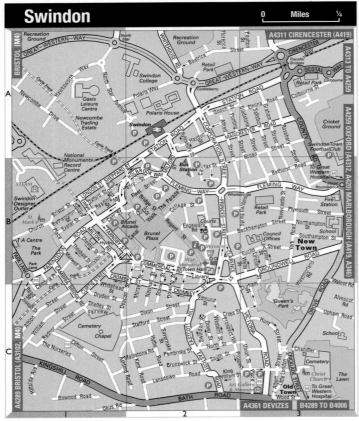

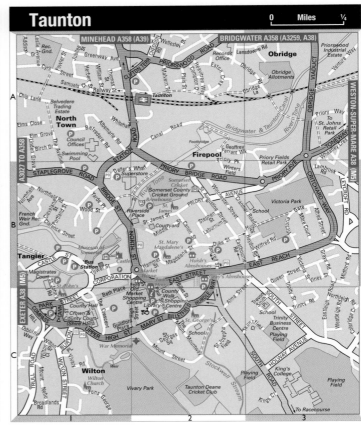

Swindon

Albert St. C3	Cross St C2	Library B2	Regent St B2
Albion St C1	Curtis St B1	Lincoln St B3	Retail Park . .A2/A3/B3
Alfred St. A2	Deacon St C2	Little London C3	Rosebery St A3
Alvescot Rd C3	Designer Outlet	London St B1	St Mark's ⛪ B1
Art Gallery &	(Great Western) . .B1	Magic Roundabout	Salisbury St A3
Museum C3	Dixon St C2	⟳ B3	Savernake St C1
Ashford Rd. C1	Dover St C2	Maidstone Rd C2	Shelley St. C1
Aylesbury St A2	Dowling St C3	Manchester Rd A3	Sheppard St B1
Bath Rd. C2	Drove Rd C3	Maxwell St B1	South St C2
Bathampton St B1	Dryden St C1	Milford St B2	Southampton St B3
Bathurst Rd B3	Durham St C3	Milton Rd B1	Spring Gardens B3
Beatrice St A2	East St B1	Morse St. C2	Stafford Street C2
Beckhampton St. . . .B3	Eastcott Hill C2	National Monuments	Staner St C2
Bowood Rd C1	Eastcott Rd C2	Record Centre A2	Station Road A2
Bristol St B1	Edgeware Rd B2	Newcastle St B3	STEAM 🏛 B1
Broad St. A3	Edmund St C1	Newcombe Drive . . .A1	Swindon College A2
Brunel Arcade. B2	Elmina Rd. A3	Newcombe	Swindon Rd C2
Brunel Plaza B2	Emlyn Square B1	Trading Estate A1	Swindon Sta 🚊 A2
Brunswick St C2	Euclid St. B3	Newhall St C2	Swindon Town
Bus Station B2	Exeter St B1	North St C2	Football Club A3
Cambria Bridge Rd. .B1	Fairview C1	North Star Ave A1	T A Centre B1
Cambria Place B1	Faringdon Rd B1	North Star ⟳ A1	Tennyson St C1
Canal Walk B2	Farnsby St B2	Northampton St B3	The Lawn C3
Carfax St B2	Fire Station B3	Oasis Leisure	The Nurseries C1
Carr St B1	Fleet St. B2	Centre A1	The Parade B1
Cemetery. C1/C3	Fleming Way B2/B3	Ocotal Way A3	The Park B1
Chandler Cl C3	Florence St A3	Okus Rd C1	Theobald St B1
Chapel C1	Gladstone St A3	Old Town C3	Town Hall B2
Chester St B1	Gooch St A2	Oxford St B1	Transfer
Christ Church ⛪ . . .C3	Graham St A2	Park Lane B1	Bridges ⟳ A3
Church Place. B2	Great Western	Park Lane ⟳ B1	Union St C2
Cirencester Way A3	Way A1/A2	Pembroke St C2	Upham Rd C3
Clarence St C2	Groundwell Rd B3	Plymouth St. B3	Victoria Rd. C2
Clifton St C1	Hawksworth Way . . .A1	Polaris House A2	Walcot Rd B3
Cockleberry ⟳ A2	Haydon St A2	Polaris Way A2	War Memorial ✚ B2
Colbourne ⟳ A3	Henry St. B2	Police Station 🏛 B2	Wells St B3
Colbourne St. A3	Hillside Ave C1	Ponting St A2	Western St C2
College St B2	Holbrook Way B2	Post Office	Westmorland Rd. B3
Commercial Rd. B2	Hunt St C3	🅿ᴼ . . .B1/B2/C1/C3	Whalebridge ⟳ B2
Corporation St A2	Hydro B1	Poulton St A3	Whitehead St C1
Council Offices. B3	Hythe Rd C1	Princes St B2	Whitehouse Rd A2
County Rd A3	Information Ctr 🅸 . . .B2	Prospect Hill C2	William St C3
Courts B2	Joseph St C1	Prospect Place C2	Wood St C3
Cricket Ground A3	Kent Rd C2	Queen St B2	Wyvern Theatre &
Cricklade Street B1	King William St C1	Queen's Park C3	Arts Centre 🎭🎵 . . .B2
Crombey St B1/C2	Kingshill Rd. C1	Radnor St. C1	York Rd. B3
	Lansdown Rd. C2	Read St. C1	
	Leicester St B3	Reading St B1	

Taunton

Addison Gr. A1	Fons George C1	Northleigh Rd C3	South Rd C3
Albemarle Rd A1	Fore St B2	Obridge Allotments A3	South St C3
Alfred St. B3	Fowler St A3	Obridge Lane A3	Staplegrove Rd. . . .B1
Alma St. C2	French Weir	Obridge Rd A3	Station Rd A1
Bath Pl B1	Recreation Grd . . .B1	Obridge Viaduct . . .A3	Stephen St. B2
Belvedere Rd. A1	Geoffrey Farrant	Old Market	Swimming Pool A1
Billet St B2	Wk. A2	Shopping Centre . .C2	Tancred St B2
Billetfield C2	Gray's	Osborne Way A3	Tauntfield Cl C3
Birch Gr A1	Almshouses 🏠 . . .B2	Park St C1	Taunton Dean
Brewhouse	Grays Rd B3	Paul St C2	Cricket Club C2
Theatre 🎭 B2	Greenway Ave A1	Plais St A2	Taunton Station 🚊. .A2
Bridge St B1	Guildford Pl C1	Playing Field C3	The Avenue A1
Bridgwater and	Hammet St B2	Police Station 🏛. . . .B1	The Crescent. C1
Taunton Canal. . . .A2	Haydon Rd A2	Portland St B1	The Mount C2
Broadlands Rd C1	Heavitree Way A2	Post Office	Thomas St A1
Burton Pl C1	Herbert St A1	🅿ᴼ B1/B2/C1	Toneway. A3
Bus Station B1	High St B2	Priorswood Industrial	Tower St B1
Canal Rd A2	Holway Ave C3	Estate A3	Trevor Smith Pl C3
Cann St C1	Hugo St B3	Priorswood Rd A2	Trinity Business
Canon St B2	Huish's	Priory Ave B2	Centre C3
Castle 🏰 B1	Almshouses 🏠 . . .B2	Priory Bridge Rd. . . .A2	Trinity Rd C3
Castle St. B1	Hurdle Way A2	Priory Fields	Trinity St B3
Cheddon Rd. A2	Information Ctr 🅸 . .C2	Retail Park. A3	Trull Rd. C1
Chip Lane A1	Jubilee St A1	Priory Park A2	Tudor House 🏠 B2
Clarence St B1	King's College. C3	Priory Way A2	Upper High St C1
Cleveland St B1	Kings Cl C3	Queen St B3	Venture Way A3
Clifton Terr A2	Laburnum St B2	Railway St A1	Victoria Gate. B3
Coleridge Cres C3	Lambrook Rd. A3	Records Office A2	Victoria Park. B3
Compass Hill C1	Lansdowne Rd A3	Recreation Grd A1	Victoria St B3
Compton Cl A2	Leslie Ave. A1	Riverside Place. A1	Viney St B3
Corporation St B1	Leycroft Rd A3	St Augustine St B2	Vivary Park C2
Council Offices. A1	Library C2	St George's 🏛 C2	Vivary Rd C1
County Hall	Linden Gr A1	St Georges Sq B2	War Memorial ✚ . . .C1
Shopping Centre .C2	Magdalene St B2	St James 🏛 B2	Wellesley St. A2
Courtyard B2	Magistrates Court . .B1	St James St B2	Wheatley Cres. A3
Cranmer Rd B2	Malvern Terr A1	St John's 🏛 C1	Whitehall. A1
Critchard Way B3	Market House 🏛 B1	St John's Rd. B1	Wilfred Rd B3
Cyril St A1	Mary St. C2	St Josephs Field C2	William St A1
Deller's Wharf B1	Middle St B2	St Mary	Wilton Church ⛪ . . .C1
Duke St B2	Midford Rd B3	Magdalene's ⛪ . . .B2	Wilton Cl C1
East Reach B3	Mitre Court B3	Samuels Ct C1	Wilton Gr C1
East St B3	Mount Nebo B1	Shire Hall & Law	Wilton St C1
Eastbourne Rd B2	Mount St C2	Courts C1	Winchester St B2
Eastleigh Rd C3	Mountway C2	Somerset County	Winters Field B2
Eaton Cres A2	Museum of	Cricket Ground B2	Wood St B1
Elm St A1	Somerset 🏛 B1	Somerset County	Yarde Pl B1
Elms Cl A1	North St B2	Hall C1	
	Northfield Ave B1	Somerset	
	Northfield Rd B1	Cricket 🏛 B2	

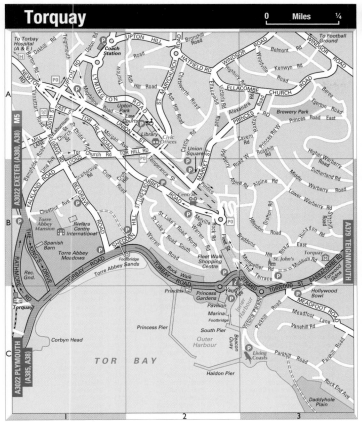

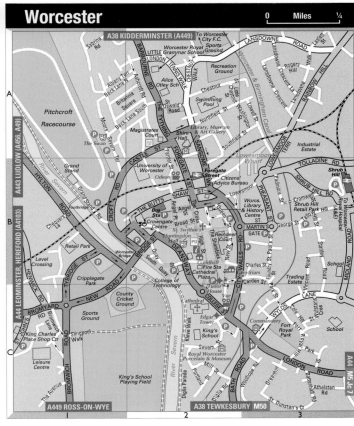

Torquay

Abbey Rd B2	Fleet St B2	Museum Rd B3	Strand B3
Alexandra Rd. A2	Fleet Walk	Newton Rd A1	Sutherland Rd. B3
Alpine Rd B3	Shopping Centre . B2	Oakhill Rd A1	Teignmouth Rd . . . A1
Ash Hill Rd A2	Grafton Rd B3	Outer Harbour C2	Temperance St B2
Babbacombe Rd . . . B3	Haldon Pier C2	Parkhill Rd. C3	The King's Drive . . . A3
Bampfylde Rd B1	Hatfield Rd A2	Pavilion C2	The Terrace B3
Barton Rd. A1	Highbury Rd A2	Pimlico. B2	Thurlow Rd A1
Beacon Quay C2	Higher Warberry	Police Station ⊠. . . A1	Tor Bay A1
Belgrave Rd. . . A1/B1	Rd A3	Post Office PO . . A1/B2	Tor Church Rd A1
Belmont Rd A3	Hillesdon Rd B3	Princes Rd A3	Tor Hill Rd A1
Berea Rd A3	Hollywood Bowl . . . C3	Princes Rd East. . . . A3	Torbay Rd. B2
Braddons Hill Rd	Hoxton Rd A3	Princes Rd West . . . A3	Torquay
East. B3	Hunsdon Rd. A3	Princess Gdns C2	Museum 🏛 B3
Brewery Park A3	Information Ctr ℹ . B2	Princess Pier. C2	Torquay Station ⇌ . C1
Bronshill Rd. A2	Inner Harbour C2	Princess Theatre 🎭 C2	Torre Abbey
Castle Rd A2	Kenwyn Rd. A2	Rathmore Rd B1	Mansion 🏛. B1
Cavern Rd A3	Laburnum St A1	Recreation Grd B1	Torre Abbey
Central ✚ B2	Law Courts A2	Riviera Centre	Meadows B1
Chatsworth Rd A2	Library A2	International B1	Torre Abbey Sands . B1
Chestnut Ave B1	Lime Ave B1	Rock End Ave. C3	Torwood Gdns B3
Church St. A1	Living Coasts 🐧 . . . C3	Rock Rd C3	Torwood St C2
Civic Offices 🏛 . . . B2	Lower Warberry Rd B3	Rock Walk B2	Union Square A1
Coach Station A1	Lucius St B1	Rosehill Rd A3	Union St A1
Corbyn Head C1	Lymington Rd A1	St Efride's Rd A1	Upton Hill. A1
Croft Hill B1	Magdalene Rd. A1	St Luke's Rd B2	Upton Park A1
Croft Rd B1	Marina C2	St Luke's Rd North . B2	Upton Rd A1
Daddyhole Plain . . . C3	Market St. B2	St Luke's Rd South . B2	Vanehill Rd C3
East St A1	Meadfoot Lane C3	St Marychurch Rd . . A2	Vansittart Rd. A1
Egerton Rd. A3	Meadfoot Rd C3	Scarborough Rd. . . . B1	Vaughan Parade . . . C2
Ellacombe Church	Melville St. B2	Shedden Hill B2	Victoria Parade C2
Rd A3	Middle Warberry	South Pier C2	Victoria Rd. A2
Ellacombe Rd A2	Rd A3	South St A1	Warberry Rd West . . B2
Falkland Rd B1	Mill Lane A1	Spanish Barn B1	Warren Rd A2
	Montpellier Rd B3	Stitchill Rd B3	Windsor Rd A2/A3
	Morgan Ave. A1		Woodville Rd. A3

Worcester

Albany Terr A1	Croft Rd B1	Little Chestnut St . . A2	Severn St C2
Alice Otley School . A2	Cromwell St. B3	Little London. A2	Shaw St B2
Angel Pl B2	Crowngate Centre . B2	London Rd C3	Shire Hall A2
Angel St B2	Deansway B2	Lowell St A3	Shrub Hill ⇌ B3
Ashcroft Rd A2	Diglis Pde. C2	Lowesmoor B2	Shrub Hill
Athelstan Rd C3	Diglis Rd. C2	Lowesmoor Terr. . . . A3	Retail Park. B3
Back Lane North. . . A1	Edgar Tower ✦ . . . C3	Lowesmoor Wharf . . B2	Shrub Hill Rd B3
Back Lane South. . . A1	Farrier St A2	Magistrates Court . . A2	Slingpool Walk C1
Barbourne Rd A2	Fire Station B2	Midland Rd B3	South Quay B2
Bath Rd. C2	Foregate St B2	Mill St C2	Southfield St A2
Battenhall Rd C3	Foregate Street ⇌ . B2	Moors Severn Terr . A1	Sports Ground . A2/C1
Bridge St B2	Fort Royal Hill C3	New Rd C1	Stanley Rd B3
Britannia Sq A1	Fort Royal Park. . . . C3	New St B2	Swan, The 🦢 A1
Broad St. B2	Foundry St B3	Northfield St A2	Swimming Pool . . . A2
Bromwich La. C1	Friar St B2	Odeon 🎬 B2	Tallow Hill B3
Bromwich Rd. C1	George St. B3	Padmore St B3	Tennis Walk A2
Bromyard Rd. C1	Grand Stand Rd. . . . B1	Park St C3	The Avenue C1
Bus Station B2	Greenhill C3	Pheasant St B3	The Butts B2
Carden St. B3	Greyfriars 🏛 B2	Pitchcroft	The Cross B2
Castle St. A2	Guildhall 🏛 B2	Racecourse. A1	The Shambles B2
Cathedral † C2	Henwick Rd B1	Police Station ⊠. . . A2	The Tything A2
Cathedral Plaza . . . B2	High St B2	Portland St C2	Tolladine Rd B3
Charles St B3	Hill St C2	Post Office PO B2	Tudor House ✦ B2
Chequers La B1	Huntingdon Hall 🎭 B2	Quay St B2	Tybridge St B1
Chestnut St A2	Hylton Rd B1	Queen St B2	University of
Chestnut Walk A2	Information Ctr ℹ . B2	Rainbow Hill A3	Worcester. B2
Citizens' Advice	King Charles Place	Recreation Ground A2	Vincent Rd B3
Bureau B2	Shopping Centre . C1	Reindeer Court. . . . B2	Vue 🎬 C2
City Walls Rd B2	King's School C2	Rogers Hill A3	Washington St A3
Cole Hill C3	King's School	Sabrina Rd A1	Woolhope Rd. C3
College of	Playing Field C2	St Dunstan's Cr C3	Worcester Bridge. . . B2
Technology B2	Kleve Walk C2	St John's C1	Worcester Library &
College St C2	Lansdowne Cr A3	St Martin's Gate . . . B3	History Centre . . . B3
Commandery 🏛 . . . C3	Lansdowne Rd A3	St Oswald's Rd A2	Worcester Porcelain
County Cricket	Lansdowne Walk . . . A3	St Paul's St. B2	Museum 🏛 C2
Ground. C1	Laslett St A3	St Swithin's	Worcester Royal
Cripplegate Park . . B1	Leisure Centre A3	Church 🏛 B2	Grammar School . A2
	Library, Museum	St Wulstans Cr C3	
	and Art Gallery 🏛 A2	Sansome Walk A2	

Index to road maps

How to use the index

Example **Middlezoy** Somerset **47** E7

- grid square
- page number
- county or unitary authority

Child Okeford 39 D6
Childrey 66 E4
Childswickham 76 E4
Chilfrome 25 A6
Chilhampton 51 E6
Chilla 32 F1
Chillaton 19 D5
Chillington
Devon 13 D6
Somerset 37 D5
Chilmark 50 E4
Chilson
Oxfordshire 72 D5
Somerset 36 F4
Chilson Common 36 F4
Chilsworthy
Cornwall 10 A4
Devon 31 E6
Chilthorne Domer 37 C8
Chilton 67 E6
Chilton Cantelo 38 B1
Chilton Foliat 60 B3
Chilton Polden 47 D7
Chilton Trinity 47 D5
Chimney 66 B4
Chimney-end 72 D5
Chipley 35 B7
Chipmans Platt 63 A7
Chippenham 58 B3
Chipping Campden 77 E6
Chipping Norton 72 B5
Chipping Sodbury 63 F6
Chipstable 45 F7
Chirton 59 E6
Chisbury 60 C2
Chiselborough 37 D7
Chiseldon 59 A8
Chiswell 25 F8
Chitterley 34 F3
Chitterne 50 C4
Chittlehamholt 33 B6
Chittlehampton 33 A5
Chittoe 58 C4
Chivelstone 13 E6
Chivenor 42 E5
Cholderton 52 C1
Cholsey 67 E8
Cholwell 56 E4
Christchurch
Dorset 28 B3
Gloucestershire 68 E5
Christian Malford 58 A4
Christon 55 E7
Christow 21 C6
Chub Tor 11 B6
Chudleigh 21 E7
Chudleigh Knighton 21 E6
Chulmleigh 33 D6
Churcham 70 D1
Churchbridge 9 D7
Church Coombe 4 B1
Church Cove 5 H2
Churchdown 70 D3
Churchend
Gloucestershire 63 A7
S Gloucestershire 63 D6
Church End
Gloucestershire 63 A6
Gloucestershire 75 E7
Oxfordshire 73 A5
Oxfordshire 73 F6
Wiltshire 59 A5
Worcestershire 75 D6
Church Enstone 73 C6
Churchfield 74 C4
Churchfields 51 F7
Church Green 23 A5
Church Hanborough 73 E7
Churchill
Devon 36 F4
Devon 43 C6
N Somerset 55 E8
Oxfordshire 72 C4
Worcestershire 75 B8
Churchill Green 55 D8
Churchinford 36 D2
Church Knowle 27 D5
Church Lench 76 B3
Church Oakley 53 A8
Churchstanton 36 D1
Churchstow 13 C5
Churchtown
Cornwall 17 E6
Devon 31 F5
Devon 43 C8
Somerset 45 D6
Church Town 4 B1
Church Westcote 72 C3
Churscombe 15 C5
Churston Ferrers 15 D6
Chute Cadley 60 F3
Chute Standen 60 F3
Chyandour 3 D5
Chyanvounder 3 F9
Chycoose 4 C4
Chynhale 3 D8
Chynoweth 3 D6
Chyvarloe 3 F9
Cicelyford 62 B2
Cinderford 69 E7
Cirencester 65 B5
Cladswell 76 A3
Claines 75 A7
Clandown 57 E5
Clanfield 66 B2
Clanville
Hampshire 52 B3
Somerset 48 E4
Wiltshire 58 A3
Clapgate 40 F3
Clapham 21 C7
Clapper 8 A3
Clapton
Somerset 37 E6
Somerset 56 F4
W Berkshire 60 B4
Clapton in Gordano 56 B1
Clapton-on-the-Hill 72 D2
Clapworthy 33 B6
Clarence Park 55 D6
Clarken Green 53 A8
Clatford 59 C8
Clatford Oakcuts 52 D3
Clatworthy 45 E8
Clavelshay 46 E5
Claverham 55 C8
Claverton 57 D7
Claverton Down 57 D7
Clawton 18 A4
Claydon 70 A4
Clayhanger
Devon 35 B5
Somerset 36 D4
Clayhidon 35 C8
Clayhill 41 E9
Clay Hill
Bristol 56 B4
W Berkshire 61 B8
Claypits
Devon 34 A4
Gloucestershire 63 A7
Clays End 57 D6
Clearbrook 11 B6
Clearwell 68 F5
Clearwood 49 B8
Cleave 36 F2
Cleddon 62 B2
Cleeve
Gloucestershire 69 E8
N Somerset 55 C9
Cleeve Hill 71 B5
Cleeve Prior 76 C4
Clements End 69 F5
Clench 59 D8
Clench Common 59 C8
Clencher's Mill 74 E4
Clerkenwater 8 B4
Clevancy 59 A6
Clevedon 55 B8
Cleveley 73 C6
Cleverton 64 E4
Clewer 47 A8
Clifford 31 B6
Clifford Chambers 77 B6
Clifford's Mesne 69 C8
Clifton
Bristol 56 B3
Devon 43 C6
Oxfordshire 73 A8
Worcestershire 75 C6
Clifton Hampden 67 C7
Clifton Maybank 38 D1
Clink 49 B7
Cloatley 64 D4
Cloatley End 64 D4
Cloford 49 C6
Cloford Common 49 C6
Closworth 38 D1
Clouds 74 E1
Clovelly 31 B6
Clowance Wood 3 D8
Clubworthy 18 B2
Clutton 56 E4
Clutton Hill 56 E4
Clyffe Pypard 59 A6
Clyst Honiton 22 B1
Clyst Hydon 35 F5
Clyst St George 22 C1
Clyst St Lawrence 35 F5
Clyst St Mary 22 B1
Coad's Green 18 E2
Coaley 63 B7
Coaley Peak 63 B7
Coalpit Heath 63 F5
Coalway 69 E5
Coarsewell 13 B5
Coat 37 B7
Coate
Swindon 65 F8
Wiltshire 59 D5
Coates 64 B4
Cobbaton 43 F7
Cobbler's Corner 75 A5
Cobbler's Plain 62 B1
Cobb's Cross 75 F5
Coberley 71 D5
Cobley 40 B3
Cockadilly 63 B8
Cock Bevington 76 B4
Cockhill 48 E4
Cockington 15 C5
Cocklake 47 B8
Cockleford 71 E5
Cocknowle 27 D5
Cocks 7 E6
Cockshoot 74 E1
Cockwells 3 D6
Cockwood
Devon 22 D1
Somerset 46 C4
Codda 17 E8
Coddington 74 D4
Codford St Mary 50 D4
Codford St Peter 50 D4
Codrington 57 A6
Codsend 44 D4
Coed-y-fedw 68 F2
Coffinswell 15 B5
Cofton 22 D1
Cog 54 C3
Cogan 54 B3
Cogges 73 F6
Colan 7 C8
Colaton Raleigh 22 C3
Colcot 54 C2
Cold Ash 61 C7
Cold Ashton 57 B7
Cold Aston 71 D8
Coldeast 21 F6
Cold Elm 70 A2
Coldharbour
Cornwall 7 F6
Devon 35 D6
Dorset 25 D8
Gloucestershire 62 B3
Cold Harbour
Dorset 27 C5
Wiltshire 50 B2
Wiltshire 58 E2
Cold Northcott 17 C9
Coldridge 33 E6
Coldvreath 8 D2
Cole 49 E5
Colebrook 35 E5
Colebrooke 20 A5
Coleford
Devon 33 F8
Gloucestershire 69 E5
Somerset 49 B5
Coleford Water 46 E2
Cole Henley 53 A6
Colehill 40 F3
Colerne 57 B8
Colesbourne 71 E5
Colesbrook 49 F8
Cole's Cross 37 F5
Coles Green 75 B5
Coleshill 66 D1
Colestocks 35 F6
Colethrop 70 E2
Coley 56 E3
Collafield 69 E7
Collamoor Head 17 B8
Collaton 13 E5
Collaton St Mary 15 D5
Colleton Mills 33 C6
Collett's Green 75 B6
Collingbourne Ducis 60 F1
Collingbourne
Kingston 60 E1
Collins Green 74 A4
Colliprest 34 D4
Colliton 35 F6
Coln Rogers 71 F7
Coln St Aldwyns 65 A7
Coln St Dennis 71 E7
Colscott 31 D7
Colthrop 61 C7
Colt's Green 63 F6
Columbjohn 21 A9
Colwall 74 D4
Colwall Green 74 D4
Colwall Stone 75 D5
Colwell 29 C6
Colyford 23 B6
Colyton 23 B6
Combe
Devon 11 E6
Devon 13 E5
Devon 14 B2
Oxfordshire 73 D7
Somerset 47 F8
W Berkshire 60 D4
Combe Almer 27 A6
Combebow 19 C6
Combe Down 57 D7
Combe Fishacre 14 C4
Combe Florey 46 E3
Combe Hay 57 E6
Combeinteignhead 15 A6
Combe Martin 43 B6
Combe Pafford 15 B6
Combe Raleigh 35 F8
Combe St Nicholas 36 D4
Combe Throop 38 B4
Combpyne 23 B7
Combrew 43 E5
Combrook 77 B9
Combwich 46 C5
Come-to-Good 4 B4
Comeytrowe 36 B2
Comford 4 C2
Comfort 4 E2
Common Hill 74 F1
Commonmoor 9 B7
Common Moor 9 B7
Common Platt 65 E7
Compass 47 E5
Compton
Devon 15 C5
Hampshire 52 F3
Plymouth 11 D5
W Berkshire 61 A7
Wiltshire 51 A7
Compton Abbas 39 C7
Compton Abdale 71 D7
Compton Bassett 59 B5
Compton Beauchamp 66 E2
Compton Bishop 55 E7
Compton
Chamberlayne 51 F5
Compton Common 56 D4
Compton Dando 56 D4
Compton Dundon 48 E1
Compton Durville 37 C6
Compton Green 69 B8
Compton Greenfield 62 F3
Compton Martin 56 E2
Compton Pauncefoot 38 A2
Compton Valence 25 B6
Conderton 76 E2
Condicote 72 B2
Coney Hill 70 D3
Congdon's Shop 18 E2
Congresbury 55 D8
Conham 56 B4
Conkwell 57 D7
Connon 9 C6
Connor Downs 3 C7
Conock 59 E6
Constantine 4 E2
Constantine Bay 16 F2
Cookbury 31 E8
Cookbury Wick 31 E7
Cookhill 76 A4
Cooksland 8 B4
Coombe
Cornwall 3 B8
Cornwall 4 B3
Cornwall 4 B4
Cornwall 8 E2
Cornwall 9 C7
Cornwall 30 D4
Devon 21 F8
Devon 35 C5
Gloucestershire 63 D7
Somerset 37 E6
Somerset 47 F5
Wiltshire 39 B7
Wiltshire 51 A8
Coombe Bissett 40 A5
Coombe Dingle 56 A3
Coombe Hill 70 B3
Coombe Keynes 26 D3
Coombs End 63 F7
Coombses 36 E4
Coped Hall 65 F6
Coppathorne 30 F4
Copperhouse 3 C7
Coppleham 45 E5
Copplestone 33 F8
Copthorne 18 B2
Corfe 36 C2
Corfe Castle 27 D6
Corfe Mullen 27 A6
Corgee 8 C3
Cornett 74 C1
Cornwell 72 B4
Cornwood 11 D8
Cornworthy 13 A7
Corscombe 37 E8
Corse 70 B1
Corse Lawn 70 A2
Corsham 58 B2
Corsley 49 B8
Corsley Heath 49 B8
Corston
Bath & NE Somerset 57 C5
Wiltshire 64 F3
Corton 50 C3
Corton Denham 38 B2
Cory 31 C7
Coryates 25 C7
Coryton 19 D6
Coscote 67 E7
Cosmeston 54 C3
Cosmore 38 E3
Cossington 47 C7
Costislost 8 A3
Coswinsawsin 3 C8
Cote
Oxfordshire 66 B3
Somerset 47 C6
Cotford St Lukes 46 F3
Cotham 56 B3
Cothelstone 46 E3
Cotheridge 75 B5
Cothill 67 C6
Cotland 62 B2
Cotleigh 36 F2
Cotmarsh 59 A6
Cotmaton 22 C4
Cotswold Community 65 C5
Cott 14 C3
Cotteylands 34 D3
Cottonworth 52 D4
Cotts 10 B4
Cottwood 32 D5
Couch Green 53 E7
Couch's Mill 9 D5
Coughton 69 C5
Coughton Fields 76 A4
Coulston 58 F4
Coultings 46 C4
Countess 51 C8
Countess Wear 21 C8
Countisbury 44 B1
Coursley 46 E2
Court Barton 21 C6
Courtway 46 E4
Cove 34 C4
Covender 74 D2
Coverack 5 G3
Coverack Bridges 4 D1
Covingham 65 E8
Cowbridge 45 C6
Cowesfield Green 41 B8
Cowgrove 27 A6
Cowhill 62 D4
Cowhorn Hill 57 B5
Cowlands 4 B4
Cowleaze Corner 66 B3
Cowley
Devon 21 A8
Gloucestershire 71 E5
Oxfordshire 67 B7
Cowleymoor 34 D4
Cowslip Green 56 D1
Coxbridge 48 D2
Coxford 17 A8
Cox Hill 4 B2
Coxley 48 C2
Coxley Wick 48 C2
Coxpark 10 A4
Crabadon 13 B6
Crab Orchard 40 E4
Crabtree 11 D6
Crackington Haven 17 A7
Craddock 35 D6
Cradley 74 C4
Crafthole 10 E3
Crahan 4 D1
Cranborne 40 D4
Cranford 31 B6
Cranham 70 E3
Cranhill 77 B5
Cranmore
Isle of Wight 29 C7
Somerset 49 C5
Crantock 7 C6
Crapstone 11 B6
Crawley
Devon 36 E3
Hampshire 53 E5
Oxfordshire 73 E5
Creacombe 34 C1
Crean 2 F3
Crediton 34 F1
Creech 27 D5
Creech Bottom 27 D5
Creech Heathfield 47 F5
Creech St Michael 36 A3
Creed 8 F1
Creegbrawse 4 B2
Creekmoor 27 B7
Creigau 62 C1
Crelly 4 D1
Cremyll 10 E5
Crendell 40 D4
Cress Green 63 B7
Crewkerne 37 E6
Crew's Hole 56 B4
Cribbs Causeway 62 F3
Crick 62 D1
Cricket Malherbie 36 D5
Cricket St Thomas 36 E5
Crickham 47 B8
Cricklade 65 D7
Crick's Green 74 B2
Criddlestyle 41 D6
Criggan 8 C3
Crimchard 36 E4
Crimp 31 C5
Crimscote 77 C7
Cripplesease 3 C6
Cripplestyle 40 D4
Critchell's Green 41 A8
Critchill 49 B7
Crizeley 68 A2
Croanford 8 A3
Crockernwell 20 B5
Crockers 43 D6
Crocker's Ash 68 D4
Crockerton 50 C2
Crockerton Green 50 C2
Crockham Heath 61 D5
Crock Street 36 D4
Crofthandy 4 B2
Croft Mitchell 4 C1
Crofton 60 D2
Cromhall 63 D5
Cromhall Common 63 E5
Crook 35 F8
Crooked Soley 60 B3
Crooked Withies 40 E4
Crookham 61 D7
Cropthorne 76 D2
Croscombe 48 C3
Cross
Devon 42 D4
Devon 43 E7
Somerset 55 F8
Cross Ash 68 D2
Cross Coombe 7 E5
Cross Green 18 C4
Cross Hill
Cornwall 17 F5
Gloucestershire 62 C3
Cross Keys 58 B2
Cross Lanes
Cornwall 4 F1
Dorset 39 F5
Cross Llyde 68 B2
Cross Roads 19 C6
Crosstown 30 C4
Crossway
Hereford 69 A6
Monmouthshire 68 D2
Crossway Green 62 D2
Crossways
Dorset 26 C2
S Gloucestershire 63 D5
Croucheston 40 A4
Crouch Hill 38 D4
Crow 41 F6
Crowan 3 D8
Crowcombe 46 D2
Crowcroft 75 B5
Crowden 19 A6
Crowder Park 14 D2
Crow Hill 69 B6
Crowlas 3 D6
Crowle 75 A8
Crowle Green 75 A8
Crown East 75 B6
Crownhill 11 D5
Crowntown 3 D8
Crows-an-wra 2 E3
Crow's Nest 9 B8
Croyde 42 D3
Croyde Bay 42 D3
Crozen 74 C1
Crudwell 64 D4
Crugmeer 16 E3
Crumplehorn 9 E7
Crumpton Hill 75 C5
Cruwys Morchard 34 D2
Crux Easton 61 E5
Cruxton 25 A7
Cubert 7 D6
Cucklington 49 F7
Cuckold's Green 58 E4
Cuckoo's Corner 59 E5
Cuckoo's Knob 59 D8
Cudlipptown 19 E7
Cudliptown 19 E7
Cudworth 37 D5
Culham 67 C7
Culkerton 64 C3
Cullompton 35 E5
Culm Davy 35 C7
Culmstock 35 D7
Culverlane 14 C2
Cumnor 67 B6
Cumnor Hill 67 A6
Cupid's Hill 68 B2
Curbridge 73 F5
Curgurrell 5 C5
Curland 36 C3
Curland Common 36 C3
Curload 47 F6
Currian Vale 8 D2
Curridge 61 B6
Curry Lane 18 B2
Curry Mallet 36 B4
Curry Rivel 37 A5
Curtisknowle 13 B5
Cury 4 F1
Cusgarne 4 B3
Cushuish 46 E3
Custards 41 E8
Cusveorth Coombe 4 B3
Cutcombe 45 D5
Cutler's Green 48 A3
Cutmadoc 8 C4
Cutmere 10 C2
Cutsdean 71 A7
Cutteslowe 73 E9
Cuttiford's Door 36 D4
Cwmcarvan 68 F3
Cyntwell 54 A2

D

Daccombe 15 B6
Daggons 40 D5
Daglingworth 64 A4
Dainton 15 B5
Dalwood 36 F3
Damerham 40 C5
Damery 63 D6
Dancing Green 69 C6
Daneway 64 B3
Dannonchapel 17 D5
Darbys Green 74 A4
Darite 9 B8
Darleyford 18 F2
Darlingscott 77 D7
Darracott
Devon 30 C4
Devon 42 D4
Darshill 48 C4
Dartington 14 C3
Dartmeet 14 A1
Dartmouth 13 B8
Dauntsey 64 F4
Dauntsey Lock 64 F4
Davidstow 17 C8
Dawlish 22 E1
Dawlish Warren 22 E1
Daw's Green 36 B1
Dawshill 75 B6
Daw's House 18 D3
Daylesford 72 B3
Dean
Devon 14 C2
Devon 42 C5
Devon 43 B7
Devon 43 B9
Dorset 40 C2
Hampshire 53 E5
Oxfordshire 73 C5
Somerset 49 C5
Dean Court 67 A6
Dean Cross 42 C5
Deane 53 A7
Deanend 40 C2
Deanland 40 C2
Dean Prior 14 C2
Deblin's Green 75 C6
Deddington 73 A8
Deepweir 62 E1
Deerhurst 70 B3
Deerhurst Walton 70 B3
Defford 75 D8
Degibna 3 E9
Delabole 17 D6
Delly End 73 E6
Demelza 8 C2
Denbury 14 B4
Denchworth 66 D4
Deptford 50 D5
Derby 43 E6
Derriford 11 D5
Derril 31 F6
Derriton 31 F6
Derry Fields 65 D5
Derry Hill 58 B4
Dertfords 49 B8
Devauden 62 C1
Deveral 3 C7
Devizes 58 D5
Devonport 10 E5
Devoran 4 C3
Dewlands Common 40 E4
Dewlish 26 A2
Dibberford 37 F7
Didbrook 71 A7
Didcot 67 E7
Diddywell 42 F4
Didley 68 A3
Didmarton 63 E8
Didworthy 14 C1
Diglis 75 B6
Dillington 37 C5
Dilton Marsh 50 B2
Dimmer 48 E4
Dimson 10 A4
Dinas 16 F3
Dinas Powys 54 B3
Dinder 48 C3
Dines Green 75 A6
Dingestow 68 E3
Dinghurst 55 E8
Dinnington 37 D6
Dinton 50 E5
Dinworthy 31 C6
Dipford 36 B2
Dippertown 19 D5
Dipple 31 C6
Diptford 14 D2
Discove 49 E5
Ditchampton 51 E6
Ditcheat 48 D4
Ditchford Hill 77 E7
Ditteridge 57 C8
Dittisham 13 B8
Dixton
Gloucestershire 71 A5
Monmouthshire 68 E4
Dizzard 17 A8
Dobwalls 9 C7
Doccombe 21 C5
Docklow 74 A1
Docton 30 B4
Dodbrooke 13 D5
Doddenham 75 A5
Doddiscombsleigh 21 C7
Doddycross 10 C2
Dodington
S Gloucestershire 63 F7
Somerset 46 C3
Dodmarsh 74 D1
Dodscott 32 C3
Dogridge 65 E6
Dog Village 22 A1
Dolemeads 57 D7
Dolton 32 D4
Dommett 36 D3
Donhead St Andrew 39 B8
Donhead St Mary 39 B8
Doniford 45 C8
Donnington
Gloucestershire 72 B2
Hereford 74 F4
W Berkshire 61 C6
Donyatt 36 D4
Dorcan 65 F8
Dorchester
Dorset 25 B8
Oxfordshire 67 D8
Dormington 74 D1
Dormston 76 A2
Dorn 77 F7
Dorn Hill 77 F6
Dorsington 77 C5
Dottery 24 A4
Doublebois 9 C6
Double Hill 57 E6
Doughton 64 D2
Doulting 48 C4
Dousland 11 B6
Doverhay 44 B4
Dowdeswell 71 D5
Dowland 32 D4
Dowlish Ford 36 D5
Dowlish Wake 37 D5
Down Ampney 65 C7
Downderry 10 E2
Downend
Gloucestershire 63 C8
S Gloucestershire 56 A4
W Berkshire 61 A6
Down End 47 C6
Downgate
Cornwall 9 A8
Cornwall 10 A3
Down Hatherley 70 C3
Downhead
Somerset 38 A1
Somerset 49 B5
Downhill 7 B8
Downicary 18 B4
Downinney 17 B9
Downs 54 B2
Down St Mary 33 F7
Downside
N Somerset 56 C1
Somerset 48 B4
Down Thomas 11 E6
Downton
Hampshire 28 B5
Wiltshire 41 B6
Dowslands 36 B2
Doynton 57 B6
Drakeland Corner 11 D7
Drake's Broughton 75 C8
Drakewalls 10 A4
Drawbridge 9 B6
Draycot Cerne 58 A3
Draycot Fitz Payne 59 D7
Draycot Foliat 59 A8
Draycott
Gloucestershire 63 B6
Gloucestershire 77 E6
Somerset 37 B8
Somerset 48 A1
Worcestershire 75 C7
Drayford 33 D8
Drayton
Oxfordshire 67 D6
Somerset 37 B6
Somerset 37 C7
Warwickshire 77 A6
Drewsteignton 20 B4
Driffield 65 C6
Drift 2 E4
Drimpton 37 E6
Drive End 38 E1
Droop 39 E5
Drope 54 A2
Druggers End 75 E5
Drybrook 69 D6
Drym 3 D8
Drynham 58 E2
Dry Sandford 67 B6
Dubbs Cross 18 B4
Duckhole 62 D4
Ducklington 73 F6
Duckswich 75 E6
Dudbridge 63 B8
Duddlestone 36 B2
Dudsbury 27 A8
Duerdon 31 C6
Dulcote 48 C3
Dulford 35 E6
Duloe 9 D7
Dulverton 45 F5
Dumbleton 76 E3
Dumpinghill 32 E1
Dunball 47 C6
Dunchideock 21 C7
Dundon 48 E1
Dundon Hayes 48 E1
Dundry 56 C3
Dunfield 65 C7
Dunge 58 F2
Dunkerton 57 E6
Dunkeswell 35 E7
Dunkirk
S Gloucestershire 63 E7
Wiltshire 58 D4
Dunmere 8 B3
Dunnington 76 B4
Dunsford 21 C6
Dunslea 9 A8
Dunstall Common 75 D7
Dunster 45 C6
Duns Tew 73 B8
Dunstone
Devon 11 E7
Devon 13 D6
Dunterton 18 E4
Dunthrop 73 B6
Duntisbourne Abbots 71 F5
Duntisbourne Leer 71 F5
Duntisbourne Rouse 64 A4
Duntish 38 E3
Dunveth 8 A2
Dunwear 47 D6
Durgan 4 E3
Durleigh 47 D5
Durley 60 D1
Durlow Common 74 E2
Durnfield 37 B7
Durns Town 29 A5
Durrington 51 C8
Dursley
Gloucestershire 63 C7
Wiltshire 58 F2
Dursley Cross 69 C7
Durston 47 F5
Durweston 39 E7
Duryard 21 B8
Dutson 18 C3
Duxford 66 C4
Dyche 46 C3

Dyer's Common 62 F3
Dymock 69 A8
Dyrham 57 A6

E

Earl's Common 76 A2
Earl's Croome 75 D7
Earlstone Common 61 D6
Earthcott Green 63 E5
Eastacombe
  Devon 32 B4
  Devon 43 F5
Eastacott 33 B5
East Allington 13 C6
East Anstey 34 A2
East Anton 52 B4
East Aston 53 B5
East Bloxworth 26 B4
East Bower 47 D6
East Brent 47 A7
Eastbrook
  Somerset 36 B2
  Vale of Glamorgan 54 B3
East Buckland 43 E8
East Budleigh 22 D3
East Burton 26 C3
Eastbury 60 A3
East Butterleigh 34 E4
East Chaldon or Chaldon Herring 26 D2
East Challow 66 E4
East Charleton 13 D6
East Chelborough 37 E9
East Chinnock 37 D7
East Chisenbury 51 A7
East Cholderton 52 B2
East Clevedon 55 B8
East Coker 37 D8
Eastcombe 64 B2
East Combe 46 E3
East Compton
  Dorset 39 C7
  Somerset 48 C4
East Cornworthy 13 A7
Eastcott
  Cornwall 31 C5
  Wiltshire 59 E5
Eastcourt
  Wiltshire 60 D1
  Wiltshire 64 D4
East Cranmore 49 C5
East Creech 27 D5
East Dean 69 C7
Eastdon 22 E1
Eastdown 13 C7
East Down 43 C7
East Dundry 56 C3
Eastend 73 C5
East End
  Dorset 27 A6
  Gloucestershire 65 B8
  Hampshire 29 A7
  Hampshire 29 A7
  Hampshire 61 D5
  N Somerset 56 B1
  Oxfordshire 73 E6
  S Gloucestershire 57 B7
  Somerset 38 A2
  Somerset 48 A3
  Somerset 49 B5
Easter Compton 62 F3
Easterton 58 F5
Easterton Sands 58 E5
Eastertown 55 F6
East Everleigh 59 F9
Eastfield 56 A3
East Fields 61 C6
East Fleet 25 D7
East Garston 60 A4
East Ginge 67 E5
East Grafton 60 D2
East Grimstead 52 F1
East Hagbourne 67 E7
East Hanney 67 D5
East Harnham 51 F7
East Harptree 56 E3
East Hatch 50 F3
East Hendred 67 E6
East Hewish 55 D7
East Holme 26 C4
East Holton 27 B6
East Horrington 48 B3
East Howe 27 A8
East Huntspill 47 C6
East Ilkerton 43 B9
East Ilsley 67 F6
Eastington
  Devon 33 E7
  Gloucestershire 63 A7
  Gloucestershire 71 E8
East Kennett 59 C7
East Kimber 19 A6
East Knighton 26 C3
East Knowstone 34 B1
East Knoyle 50 E2
East Lambrook 37 C6
Eastleach Martin 65 A9
Eastleach Turville 65 A8
Eastleigh 42 F4
East Leigh
  Devon 12 B4
  Devon 33 E6
East Lockinge 67 E5
East Looe 9 E8
East Lulworth 26 D4
East Lydeard 46 F3
East Lydford 48 E3
East Lyng 47 F6
East Martin 40 C4
East Melbury 39 B7
East Mere 34 C4
East Moors 54 A4
East Morden 27 A5
Eastnor 74 E4
East Nynehead 35 B8
East Oakley 53 A8
East Ogwell 14 A4
Easton
  Bristol 56 B4
  Devon 12 C4
  Devon 20 C4
Easton
  Dorset 24 D2
  Hampshire 53 E7
  Isle of Wight 29 C6
  Somerset 48 B2
  W Berkshire 61 B5
  Wiltshire 58 B2
Easton Grey 64 E2
Easton Royal 59 D9
Easton Town
  Somerset 48 E3
  Wiltshire 64 E2
East Orchard 39 C6
Eastover 47 D6
East Panson 18 B4
East Parley 28 A2
East Pennard 48 D3
East Portholland 5 B7
East Portlemouth 13 E5
East Prawle 13 E6
East Pulham 38 E4
East Putford 31 C7
East Quantoxhead 46 C2
Eastrip 57 B8
East Rolstone 55 D7
East Stoke
  Dorset 26 C4
  Somerset 37 C7
East Stour 39 B6
East Stour Common 39 B6
East Stratton 53 D7
East Street 48 E7
East Taphouse 9 C6
East-the-Water 32 A2
East Town
  Somerset 46 E2
  Somerset 48 C4
  Wiltshire 58 E2
East Tuelmenna 9 B7
East Tytherley 52 F2
East Tytherton 58 B4
East Village 34 E1
Eastville 56 B4
East Water 48 A2
East Week 20 B3
East Wellow 41 B9
East Winterslow 52 E1
Eastwood 74 D2
East Woodhay 61 D5
East Woodlands 49 C7
East Worlington 33 D8
East Youlstone 31 C5
Eaton 67 B5
Eaton Hastings 66 C2
Ebberly Hill 32 C4
Ebbesbourne Wake 40 B2
Ebblake 40 E5
Ebdon 55 D7
Ebford 22 C1
Ebley 63 A8
Ebrington 77 D6
Ecchinswell 61 A5
Eccliffe 39 A5
Eckington 75 D8
Eckworthy 31 C8
Edbrook 46 C4
Eddington 60 C3
Eddistone 31 B5
Eden Vale 50 A2
Edford 49 B5
Edgarley 48 D2
Edgcott 44 D3
Edgcumbe 4 D2
Edge 70 F2
Edge End 69 E5
Edgeworth 64 A3
Edginswell 15 B5
Edington
  Somerset 47 C7
  Wiltshire 50 A3
Edingworth 55 F7
Edistone 30 B4
Edithmead 47 B6
Edmondsham 40 D4
Edmonton 8 A2
Edvin Loach 74 A3
Edwyn Ralph 74 A2
Efford
  Devon 34 F2
  Plymouth 11 D6
Egbury 53 A5
Egdon 75 B8
Egford 49 B7
Eggbeare 18 C3
Eggbuckland 11 D6
Eggesford Station 33 D6
Egloshayle 8 A2
Egloskerry 18 C2
Egypt
  Hampshire 53 C6
  W Berkshire 61 A5
Elberton 62 E4
Elborough 55 E7
Elburton 11 E6
Elcombe
  Gloucestershire 63 C7
  Swindon 65 F7
Elcot 60 C4
Eldene 65 F8
Eldersfield 70 A2
Eling 61 A7
Elkstone 71 E5
Ellacombe 15 C6
Ellenglaze 7 D6
Ellerhayes 34 F4
Ellicombe 45 C6
Ellingham 41 E5
Elliots Green 49 B7
Ellwood 69 F5
Elmbridge 70 D3
Elm Cross 59 A7
Elm Hill 39 A6
Elmley Castle 76 D2
Elmore 70 D1
Elmore Back 70 D1
Elmscott 30 B4
Elmstone Hardwicke 70 B4
Elston
  Devon 33 F8
  Wiltshire 51 C6
Elstone 33 C6
Elton 69 E8
Elwell
  Devon 43 E8
  Dorset 25 D8
Elworthy 45 E8
Ely 54 A2
Emborough 48 A4
Emerson's Green 57 D8
Emery Down 41 E8
Enborne 61 C5
Enborne Row 61 D5
Enford 51 A7
Engine Common 63 F5
English Bicknor 69 D5
Englishcombe 57 D6
Engollan 7 A8
Enham Alamein 52 B4
Enis 32 A4
Enmore 46 E4
Enmore Green 39 B7
Enniscaven 8 D2
Ensbury 27 A8
Ensbury Park 27 B8
Ensis 32 A4
Enslow 73 D8
Enstone 73 C6
Epney 70 E1
Erlestoke 58 F4
Ermington 11 E8
Ernesettle 10 D4
Escott 46 D1
Estover 11 D6
Etchilhampton 59 D5
Etloe 63 A5
Ettington 77 C8
Evendine 75 D5
Evenlode 72 B3
Even Pits 74 E1
Even Swindon 65 E7
Evercreech 48 D4
Everleigh 59 F9
Evershot 38 F1
Everton 29 B5
Evesbatch 74 C3
Evesham 76 D3
Ewen 64 C5
Eworthy 19 B6
Ewyas Harold 68 B1
Exbourne 32 F5
Exbury 29 A8
Exebridge 34 B3
Exeter 21 B8
Exford 44 D4
Exhall 76 A5
Exminster 21 C8
Exmouth 22 D2
Exton
  Devon 22 C1
  Somerset 45 E5
Exwick 21 B8
Eynsham 73 F7
Eype 24 B4

F

Faberstown 52 A2
Faccombe 60 E4
Failand 56 B2
Fairfield 76 D3
Fairfield Park 57 C7
Fairfields 69 A8
Fairford 65 B8
Fairmile
  Devon 22 A3
  Dorset 28 B3
Fair Oak 61 D8
Fairview 71 C5
Fairwater 54 A2
Fairwood 50 A1
Fairy Cross 31 B8
Falcon 69 A6
Falfield 63 D5
Falmouth 4 D4
Far Green 63 B7
Faringdon 66 C2
Farleigh 56 C1
Farleigh Hungerford 57 E8
Farleigh Wick 57 D8
Farley
  Bristol 55 B8
  Wiltshire 52 F1
Farleys End 70 D1
Farmborough 57 D5
Farmcote 71 B7
Farmington 71 D8
Farmoor 73 F7
Farms Common 4 D1
Farnborough 67 F5
Farnham 40 C2
Far Oakridge 64 B3
Farrington 22 B2
Farrington 39 C6
Farrington Gurney 56 E4
Far Thrupp 64 B2
Farway 23 A5
Farway Marsh 36 F4
Faulkland 57 F6
Fawler
  Oxfordshire 66 E3
  Oxfordshire 73 D6
Fawley 66 F4
Fawley Chapel 69 B5
Feltham 36 C2
Felton
  Hereford 74 C1
  N Somerset 56 C2
Feniton 22 A4
Fennington 46 F3
Fenny Bridges 22 A4
Fenny Castle 48 C2
Fentonadle 17 E6
Fenton Pits 8 C4
Feock 4 C4
Ferndown 40 F4
Ferne 39 B8
Fernham 66 D2
Fernhill Heath 75 A7
Fernsplatt 4 B3
Fiddington
  Gloucestershire 70 A4
  Somerset 46 C4
Fiddington Sands 58 F5
Fiddleford 39 D6
Fiddler's Green
  Gloucestershire 70 C5
  Hereford 74 C4
Field 48 C4
Field Assarts 72 E5
Fifehead Magdalen 39 B5
Fifehead Neville 39 D5
Fifehead St Quintin 39 D5
Fifield
  Oxfordshire 72 D3
  Wiltshire 51 A7
Fifield Bavant 40 A3
Figheldean 51 B8
Filands 64 E3
Filchampstead 67 A6
Filham 11 D8
Filkins 66 B1
Filleigh
  Devon 33 D7
  Devon 43 F8
Filton 56 A4
Filwood Park 56 C3
Finstock 73 D6
Firsdown 52 E1
Fisherton de la Mere 50 D5
Fishleigh 32 E3
Fishleigh Barton 32 B4
Fishleigh Castle 32 E3
Fishponds 56 A4
Fishpool 69 B7
Fittleton 51 B7
Fitzhead 46 F2
Five Acres 69 E5
Five Bells 45 C8
Five Bridges 74 C3
Fivehead 36 B5
Five Houses 29 C8
Fivelanes 18 D1
Fladbury 76 C2
Fladbury Cross 76 C2
Flaggoners Green 74 B2
Flax Bourton 56 C2
Flaxley 69 D7
Flaxpool 46 D2
Fleet 25 D7
Fletchersbridge 9 B5
Flexbury 30 E4
Flood Street 41 C5
Flushing
  Cornwall 4 D4
  Cornwall 4 E3
Flyford Flavell 76 B2
Foddington 48 F3
Folke 38 D3
Folly 38 F4
Folly Cross 32 E2
Folly Gate 19 A8
Fonston 18 B1
Fonthill Bishop 50 E3
Fonthill Gifford 50 E3
Fontmell Magna 39 C7
Fontmell Parva 39 D6
Footbridge 71 B6
Ford
  Devon 11 E8
  Devon 13 D6
  Devon 31 B8
  Devon 36 F2
  Gloucestershire 71 B7
  Plymouth 10 D5
  Somerset 46 F1
  Somerset 56 F3
  Wiltshire 51 E8
  Wiltshire 58 B1
Forda
  Devon 19 B7
  Devon 42 D4
Forder 10 D4
Forder Green 14 B3
Fordgate 47 E6
Fordingbridge 41 D5
Ford Street 35 C8
Fordton 21 A6
Fordwater 36 F4
Fordwells 72 E5
Forest Green 64 B1
Forest Hill 59 C9
Forestreet 31 D7
Forewoods Common 58 D1
Forge 4 A1
Forrabury 17 B6
Forston 25 A8
Forthampton 70 A3
Forthay 63 C6
Forton
  Hampshire 53 C5
  Somerset 36 E4
Fortuneswell 25 F8
Forwood 64 B2
Fosbury 60 E3
Foscot 72 C3
Foscote 58 A2
Foss Cross 71 F7
Fossebridge 71 E7
Foulford 41 E6
Foundry 3 C7
Four Elms 36 E3
Four Foot 48 E3
Four Forks 46 D4
Four Lanes 4 C1
Four Mile Elm 70 E2
Four Oaks 69 B7
Four Points 61 A8
Four Pools 76 D3
Fovant 50 F5
Fowey 9 E5
Fowler's Plot 47 E3
Fownhope 74 F1
Foxcombe Hill 67 B6
Foxcote
  Gloucestershire 71 D6
  Somerset 57 E6
Foxdown 53 A7
Foxham 58 A4
Fox Hill
  Bath & NE Somerset 57 D7
  Hereford 74 C3
Foxhole 8 E2
Fox Holes 50 C2
Foxley 64 E2
Foy 69 B5
Fraddam 3 D7
Fraddon 8 D1
Frampton 25 A7
Frampton Cotterell 63 F5
Frampton Court 71 A6
Frampton End 63 F5
Frampton Mansell 64 B3
Frampton on Severn 69 F8
France Lynch 64 B3
Freathy 10 E4
Freefolk 53 B6
Freeland 73 E7
Fremington 42 E5
Frenchay 56 A4
Frenchbeer 20 C3
Frenchmoor 52 F2
Freshbrook 65 F7
Freshford 57 D7
Freshwater 29 C6
Freshwater Bay 29 C6
Fretherne 69 F8
Friarn 46 D3
Friars Cliff 28 B3
Frieze Hill 36 A2
Frilford 67 C5
Frilford Heath 67 C5
Frilsham 61 B7
Fritham 41 D7
Frithelstock 32 C2
Frithelstock Stone 32 C2
Frittiscombe 13 D7
Frocester 63 B7
Frogham 41 D6
Frogland Cross 62 F4
Frogmore 13 D6
Frogpool 4 B3
Frogwell 10 B2
Frome 49 B7
Fromebridge 70 F1
Fromefield 49 B7
Frome St Quintin 38 F1
Fromes Hill 74 C3
Frost 33 E8
Frost Hill 55 D8
Froxfield 60 C2
Fugglestone St Peter 51 E7
Fulbrook 72 E4
Fulflood 53 F6
Fulford 46 F4
Fullabrook 43 C5
Fullerton 52 D4
Fulready 77 C8
Fulwell 73 C6
Fulwood 36 B2
Furley 36 F3
Furnham 36 E4
Furze 33 A5
Furzebrook 27 D5
Furzedown 52 F4
Furzehill
  Devon 44 B1
  Dorset 40 F3
Furze Hill 41 D6
Furzley 41 C8
Fyfett 36 D2
Fyfield
  Gloucestershire 65 B9
  Hampshire 52 B2
  Oxfordshire 67 C5
  Wiltshire 59 C8
  Wiltshire 59 D8

G

Gabalfa 54 A3
Gadfield Elm 70 A1
Gagingwell 73 B7
Gainfield 66 C3
Galhampton 48 F4
Galmington 36 B2
Galmpton
  Devon 12 D4
  Torbay 15 D5
Gam 17 E6
Gammaton 32 A2
Gammaton Moor 32 B2
Ganarew 68 D4
Ganders Green 69 C8
Gang 10 B2
Gannetts 39 C5
Gappah 21 E7
Gare Hill 49 C7
Garford 67 C5
Garker 8 E3
Garlandhayes 35 C8
Garliford 33 A8
Garras 4 F2
Garsdon 64 E4
Garsington 67 B8
Garway 68 C3
Garway Hill 68 B2
Gasper 49 E7
Gastard 58 C2
Gatherley 18 D4
Gatwick 69 E8
Gaunt's Common 40 F4
Gaunt's Earthcott 62 B1
Geat Wolford 77 F7
Georgeham 42 D4
George Nympton 33 B7
Georgia 3 C5
Germansweek 19 B5
Germoe 3 E7
Gerrans 5 C5
Gibraltar 73 D8
Giddeahall 58 B2
Giddy Green 26 C3
Gidleigh 20 C3
Gilbert's Coombe 4 D6
Gilbert's End 75 D6
Gillan 4 F3
Gillingham 39 A6
Gilver's Lane 75 F3
Girt 38 B2
Gittisham 22 A4
Glanvilles Wootton 38 E3
Glasshouse 69 C8
Glasshouse Hill 69 C8
Glastonbury 48 D2
Glenholt 11 C6
Glewstone 68 C5
Gloucester 70 D2
Glowth 4 B3
Gluvian 8 C1
Glympton 73 C7
Glyn 62 C1
Goatacre 58 A5
Goathill 38 C3
Goathurst 46 E5
Godmanstone 25 A8
Godney 48 C1
Godolphin Cross 3 D8
God's Blessing Green 40 D3
Godshill 41 D6
Godswinscroft 28 A3
Godwell 11 D8
Godwinscroft 28 A3
Golant 9 E5
Golberdon 10 A2
Golden Balls 67 C8
Golden Hill
  Bristol 56 A3
  Hampshire 28 A5
Golden Park 30 B4
Golden Valley
  Gloucestershire 70 C4
  Hereford 74 C3
Goldfinch Bottom 61 D7
Gold Hill 39 D6
Gold's Cross 56 B7
Goldsithney 3 D6
Goldworthy 31 B3
Gollawater 7 E6
Golsoncott 45 D7
Gomeldon 51 D8
Gonamena 9 A8
Goodleigh 43 E7
Goodrich 69 D5
Goodrington 15 D5
Goodstone 14 A3
Goodworth Clatford 52 C4
Goom's Hill 76 C4
Goonabarn 8 E2
Goonbell 7 F5
Goon Gumpas 4 B2
Goonhavern 7 E6
Goonhusband 4 E1
Goonlaze 4 C2
Goonown 7 E5
Goon Piper 4 C4
Goonvrea 6 F5
Gooseford 20 B3
Goose Green
  Hampshire 41 E9
  S Gloucestershire 63 F6
Gooseham Mill 30 E2
Goose Hill 61 D7
Goosenford 46 F4
Goosewell 43 B6
Goosey 66 D4
Gore 38 C1
Gore Cross 50 A5
Gore End 61 D5
Gorran Churchtown 5 B7
Gorran Haven 5 B8
Gorran High Lanes 5 B7
Gorse Hill 65 E8
Gorsley 69 B7
Gorsley Common 69 B7
Gosford 73 E8
Gossington 63 B6
Gotham 40 D4
Gothelney Green 46 D5
Gotherington 71 B5
Gothers 8 D2
Gotton 46 F4
Goveton 13 C6
Gozzard's Ford 67 C6
Gracca 8 D3
Grade 5 H2
Grafton
  Oxfordshire 66 B2
  Worcestershire 76 E2
Grafton Flyford 76 A2
Grampound 8 F1
Grampound Road 8 E1
Grandpont 67 A7
Grange 40 F3
Grange Estate 40 E5
Grange Park 65 F7
Grangetown 54 B3
Grange Village 69 E7
Grateley 52 C2
Gratton 31 D7
Great Alne 76 A5
Great Ashley 57 D8
Great Barrington 72 E3
Great Bedwyn 60 D2
Great Bosullow 2 D4
Great Chalfield 58 D2
Great Cheverell 58 F4
Great Comberton 76 D2
Great Coxwell 66 D2
Great Doward 68 D5
Great Durnford 51 D7
Great Elm 49 B6
Greater Doward 68 D5
Greatfield 65 E6
Great Hinton 58 E3
Great Malvern 75 C5
Great Rissington 72 D2
Great Rollright 72 A5
Great Shefford 60 B4
Great Shoddesden 52 B2
Great Somerford 64 F4
Great Stoke 62 F4
Great Tew 73 B6
Great Torrington 32 C2
Great Tree 9 D8
Great Washbourne 76 F2
Great Weeke 20 C4
Great Wishford 51 D6
Great Witcombe 70 E4
Great Wolford 77 F7
Green Bottom
  Cornwall 4 A3
  Gloucestershire 69 D7
Greendown 56 F3
Green Down 36 F3
Greenend 73 C5
Green Gate 35 C5
Greenham
  Dorset 37 F6
  Somerset 35 B6
  W Berkshire 61 C6
Greenhill
  Hereford 74 C4
Greenhill
  Worcestershire 76 C3
Green Hill 65 E6
Green Lane
  Devon 21 E5
  Hereford 74 C2
Greenman's Lane 64 F4
Greenmeadow 65 E7
Green Ore 48 A3
Green Parlour 57 F6
Greensplat 8 D2
Green Street
  Gloucestershire 63 B7
  Gloucestershire 70 D3
  Worcestershire 75 C7
  Worcestershire 75 D7
Greenway
  Hereford 74 F4
  Somerset 46 F3
Greenwich 50 E3
Greenwith Common 4 B3
Greet 71 A6
Greinton 47 D8
Grendon Bishop 74 A1
Grendon Green 74 A1
Grenofen 11 A5
Gretton 71 A6
Gretton Fields 71 A6
Greyfield 56 E4
Greylake 47 E7
Greylake Fosse 47 D8
Greystones 76 C4
Greytree 69 B5
Gribb 37 F5
Gridley Corner 18 B4
Grillis 4 C1
Grilstone 33 B7
Grimscott 31 E5
Grimstone 25 B7
Grinacombe Moor 19 B5
Grittenham 65 F5
Grittlesend 74 C4
Grittleton 64 F2
Grosmont 68 C2
Grove
  Dorset 24 D3
  Hereford 74 D2
  Oxfordshire 67 D5
Grove End 77 E9
Grumbla 2 E4
Guarlford 75 C6
Guineaford 43 D6
Guiting Power 71 C7
Guller's End 75 E7
Gulval 3 D5
Gulworthy 10 A4
Gummow's Shop 7 D8
Gundenham 35 B7
Gunn 43 E7
Gunnislake 10 A4
Gunwalloe 3 F9
Gunwalloe Fishing Cove 3 F9
Gupworthy 45 D6
Gurney Slade 48 B4
Gussage All Saints 40 D3
Gussage St Andrew 40 D2
Gussage St Michael 40 D2
Guy's Marsh 39 B6
Gwallon 3 D6
Gwavas
  Cornwall 3 E9
  Cornwall 5 H2
Gwedna 3 D8
Gweek 4 E2
Gwennap 4 C2
Gwenter 5 G2
Gwills 7 D7
Gwinear 3 C7
Gwinear Downs 3 D8
Gwithian 3 B7

H

Haccombe 15 A5
Hackness 47 B6
Hackthorn 51 B8
Haddacott 32 B3
Hadspen 49 E5
Hagginton Hill 43 B6
Hagloe 63 A5
Hailes 71 A6
Hailey 73 E6
Hailstone Hill 65 D6
Hains 39 C5
Hakeford 43 D7
Halabezack 4 D2
Halamanning 3 D7
Halberton 35 D5
Halcon 36 A2
Hale
  Hampshire 41 C6
  Somerset 49 F7
Hale Coombe 55 E8
Hale Mills 4 B3
Hales Bank 74 B2
Hales Wood 69 A6
Half Moon Village 21 A7
Halford 77 C8
Halfway
  W Berkshire 61 C5
  Wiltshire 50 B2
Halgabron 17 C6
Hallatrow 56 E4
Hallen 62 F3
Hall End 63 E6
Hallew 8 D3
Hallow 75 A6
Hallow Heath 75 A6
Hallsands 13 E7
Hallspill 32 B2
Hallwood Green 74 F3
Hallworthy 17 C8
Halmond's Frome 74 C3
Halmore 63 B5
Halse 46 F2
Halsetown 3 C6
Halsfordwood 21 B7
Halsinger 42 D5

King's Nympton 33 C6
King's Somborne 52 E4
King's Stag 38 D4
King's Stanley 63 B8
King's Tamerton 10 D5
Kingsteignton 15 A5
King's Thorn 68 A4
Kingston
Devon 11 F8
Devon 15 E6
Dorset 27 E6
Dorset 39 E5
Hampshire 41 F6
Kingston Bagpuize 67 C5
Kingston Deverill 50 D1
Kingstone
Hereford 69 C6
Somerset 37 D5
Kingstone Winslow 66 E2
Kingston Lisle 66 E3
Kingston Maurward 26 B1
Kingston Russell 25 B6
Kingston St Mary 46 F4
Kingston Seymour 55 C8
Kingsway 57 D6
Kingswear 13 B8
Kingswood
Gloucestershire 63 D6
S Gloucestershire 56 B4
Somerset 46 D2
Kings Worthy 53 E6
Kington
S Gloucestershire 62 D4
Worcestershire 76 A2
Kington Langley 58 A3
Kington Magna 39 B5
Kington St Michael 58 A3
Kingweston 48 E2
Kinnersley 75 D7
Kinsham 75 E8
Kinson 27 A8
Kintbury 60 C4
Kirtlington 73 D8
Kitbridge 36 F4
Kitebrook 72 A3
Kit Hill 39 C6
Kitlye 64 B2
Kittisford 35 B6
Kittwhistle 37 F5
Kivernoll 68 A3
Knap Corner 39 B6
Knapp
Somerset 36 A4
Wiltshire 40 A3
Knapp Hill 50 F2
Knightacott 43 D8
Knightcott 55 E7
Knighton
Devon 11 F6
Dorset 38 D2
Oxfordshire 66 E2
Poole 27 A7
Somerset 46 C3
Wiltshire 60 B2
Worcestershire 76 A3
Knightor 8 D3
Knightsbridge 70 B3
Knights Enham 52 B4
Knightsmill 17 D6
Knightwick 74 A4
Knockdown 63 E8
Knole 37 A7
Knoll Green 46 D4
Knook 50 C3
Knott Oak 37 D5
Knotty Corner 31 A8
Knowle
Bristol 56 B4
Devon 22 D3
Devon 33 F8
Devon 35 E5
Devon 42 D4
Somerset 47 D6
Wiltshire 59 D8
Knowle Fields 76 A3
Knowle St Giles 36 D4
Knowles Hill 15 A5
Knowlton 40 D3
Knowstone 34 B1
Kuggar 5 G2
Kymin
Hereford 74 C1
Monmouthshire 68 E4
Kynaston 68 B4

L

Lacock 58 C3
Laddenvean 4 F3
Ladock 7 E8
Ladycross 18 C3
Ladyridge 69 A5
Laira 11 D6
Laity Moor 4 A1
Lake
Devon 19 C7
Devon 32 E1
Devon 43 E6
Poole 27 B6
Wiltshire 51 D7
Lamanva 4 D3
Lambourn 60 A3
Lambourne 7 E6
Lambourn Woodlands 60 A3
Lambridge 57 C7
Lambs' Green 27 A6
Lamellion 9 C7
Lamerton 19 E6
Lamledra 5 B8
Lamorick 8 C3
Lamorna 2 F4
Lamorran 5 B5
Lamyatt 49 D5
Lana
Devon 18 A3
Devon 31 E6
Landcross 32 B2
Landewednack 5 H2
Landford 41 C8
Landford Manor 41 B8
Landfordwood 41 B8
Landhill 19 A5
Landkey 43 E6
Landkey Newland 43 E6
Landrake 10 C3
Landscove 14 B3
Landulph 10 C4
Lane 7 C7
Laneast 18 D1
Lane-end 8 B3
Lane End
Devon 31 F8
Dorset 26 B4
Gloucestershire 69 D6
Wiltshire 49 B8
Lanehouse 25 E8
Lanescot 8 D4
Langaford 19 A5
Langage 11 E7
Langaller 36 A3
Langdon 18 C3
Langford
Devon 21 A8
Devon 35 F5
Oxfordshire 66 B1
Somerset 36 A2
Langford Budville 35 B7
Langford Green
Devon 35 F5
N Somerset 56 E1
Langham
Dorset 39 A5
Somerset 36 D4
Langley
Gloucestershire 71 B6
Oxfordshire 72 D5
Somerset 45 F8
Langley Burrell 58 A3
Langley Marsh 45 F8
Langore 18 C3
Langport 47 F8
Langridge 57 C6
Langridge Ford 32 B4
Langstone 20 D4
Langton Herring 25 D7
Langton Long
Blandford 39 E7
Langton Matravers 27 E7
Langtree 32 C2
Langtree Week 32 C2
Lanivet 8 C3
Lanjeth 8 E2
Lanjew 8 C2
Lank 17 E6
Lanlivery 8 D4
Lanner 4 C2
Lanreath 9 D6
Lansallos 9 E6
Lansdown
Bath & NE Somerset 57 C6
Gloucestershire 70 C4
Lanstephan 18 C3
Lanteglos 17 D6
Lanteglos Highway 9 E6
Lantuel 8 B2
Lantyan 9 D5
Lapford 33 E7
Lapford Cross 33 E7
Larkhall 57 C7
Larkhill 51 C7
Larport 74 E1
Larrick 18 E3
Lasborough 63 D8
Lassington 70 C1
Latcham 47 B8
Latchbrook 10 D4
Latchley 19 F5
Latteridge 63 F5
Lattiford 38 A3
Latton 65 C6
Laughern Hill 75 A5
Launcells 30 E4
Launcells Cross 31 E5
Launceston 18 D3
Launcherley 48 C2
Laverley 48 D3
Lavernock 54 C3
Laverstock 51 E8
Laverstoke 53 B6
Laverton
Gloucestershire 76 E4
Somerset 49 A7
Lavington Sands 58 E5
Lavrean 8 D3
Lawford 46 D2
Lawhitton 18 D4
Lawn 65 F8
Lawrence Weston 56 A2
Laymore 37 F5
Lea
Hereford 69 C7
Wiltshire 64 E4
Leafield
Oxfordshire 72 D5
Wiltshire 58 C2
Leagreen 29 B5
Lea Line 69 C7
Leathern Bottle 63 B6
Leburnick 18 D4
Lechlade-on-Thames 66 C1
Leckford 52 D4
Leckhampstead 61 A5
Leckhampstead
Thicket 61 A5
Leckhampton 70 C4
Leckwith 54 B3
Ledbury 74 E4
Leddington 74 F3
Ledstone 13 C5
Ledwell 73 B7
Lee
Devon 42 B4
Devon 43 B6
Leechpool 62 E2
Leedstown 3 D8
Leeford 44 B2
Lee Mill 11 D8
Lee Moor 11 C7
Leigh
Devon 33 D7
Dorset 27 A7
Dorset 38 E2
Dorset 39 E5
Gloucestershire 70 B3
Wiltshire 65 D6
Leigh
Worcestershire 75 B5
Leigham 11 D6
Leigh Common 49 F6
Leigh Delamere 58 A2
Leighland Chapel 45 D7
Leigh Sinton 75 B5
Leighterton 63 D8
Leighton 49 C6
Leigh upon Mendip 49 B5
Leigh Woods 56 B3
Lelant 3 C6
Lelant Downs 3 C6
Lenchwick 76 C3
Leonard Stanley 63 B8
Lepe 29 A9
Lerryn 9 D5
Lesnewth 17 B7
Letcombe Bassett 66 E4
Letcombe Regis 66 E4
Lettaford 20 D4
Levalsa Meor 8 F3
Leverton 60 B3
Lew 66 A3
Lewannick 18 D2
Lewcombe 37 E9
Lewdown 19 C5
Leworthy
Devon 31 F6
Devon 43 D8
Lewthorn Cross 21 E5
Lewtrenchard 19 C6
Ley
Cornwall 9 B6
Somerset 44 D3
Leyhill 63 D5
Leys Hill 69 D5
Lezant 18 E3
Lezerea 4 D1
Libbery 76 A2
Liddaton 19 D6
Liddington 65 F9
Liden 65 F8
Lidstone 73 C6
Lifton 18 C4
Liftondown 18 C4
Lightpill 64 B1
Lillesdon 36 B4
Lilley 61 A5
Lillington 38 D2
Lilliput 27 B7
Lilstock 46 C3
Limerstone 29 D8
Lime Street 70 A2
Limington 37 B8
Limpers Hill 49 E8
Limpley Stoke 57 D7
Lincombe
Devon 14 D2
Devon 42 B4
Linden 70 D2
Liney 47 D7
Linford 41 E6
Link 56 E1
Linkend 70 A2
Linkenholt 60 E4
Linkinhorne 10 A2
Linley Green 74 B3
Linton 69 B7
Linton Hill 69 C7
Lintridge 69 A8
Linwood 41 E6
Liscombe 44 E4
Liskeard 9 C8
Listock 36 B4
Litchfield 61 F6
Little Ann 52 C3
Little Ansty or Pleck 39 F5
Little Ashley 57 D8
Little Atherfield 29 D9
Little Badminton 63 F8
Little Barrington 72 E3
Little Beckford 76 F2
Little Bedwyn 60 C2
Little Birch 68 A4
Littleborough 34 D1
Little Bosullow 2 D4
Little Bray 43 D8
Littlebredy 25 C6
Little Bristol 63 D6
Little Britain 76 B5
Little Canford 27 A7
Little Chalfield 58 D2
Little Cheverell 58 F4
Little Clanfield 66 B2
Little Comberton 76 D2
Little Comfort 18 D3
Little Compton 72 A4
Littlecott 51 A7
Little Cowarne 74 B2
Little Coxwell 66 D2
Littledean 69 E7
Littledean Hill 69 E7
Little Dewchurch 68 A4
Little Doward 68 D4
Littledown
Bournemouth 28 B2
Hampshire 60 E3
Little Drybrook 69 F5
Little Durnford 51 E7
Little Eastbury 75 A6
Little Faringdon 66 B1
Little Gorsley 69 B7
Little Green 49 B6
Littleham
Devon 22 D2
Devon 31 B8
Little Haresfield 70 F2
Littlehempston 14 C4
Little Herbert's 71 D5
Little Hill
Hereford 68 B3
Somerset 36 D3
Little Horton 59 D5
Little Hungerford 61 B7
Little Inkberrow 76 A3
Little Keyford 49 B7
Little Langford 51 D5
Little Load 37 B7
Little London
Gloucestershire 69 D8
Hampshire 52 B4
Oxfordshire 67 B7
Little London
Somerset 48 B4
Little Malvern 75 D5
Little Marcle 74 E3
Little Marsh 58 E2
Little Minster 72 E5
Littlemoor 25 D8
Littlemore 67 B7
Little Norton 37 C7
Little Petherick 8 A1
Little Rissington 72 D2
Little Rollright 72 A4
Little Salisbury 59 D8
Little Shoddesden 52 B2
Little Shurdington 70 D4
Little Silver
Devon 34 E3
Devon 43 C5
Little Sodbury 63 F7
Little Sodbury End 63 F6
Little Somborne 52 E4
Little Somerford 64 F4
Little Stoke 62 F4
Little Tarrington 74 D2
Little Tew 73 B6
Littleton
Bath & NE Somerset 56 D3
Dorset 39 F7
Hampshire 53 E6
Somerset 48 E1
Wiltshire 58 D3
Littleton Drew 63 F8
Littleton-on-Severn 62 E3
Littleton Panell 58 F4
Littleton-upon-
Severn 62 D3
Little Torrington 32 C2
Little Washbourne 76 F2
Little Welland 75 E6
Little Weston 38 A2
Little Whitehouse 29 B9
Littlewindsor 37 F6
Little Wishford 51 D6
Little Witcombe 70 D4
Little Wittenham 67 D8
Little Wolford 77 E8
Little Woolgarston 27 D6
Littleworth
Gloucestershire 64 B1
Gloucestershire 77 E5
Oxfordshire 66 C3
Oxfordshire 67 A8
Wiltshire 59 D8
Worcestershire 75 B7
Litton 56 F3
Litton Cheney 25 B6
Livermead 15 C6
Liverton 21 E6
Livingshayes 34 F4
Lizard 5 H2
Llancloudy 68 C3
Llandaff 54 A3
Llandaff North 54 A3
Llandinabo 68 B4
Llandogo 62 B2
Llandough 54 B3
Llanfaenor 68 D2
Llangarron 68 C4
Llangattock-Vibon-
Avel 68 D3
Llangrove 68 D4
Llangua 68 B1
Llanishen 62 B1
Llanmaes 54 A2
Llanrothal 68 D3
Llantilio Crossenny 68 E1
Llanvihangel-Ystern-
Llewern 68 E2
Llanwarne 68 B4
Lobb 42 D4
Lobhillcross 19 C6
Lockengate 8 C3
Lockeridge 59 C7
Lockeridge Dene 59 C7
Locking 55 E7
Lockinge 67 E5
Lockleaze 56 A4
Locksbrook 57 D6
Locksgreen 29 B8
Loddiswell 13 C5
Loders 24 B4
Lodge Hill 9 C7
Lodway 56 A2
London Apprentice 8 E3
London Minstead 41 D8
Long Ashton 56 B3
Longborough 72 B2
Long Bredy 25 B6
Longbridge 11 D6
Longbridge Deverill 50 C2
Longburton 38 D3
Longcause 14 C3
Long Compton 72 A4
Longcot 66 D2
Long Crichel 40 D2
Longcross 19 E5
Long Cross 49 E7
Long Dean 58 A2
Longdon 75 E6
Longdon Heath 75 E6
Longdon Hill End 75 E6
Longdown 21 B7
Longdowns 4 D2
Longfield 58 E2
Longfleet 27 B7
Longford 70 C2
Long Green 75 F6
Longham 27 A8
Long Hanborough 73 E7
Longhedge 49 C8
Longhope 69 D7
Longhouse 57 D6
Longlane 61 B6
Longlevens 70 C3
Longley Green 74 B4
Long Load 37 B7
Long Marston 77 C6
Long Newnton 64 D3
Longney 70 E1
Longparish 53 C5
Long Park 53 E5
Longridge 70 F3
Longridge End 70 C2
Longrock 3 D5
Longstock 52 D4
Longstone
Cornwall 3 C6
Cornwall 17 F6
Somerset 47 F7
Longstreet 51 A7
Long Sutton 37 A7
Longwell Green 57 B5
Long Wittenham 67 D7
Longworth 66 C4
Looe 9 E8
Looe Mills 9 C7
Lopcombe Corner 52 D2
Lopen 37 D6
Lopen Head 37 D6
Lopwell 11 C5
Loscombe 24 A5
Lostwithiel 9 D5
Lottisham 48 E3
Lovaton 11 B6
Lover 41 B7
Lovington 48 E3
Lowbands 70 A1
Low Bridge 58 B4
Lower Aisholt 46 D4
Lower Amble 16 F4
Lower Ansty 39 F5
Lower Ashton 21 D6
Lower Berry Hill 69 E5
Lower Binton 77 B5
Lower Blandford St
Mary 39 E7
Lower Blunsdon 65 D7
Lower Bockhampton 26 B1
Lower Bodinnar 2 D4
Lower Boscaswell 2 D3
Lower Broadheath 75 A6
Lower Brook 52 F3
Lower Brynn 8 C2
Lower Buckenhill 74 F2
Lower Buckland 29 A6
Lower Bullington 53 C6
Lower Burgate 41 C6
Lower Burrow 37 B6
Lower Cam 63 B6
Lower Canada 55 E7
Lower Cator 20 E3
Lower Chedworth 71 E7
Lower Cheriton 35 F7
Lower Chicksgrove 50 E4
Lower Chute 52 A3
Lower Clicker 9 C8
Lower Clopton 77 A6
Lower Creedy 34 F1
Lower Croan 8 A3
Lower Daggons 40 D4
Lower Dean 14 C2
Lower Denzell 7 B8
Lower Dowdeswell 71 D6
Lower Drift 2 E4
Lower Durston 47 F5
Lower Egleton 74 C2
Lower End
Gloucestershire 64 B4
Oxfordshire 73 D5
Lower Everleigh 59 F8
Lower Failand 56 B2
Lower Gabwell 15 B6
Lower Godney 48 C1
Lower Green 60 D4
Lower Grove
Common 68 B5
Lower Halstock Leigh 37 E8
Lower Hamswell 57 B6
Lower Hamworthy 27 B7
Lower Hazel 62 E4
Lower Heyford 73 C8
Lower Holditch 36 F4
Lower Holwell 40 D4
Lower Hook 75 D6
Lower Hookner 20 D4
Lower Howsell 75 C5
Lower Kilcott 63 E7
Lower Kingcombe 25 A6
Lower Knapp 36 A4
Lower Knowle 56 B3
Lower Langford 56 D1
Lower Lemington 77 F7
Lower Lode 70 A3
Lower Lovacott 43 F5
Lower Loxhore 43 D7
Lower Lydbrook 69 D5
Lower Mannington 40 E4
Lower Marsh 38 B4
Lower Marston 49 C7
Lower Meend 62 B3
Lower Menadue 8 D3
Lower Merridge 46 E4
Lower Mill 5 C6
Lower Milton 48 B2
Lower Moor
Wiltshire 65 D5
Worcestershire 76 C2
Lower Morton 62 D4
Lower Netherton 15 A5
Lower Ninnes 2 D5
Lower Nyland 38 B4
Lower Odcombe 37 C8
Lower Oddington 72 B3
Lower Penarth 54 C3
Lower Pennington 29 B6
Lower Porthpean 8 E3
Lower Quinton 77 C6
Lower Radley 67 C7
Lower Rea 70 D2
Lower Ridge 36 F2
Lower Roadwater 45 D7
Lower Rose 7 E6
Lower Row 40 F3
Lower Seagry 64 F4
Lower Slade 42 B5
Lower Slaughter 72 C2
Lower Soudley 69 F7
Lower Southfield 74 D3
Lower Stanton St
Quintin 64 F3
Lower Stone 63 D5
Lower Stratton
Somerset 37 C6
Swindon 65 E8
Lower Strensham 75 D8
Lower Studley 58 E2
Lower Swainswick 57 C7
Lower Swell 72 B2
Lower Tale 35 F6
Lowertown
Cornwall 3 E9
Cornwall 8 C4
Devon 19 D6
Lower Town
Devon 35 D5
Hereford 74 D2
Worcestershire 75 A7
Lower Trebullett 18 E3
Lower Tregunnon 18 D1
Lower Treworrick 9 B7
Lower Tuffley 70 E2
Lower Turmer 41 E5
Lower Twitchen 31 C7
Lower Vexford 46 D2
Lower Wanborough 66 F1
Lower Weacombe 46 C2
Lower Wear 21 C8
Lower Weare 55 F8
Lower Westholme 48 C3
Lower Westmancote 75 E8
Lower Weston 57 C6
Lower Whatcombe 39 F6
Lower Whatley 49 B6
Lower Wick
Gloucestershire 63 C6
Worcestershire 75 B6
Lower Wolverton 75 B8
Lower Woodford 51 E7
Lower Woodley 8 B3
Lower Woolston 49 F5
Lower Woon 8 C3
Lower Wraxall
Dorset 38 F1
Somerset 48 D4
Wiltshire 57 D8
Lower Wyche 75 D5
Lower Yelland 42 E4
Lower Zeals 49 E7
Low Ham 47 F8
Lowton 36 C1
Loxbeare 34 C3
Loxhore 43 D7
Loxhore Cott 43 D7
Loxley 77 B8
Loxter 74 D4
Loxton 55 E7
Luccombe 45 C5
Luckett 18 F4
Luckington 63 F8
Luckwell Bridge 45 D5
Ludbrook 11 E9
Luddington 77 B6
Ludgershall 52 A2
Ludgvan 3 D6
Ludney 37 D5
Ludstock 74 E3
Ludwell 39 B8
Luffincott 18 B3
Lufton 37 C8
Lullington 49 A7
Lulsgate Bottom 56 C2
Lulsley 74 A4
Lulworth Camp 26 D3
Lumburn 19 F6
Luppitt 35 E8
Lupridge 13 B5
Lurley 34 D3
Luson 11 F8
Lustleigh 21 D5
Lustleigh Cleave 20 D5
Lusty 49 E5
Luton
Devon 21 E8
Devon 35 F6
Lutsford 31 C5
Lutton
Devon 11 D7
Devon 14 C1
Lutworthy 33 C8
Luxborough 45 D6
Luxley 69 C7
Luxton 36 D2
Luxulyan 8 D4
Lyatts 37 D8
Lydcott 43 D8
Lydeard St Lawrence 46 E2
Lyde Green 57 A5
Lydford 19 D7
Lydford Fair Place 48 E3
Lydford-on-Fosse 48 E3
Lydiard Green 65 E6
Lydiard Millicent 65 E6
Lydiard Plain 65 E6
Lydiard Tregoze 65 F7
Lydlinch 38 D4
Lydmarsh 36 E5
Lydney 62 B4
Lye Cross 56 D1
Lye Green 57 E8
Lye Hole 56 D2
Lyford 66 D4
Lyme Regis 24 B1
Lymington 29 A6
Lymore 29 B5
Lympsham 55 F6
Lympstone 22 D1
Lynbridge 44 B1
Lynch
Hampshire 53 B7
Somerset 45 B5
Lynch Hill 53 B6
Lyndhurst 41 E9
Lyne Down 69 A6
Lyneham
Oxfordshire 72 C4
Wiltshire 58 A5
Lyng 47 F6
Lyngford 36 A2
Lynmouth 44 B1
Lynstone 30 E4
Lynton 44 B1
Lynworth 71 C5
Lyon's Gate 38 E3
Lypiatt 70 F4
Lytchett Matravers 27 A5
Lytchett Minster 27 B6

M

Mabe Burnthouse 4 D3
Mackham 35 E8
Mackney 67 E8
Maddington 51 C6
Maders 10 A2
Madford 35 D7
Madjeston 39 A6
Madresfield 75 C6
Madron 2 D5
Maenporth 4 E3
Maer 30 E4
Maiden Bradley 49 D8
Maidencombe 15 B6
Maiden Head 56 C3
Maiden Newton 25 A6
Maidenwell 9 A5
Maindy 54 A3
Maisemore 70 C2
Malborough 13 E5
Malmesbury 64 E3
Malmsmead 44 B2
Malpas 4 B4
Malswick 69 B8
Malvern Common 75 D5
Malvern Link 75 C5
Malvern Wells 75 D5
Manaccan 4 F3
Manadon 11 D5
Manaton 20 D5
Mangotsfield 57 A5
Manhay 4 D1
Manley 34 D4
Mannamead 11 D5
Manningford Abbots 59 E7
Manningford Bohune 59 E7
Manningford Bruce 59 E7
Mannington 40 E4
Manor Bourne 11 F5
Manor Parsley 4 A2
Manston 39 C6
Manswood 40 E2
Manton 59 C8
Maperton 38 A3
Mapperton
Dorset 24 A5
Dorset 27 A5
Mappowder 38 E4
Marazanvose 7 E7
Marazion 3 D6
Marcham 67 C6
Marden 59 E6
Margaret Marsh 39 C6
Marhamchurch 30 F4
Mariansleigh 33 B7
Mark 47 B7
Mark Causeway 47 B7
Market Lavington 58 F5
Marksbury 57 D5
Marlas 68 B2
Marl Bank 75 D5
Marlborough 59 C8
Marlcliff 76 B4
Marldon 15 C5
Marle Hill 71 C5
Marnhull 39 C5
Marr Green 60 D1
Marsh 36 D3
Marshall's Elm 48 E1
Marshalsea 37 F5
Marsh Baldon 67 C8
Marsh Benham 61 C5
Marsh Common 62 F3
Marsh End 75 E6
Marshfield 57 B7
Marshgate 17 B8
Marsh Gate 60 C3
Marsh Green 22 B2
Marsh Lane 69 F5
Marsh Mills 46 D3
Marsh Street 45 C6
Marshwood 24 A2
Marston 58 E4
Marston Bigot 49 C7
Marston Gate 49 B7
Marston Hill 65 C7
Marston Magna 38 B1
Marston Meysey 65 C7
Marston Stannett 74 A1
Marstow 68 D5
Marten 60 E2
Martin 40 C4
Martin Drove End 40 B4
Martinhoe 43 B8
Martinhoe Cross 43 B8
Martinstown 25 C7
Martinstown or
Winterbourne St
Martin 25 C7
Martock 37 C7
Martyr Worthy 53 E7
Marwood 43 D5
Maryfield 10 D4
Maryland 62 A2
Mary Tavy 19 E7
Mathern 62 D2
Mathon 74 C4
Matson 70 D2
Maudlin
Cornwall 8 C4
Dorset 37 E5
Maudlin Cross 37 E5
Maugersbury 72 B3
Maundown 45 F8
Mawgan 4 E2
Mawgan Porth 7 B8
Mawla 4 A2
Mawnan 4 E3
Mawnan Smith 4 E3
Maxworthy 18 B2
May Hill 68 E4
May Hill Village 69 C8
Mayon 2 E3
Maypole
Monmouthshire 68 D3
Scilly 6 B3
May's Green 55 D7